THE LEGACY OF ERIC WILLIAMS

The University of the West Indies Press
7A Gibraltar Hall Road, Mona
Kingston 7, Jamaica
www.uwipress.com

A catalogue record of this book is available
from the National Library of Jamaica.

ISBN: 978-976-640-556-4 (print)
978-976-640-565-6 (Kindle)
978-976-640-574-8 (ePub)

Cover photograph courtesy of Balisier House, Port of Spain, Trinidad.
Cover and book design by Robert Harris
Set in Scala 10.25/15 x 27

Printed in the United States of America

THE LEGACY OF
ERIC WILLIAMS

Caribbean Scholar and Statesman

e d i t e d   b y

COLIN A. PALMER

THE UNIVERSITY OF THE WEST INDIES PRESS
Jamaica • Barbados • Trinidad and Tobago

Dedicated to the memory of Barbara Solow

Contents

Acknowledgements

This volume of essays commemorates the centenary of the birth of Eric Williams. They were originally presented as papers at a conference held at St Catherine's College, Oxford University, 24–25 September 2011. It was conceived by Erica Williams Connell, who also procured the requisite funding from the Eric Williams Memorial Collection in Trinidad and Tobago, the government of Trinidad and Tobago, and the W.E.B. Dubois Institute at Harvard University. Most of the papers presented at the conference are included in the volume, some having undergone significant revisions. It is dedicated to the memory of Barbara L. Solow, the co-organizer of the conference, who passed away in February 2014. The contributors to the volume and the funders of the conference deserve our gratitude. Jobert Bienvenue provided essential support in typing major parts of the manuscript and rendering valuable editorial assistance. It is fitting that the University of the West Indies Press is the volume's publisher since Eric Williams served the university with distinction as one of its pro-vice-chancellors.

Abbreviations

CARICOM	Caribbean Community
CARIFTA	Caribbean Free Trade Agreement
CPUSA	Communist Part of the United States of America
IAFE	International African Friends of Ethiopia
IAO	*International African Opinion*
IASB	International African Service Bureau
ILP	Independent Labour Party
ISI	import-substitution industrialization
ITUCNW	International Trade Union Committee of Negro Workers
LCP	League of Coloured Peoples
NWA	Negro Welfare Association
PNM	People's National Movement
WASU	West African Student's Union

Introduction

COLIN A. PALMER

Eric Eustace Williams occupies a uniquely important place in the history and historiography of the anglophone Caribbean. Born in Trinidad and Tobago in 1911, the intellectually gifted young man attended Queens Royal College and compiled a distinguished academic record, winning the prestigious Island Scholarship in 1931. Entering Oxford University in the fall of 1932, he read for a degree in history. His father would have preferred his son to pursue the traditional academic paths of medicine or law, but Eric followed his own drummer, excelled at his studies and graduated with the highly coveted first-class degree.[1]

Having completed his undergraduate degree, Williams decided to pursue a doctorate in history. He chose colonial history as his field of specialization. This was, in retrospect, both a predictable and an inspired choice. As a student in Trinidad and Tobago, Williams recalled that the high school he attended was designed "to produce coloured Englishmen in the West Indies".[2] He further observed: "the intellectual equipment with which I was endowed by the Trinidad school system had two principal characteristics – quantitatively it was rich, qualitatively it was British. 'Be British' was the slogan not only of the Legislature but also of the school."[3]

Placed in this context, it is not surprising that Williams wanted to devote his intellectual and political lives to challenging, opposing and undermining colonialism. During his tenure at Oxford, he embraced and espoused a virulent anti-colonialism, an ideological prism through which he filtered the developments of his time. He interacted in England with young black intellectuals who shared his views, including his countrymen George

Padmore and C.L.R. James. The Second Italo-Ethiopian War, which began in 1935, sharpened his political consciousness and helped to make of him an eloquent and indefatigable critic of imperialism in all of its manifestations. The intellectual questions to which his doctoral research and study exposed him most certainly helped to shape his career as a historian and statesman.

Williams submitted his doctoral dissertation to the Oxford faculty in 1938. Entitled "The Economic Aspect of the Abolition of the West Indian Slave Trade and Slavery", it was a work of conceptual brilliance, provocative and groundbreaking. The revised dissertation was submitted to the University of North Carolina Press in 1943. The readers for the press recommended its publication but failed to appreciate the work's originality. One reader, for example, thought the manuscript was "really a study of slavery in the West Indies rather than of capitalism and slavery".[4] Williams resisted the suggestion that he change the title of the proposed book. He told the director of the press that "with respect to the change of title suggested by your readers, I am wholly in disagreement".[5] After considering and rejecting various potential titles, Williams insisted on his original title and *Capitalism and Slavery* was born.

Eric Williams had ambitious goals for his book. He wanted to "place in historical perspective the relationship between early capitalism as exemplified by Great Britain, and the Negro slave trade, Negro slavery, and the general colonial trade of the seventeenth and eighteenth centuries". The young West Indian scholar further characterized his book as "strictly an economic study of the role of Negro slavery and the slave trade in providing the capital which financed the Industrial Revolution in England and of mature industrial capitlism in destroying the slave system". The book, he said, "was first a study in English economic history and second in West Indian and Negro history". He insisted that it was not a study of the institution of slavery but of the contribution of slavery to the development of British capitalism.[6]

The publication of *Capitalism and Slavery* was a landmark event in the historiography of British capitalism, slavery and the anglophone Caribbean. Williams's book appeared to be conceptually fresh, and he wrote from the perspective of a colonial West Indian and the descendant of enslaved Africans. His objective was not to celebrate Britain's economic growth and power but to discover the roots of England's Industrial Revolution. Methodologically,

Williams maintained that such scholarship should address "the worldwide and interrelated nature of the commerce" that contributed to the Industrial Revolution.[7] This led him to focus on the roles of the British in the Atlantic slave trade and on slavery in the anglophone Caribbean. He argued that these economic enterprises made fundamental contributions to the construction of British capitalism.

This was a bold and contentious conclusion. The assertion that Britain's wealth was based significantly upon the trade in enslaved Africans and their exploitation in the Caribbean was greeted with scepticism by white scholars in particular. The prominent economic historian D.A. Farnie denounced Williams's argument, charging that it provided the black author's "own community with the sustaining myth that 'capitalism' was responsible for their condition, a view that has not found favour in Western Europe, where history has been separated from its tap-root in myth, but has been found highly acceptable to the educated elites in Africa and Asia".[8]

This dismissive and patronizing comment did not address the historical validity of Williams's conclusions, but accused him of promoting a myth that had resonance in Africa and Asia. Williams's argument was particularly unacceptable to those who saw the Caribbean colonies as the recipients of the mother country's benevolence rather than their enslaved African ancestors being the indispensable engines of Britain's economic growth.

Williams also rejected the traditional argument that the emancipation of the slaves was primarily a function of the efficacy of British humanitarianism. British imperial historians had consistently advanced this position. Williams maintained, however, that the importance of the humanitarians in the struggle to end slavery "has been seriously misunderstood and grossly exaggerated by men who have sacrificed scholarship to sentimentality and, like the scholastics of old, placed faith before reason and evidence".[9] He credited the enslaved peoples with playing a significant role in their emancipation. Recognizing that the slaves were employing violence to resist their condition with increasing frequency, the imperial authorities, Williams argued, abolished the institution of slavery as an act of self-preservation. Williams wrote that in 1833, "the alternatives were clear: emancipation from above, or emancipation from below. But EMANCIPATION."[10] These and other provocative conclusions have provoked much scholarly debate, and *Capitalism and Slavery* became, over time, the most widely read and criticized historical work by a historian of the anglophone Caribbean.

The criticism has come mainly from two fronts. The first is the denial that the slave/sugar complex made a crucial contribution to the Industrial Revolution in England.[11] The second is that the abolition of the slave trade inflicted damage on the British economy that amounted to "econocide".[12] They cannot both be right. If the slave/sugar complex was as insignificant to an industrializing Britain as Williams's critics claim, then abolition of the slave trade could hardly have caused that nation's economy any major damage. Some recent research suggests that both criticisms are questionable and provides support for Williams's conclusions.[13]

When Eric Williams left Trinidad and Tobago for Oxford University in 1931, he lacked the tools of modern economic analysis, the databases and archival materials that are now available to scholars. He did possess, however, an original and comprehensive view of the roles of the slave trade and slavery in helping to create the modern world. Eric Williams's contribution to our understanding of the rise of an international trade that was the catalyst for the industrialization of England must be assessed not by a minute examination of the supporting arguments and data that he provided for his insights, but by the validity of the insights themselves.

Capitalism and Slavery remains Eric Williams's most distinguished and celebrated contribution to scholarship. His other writing reflected his anti-colonial sentiments but lacked the searing originality of this classic work. Returning to Trinidad and Tobago in 1954, the public-spirited scholar began to give a series of lectures to generate a feeling of West Indian nationalism among his people. These lectures, initially, were delivered at the Trinidad Public Library in Port of Spain. In order to reach a larger audience, he converted Woodford Square into an "open-air" lecture hall, educating the thousands who came to hear him on a variety of political, historical and contemporary issues.

This remarkable exercise in public education earned Dr Williams considerable respect and popularity. Not surprisingly, he began to contemplate playing an active role in the political life of the colony. In January 1956, Williams and some of his associates founded the People's National Movement, the first modern political party in Trinidad and Tobago. Several months later, the party won the general elections and Williams was named the chief minister.

As a politician, Eric Williams kept faith with the philosophical positions that informed his scholarship. He led the fight for the independence of the short-lived West Indies Federation when it was founded by ten British colonies in 1958. He launched an aggressive campaign against the existence of the American naval base at Chaguaramas, a short distance from Port of Spain. The British had leased the land to the Americans in 1942 for ninety-nine years. Williams argued, with considerable passion, that the residents of the colony had never been consulted when their soil was leased. The acrimonious dispute continued for several years until 1966, when the Americans acquiesced to his demands to vacate the base. It had become of declining importance to the defence of American interests in the hemisphere. In a further pugnacious display of his political independence, Williams initially rejected the "golden handshake" or parting gift that the imperial country gave to its former colonies. He found the amount of money England offered to Trinidad and Tobago to be unacceptably small. "The [British] offer is quite unacceptable and we would prefer not to have it", he told a meeting of West Indian students in London.[14] In the end, the economic pressures that Trinidad and Tobago faced forced Williams to reach a compromise with the former imperial overlords.

As a politician, Williams clung tenaciously to the position that Britain had a moral obligation to be financially generous to her colonies and former colonies. This was a logical extension of the conclusions that he articulated in *Capitalism and Slavery*. The West Indian islands deserved special treatment, Williams maintained, because the profits from the slave trade and the labour of the enslaved peoples had contributed so much to the growth of the British economy.

Eric Williams served as the head of his country's government from 1956 to 1981. He successively held the positions of chief minister, premier and prime minister. Williams presided over a country with acute racial divisions, particularly between the peoples of African and Indian descent, but he was able to maintain a fragile racial balance. His commitment to the creation of a non-racial nationalism in his country remains an enduring but still contested legacy. A bold and self-assured leader, Williams dominated the political life of Trinidad and Tobago during the twenty-five years that he served as the head of its government. He modernized the country's infrastructure, introduced significant changes to its educational system, expanded the production and delivery of social services, and promoted policies to enhance economic growth and development. But the Williams administration faced a major crisis in 1970 when the proponents of Black Power rebelled, accusing him of inattention to the economic plight of the dispossessed peoples and the nation.

The historiography of Eric Williams, the politician and statesman, remains in its infancy. Selwyn Ryans's *Eric Williams: The Myth and the Man* is a comprehensive discussion of the life and times of his subject. More limited in its scope is Ken Boodhoo's *The Elusive Eric Williams*, published in 2001. Appearing in 2006, Colin Palmer's *Eric Williams and the Making of the Modern Caribbean* examines his subject's role on the larger Caribbean stage. As well, several of Williams's colleagues have published their memoirs, and these provide useful and controversial accounts of his work in office and leadership style.[15]

This volume consists of some of the papers that were presented at a conference held at St Catherine's College, Oxford University, in September 2011. The conference commemorated the centenary of Williams's birth, with St Catherine's College, his undergraduate alma mater, being a fitting venue. The conference attracted many of the world's leading scholars who have studied *Capitalism and Slavery* and the debate that it has produced over the years. It also brought together scholars who have examined Williams's tenure as head of his country's government.[16] Taken together, the chapters on *Capitalism and Slavery* provide fascinating examinations of how Williams, the coloured subject, reshaped the history of the metropolitan country by centring slavery, the colonies and colonial trade in its economic growth and development. The other chapters go beyond *Capitalism and Slavery* and address Williams's place in the historiography of the Caribbean. They also discuss aspects of his life as a political figure, showing how the ideas that informed his work as a historian influenced his practice of the art of politics.

Arnold Rampersad's keynote address, reproduced in chapter 1, established the intellectual tone for the proceedings. Speaking personally at times, he recalled that "single-handedly and single-mindedly, Eric Williams transformed our lives. He swept away the old and inaugurated the new. He made us proud to be who we were, and optimistic as never before about what we were going to be, or could be." Focusing on Williams's "reputation and legacy", Rampersad examines his controversial place in the national conscious-ness of Trinidad and Tobago. "For all his flaws", Rampersad concludes, "Trini-dad and Tobago was fortunate to have him as one of its children in the early days of the century, just as the history profession was fortunate to have him join its ranks when, as a young, brown-skinned man from a distant tropical island, he first appeared at the gates of Oxford University in 1932 and sought admission to its treasures."

Chapters 2 to 5 provide assessments of Eric Williams's impact on the historiography of the Caribbean and aspects of his twenty-five-year role as the head of the government of Trinidad and Tobago. Lydia Lindsey's contribution is a richly detailed discussion of Williams's formative years as a student in England and of his interactions with his countrymen, such as C.L.R. James and George Padmore as well as other young people from various parts of the British Empire. She explores the intellectual currents that shaped the emer-ging scholar, especially his embrace of a virulent anti-colonialism.

Eric Williams was not only a brilliant scholar but also a "man of culture", as Selwyn Cudjoe fittingly describes him. His chapter stresses the scholar's familiarity with the major poets of the Eastern and Western worlds, his admiration for the poetry of Rabindranath Tagore and his respect for the thought of Mahatma Gandhi and Jawaharlal Nehru. Cudjoe notes that, as a leader, Williams believed that the "struggle for the national culture today is not only a part of the struggle for political independence but also a struggle for building a new social order as well". Thoroughly familiar with Williams's writings and speeches, Cudjoe introduces the reader to the ways in which Williams used the insights he learned from literature to educate his people and to create a nationalist movement.

In his chapter, Colin Palmer describes Williams's efforts to achieve the economic integration of the Caribbean region. Williams had been an ardent proponent of the federation of the West Indian islands and the independence of the colonies. When the West Indies Federation failed in 1962, he turned his energies to conceptualizing an economic union of all the territories. The strong, comprehensive, powerful and effective body that he envisioned, how-ever, remained disappointingly elusive. A frustrated Eric Williams, Palmer suggests, seemed to have lost much of his fervour for the economic integra-tion of the area towards the end of his political career.

The final chapter in this section enlarges our understanding of the work of Eric Williams the historian. Franklin Knight provides us with "a general examination" of his role "in the development of modern Caribbean historiography". Knight's conclusion that Williams's contribution was "extraordinarily important" is an assessment with which many contemporary scholars will readily agree.

Chapters 6 to 9 represent the most recent and sophisticated research and discussion of the economic questions that Williams raised and sought to answer in *Capitalism and Slavery*. The contributors have eschewed the partisan, nationalistic and vituperative responses of some of Williams's early critics and have grounded their work in solid archival research. These scholars are noted for their previous publications of distinction, and their chapters elucidate, to a considerable degree, the continuing importance and relevance of the work of the West Indian scholar. These and other scholars are now applying Williams's arguments to other historical periods and economies such as the United States and Brazil. Their papers address, to varying degrees, the crucially important ways in which an ever-expanding Atlantic commerce contributed to England's industrialization, roughly between 1650 and 1850. African slaves provided the engines upon which the commodities that were produced in the Americas depended, as Williams had argued. Although there is no consensus on this aspect of the "Williams thesis", the interpretive tide appears to be moving in its favour.[17] P.K. O'Brien and Stanley Engerman concluded, for example, that "without the enforced and cheap labor of Africans, the rate of growth of transnational commerce between 1660 and the [British] abolition of the slave trade in 1808 would have been far slower". They argue that "it is difficult to envisage an alternative path of development that might have carried both international and British trade to the level attained by the early nineteenth century".[18]

Dale Tomich devotes his chapter to a discussion of the methodological assumptions underlying the "Williams thesis". He reconfigures the debate by examining the political and economic restructuring in the Atlantic economy after the independence of the United States and the Haitian Revolution. In chapter 7, Ronald Findlay and Kevin O'Rourke support the conclusion that the export of British manufactured goods to the Americas and the importation of colonial products had positive effects on the economy of the metropolitan country in the eighteenth century. The authors maintain that slavery remained important to the British economy during the nineteenth century, primarily as a result of that nation's trade with the slave-owning societies of the United States, Cuba and Brazil.

Rafael Marquese provides a lengthy discussion of the impact of *Capitalism and Slavery* on the historiography of Brazil. He situates the growth of the Brazilian coffee industry in the context of Williams's arguments, embedding his narrative in interregional developments in Brazil and in the international capitalist world economy. In the final chapter, Joseph Inikori argues that a study of England's counties from the medieval period to the mid-nineteenth century convincingly shows that the nation's Atlantic trade was the engine of the Industrial Revolution.

Eric Williams's place in the historiography of African slavery, the history of the anglophone Caribbean and the rise of British capitalism is secure. The issues that he addressed in *Capitalism and Slavery* will probably never be completely resolved, as future generations of historians will continue to ask new questions, discover fresh evidence and employ innovative methodologies. *Capitalism and Slavery* remains a work of innovative scholarship and enormous intellectual significance with a lasting impact on the historiography of slavery. Its endurance is testimony to the provocative nature of the questions that the author posed and the answers he provided. Williams had not said the last word on any of the issues he identified and discussed. His monumental achievement was to open a timeless debate on a major aspect of the human experience. As Ronald Findlay and Kevin O'Rourke assert in this volume,

> the legacy of Eric Williams . . . is alive and well . . . not just as an act of piety towards a creative researcher and stalwart fighter on behalf of the oppressed people of the Caribbean, who overcame incredible odds of racial prejudice and blatant discrimination, but as the author of an enduring masterpiece in the historiography of the British Industrial Revolution and its relationship to the fateful trade across the Atlantic in capital, goods and, above all, people.

Eric Williams's legacy is not confined to his contribution to historical scholarship. His intellectual pugnacity was matched by that which he displayed as a politician, whether he was denouncing colonialism or demanding that the Americans abandon their naval base at Chaguaramas. Williams's

debut on the political stage of Trinidad and Tobago and the content of his elec-
trifying speeches gave to the people a sense of their own worth and boundless
possibilities. Acknowledged as the founding architect of his nation, Williams
also played a prominent role in the construction of the modern Caribbean.
But he is not a candidate for either intellectual or political deification. As with
Capitalism and Slavery, the significance of his variegated political roles in the
Caribbean will continue to be the subject of vigorous debate.

NOTES

1.   For a discussion of his early life and education, see Eric Williams, *Inward Hunger:
     The Education of a Prime Minister* (London: Andre Deutsch, 1969).
2.   This comment is found in the unpublished version of Eric Williams's memoirs.
     See the Eric Williams Memorial Collection, University of the West Indies, St
     Augustine, Trinidad, vol. 139.
3.   Williams, *Inward Hunger*, 33.
4.   Colin A. Palmer, Introduction, in Eric Williams, *Capitalism and Slavery* (1944;
     reprint, Chapel Hill, NC: University of North Carolina Press, 1994), xiii. The
     dissertation has recently been published since it differs in many respects from
     Capitalism and Slavery. See Eric Williams, *The Economic Aspect of the Abolition of
     the West Indian Slave Trade and Slavery*, ed. Dale W. Tomich (New York: Rowman
     and Littlefield, 2014).
5.   Ibid., xv.
6.   Ibid., ix.
7.   Ibid., ix. William Darity has argued that Williams was influenced by earlier
     scholars. See his "The Williams Abolition Thesis before Williams", *Slavery and
     Abolition* 9, no. 1 (1988): 29–41.
8.   D.A. Farnie, "The Commercial Empire of the Atlantic, 1607–1783", *Economic
     History Review* 15, no. 2 (1962): 212.
9.   Williams, *Capitalism and Slavery*, 178.
10. Ibid., 208.
11. See, for example, David Eltis and Stanley Engerman, "The Importance of Slavery
     and the Slave Trade to Industrializing Britain", *Journal of Economic History* 60,
     no. 1 (March 2000): 123–44; Stanley Engerman, "The Slave Trade and British
     Capital Formation in the Eighteenth Century: A Comment on the Williams
     Thesis", *Business History Review* 46 (Winter 1972): 430–43.

12. Seymour Drescher, *Econocide: British Slavery in the Era of Abolition* (Pittsburgh: University of Pittsburgh Press, 1977).

13. See Ronald Findlay and Kevin H. O'Rourke, *Power and Plenty: Trade, War, and the World Economy in the Second Millennium* (Princeton, NJ: Princeton University Press, 2009); Joseph E. Inikori, *Africans and the Industrial Revolution in England: A Study in International Trade and Economic Development* (Cambridge: Cambridge University Press, 2002); Selwyn H.H. Carrington, *The Sugar Industry and the Abolition of the Slave Trade, 1775–1810* (Gainesville: University of Florida Press, 2003).

14. Colin A. Palmer, *Eric Williams and the Making of the Modern Caribbean* (Chapel Hill: University of North Carolina Press, 2006), 149.

15. Selwyn Ryan, *Eric Williams: The Myth and the Man* (Kingston: University of the West Indies Press, 2009); Ken Boodhoo, *The Elusive Eric Williams* (Kingston: Ian Randle, 2002); Colin Palmer, *Eric Williams and the Making of the Modern Caribbean* (Chapel Hill: University of North Carolina Press, 2006); Winston Mahabir, *In and Out of Politics: Tales of the Government of Dr Eric Williams from the Notebooks of a Former Minister* (Port of Spain: Imprint Caribbean, 1975); Patrick Solomon, *An Autobiography* (Port of Spain: Imprint Caribbean, 1981).

16. The conference was organized by Colin A. Palmer and Barbara Solow. St Catherine's College and its master, Roger Ainsworth, served as the host. The Eric Williams Memorial Collection, located at the University of the West Indies, St Augustine, provided the main funding. The conference was conceived by Erica Williams Connell, who worked indefatigably to make it a success.

17. See, for example, Inikori's outstanding *Africans and the Industrial Revolution*; Findlay and O'Rourke, *Power and Plenty.*

18. P.K. O'Brien and S.L. Engerman, "Exports and the Growth of the British Economy from the Glorious Revolution to the Peace of Amiens", in *Slavery and the Rise of the Atlantic System*, ed. Barbara Solow (Cambridge: Cambridge University Press, 1991), 181, 182, 187.

Chapter 1

The Life and Work of Eric Williams

ARNOLD RAMPERSAD

Since I am neither a historian nor an economist, but a professor of English with a special interest in African American biography, you will perhaps think of me as an odd choice for the lead chapter. I can think of only two professional qualifications on my part. The first qualification has to do with the extent to which Dr Williams was a man of letters. More than merely comfortable with *belles-lettres*, he was capable of respectfully invoking the words of writers such as Shakespeare, Dante, Wordsworth and Tagore. He showed a greater familiarity with the work of eminent writers than one would find merely by thumbing through Bartlett's *Quotations*. The other main connection between his world and mine has to do with the years he spent in America, especially at Howard University. Despite an essay on the subject by no less a historian than John Hope Franklin, I am not sure that the importance of that time has been fully appreciated – especially the extent to which Williams's consciousness was shaped by his exposure to racial segregation and, inevitably, a degree of racial humiliation in Washington, DC, and also his exposure to the African American near-obsession with race as a category. But that discussion is for another day.

A few years ago, when Selwyn Cudjoe asked me to comment on his volume *Eric E. Williams Speaks: Essays on Colonialism and Independence*, my mind flashed back to my early years. I wrote then, about the essays in the book, that

> to someone like [me] who was a teenager in Trinidad when Eric Williams
> burst onto the public scene there around 1955, certain of these pieces have an

emotional power far beyond their considerable force as political analysis and argument. Single-handedly and single-mindedly, Eric Williams transformed our lives. He swept away the old and inaugurated the new. He made us proud to be who we were, and optimistic as never before about what we were going to be, or could be. "Bliss was it in that dawn to be alive", and nothing that has transpired since in Trinidad can negate Williams' gift to his people, or his triumph of intellect and spirit.[1]

I stand by that statement today.

My emphasis on the personal thus far probably seems at variance with the central goal of this conference, which should lead to another excellent volume to complement *British Capitalism and Caribbean Slavery: The Legacy of Eric Williams*, published in 1987 by Barbara Solow and Stanley Engerman, and *Capitalism and Slavery Fifty Years Later: Eric Eustace Williams – A Reassessment of the Man and His Work*, edited by Heather Cateau and Selwyn Carrington and published in 2000. To quote from Cateau and Carrington about Williams and the span of fifty years since *Capitalism and Slavery* was published: "The 'man' and his ideas are still very much alive. We must not only embrace the new, but place it on the foundation laid by the old. As a result, the foundation must be constantly reinforced to ensure that it can withstand the weight that the future is destined to place on it."[2]

And indeed the work continues. Recently, for example, Seymour Drescher and Pieter C. Emmer demonstrated the ongoing vitality of one of the basic subjects underlying *Capitalism and Slavery* when they published *Who Abolished Slavery? Slave Revolts and Abolitionism: A Debate with João Pedro Marques*. In his own essay in the book, Drescher outlines Marques's attempt at "deflating a new master narrative that places insurgent slave revolts at the center of the story".[3] Having done so, Drescher continues: "I will concentrate on two events Marques designates as examples of *his* 'new equation,' the slave revolts that broke out . . . in Saint-Domingue, Barbados, Demerara, and Jamaica." The phrase "*his* new equation" seems to me essentially a droll way to point to the almost endless variety of ideas having to do with slavery, slave revolts, abolition, Europe, capitalism and the Caribbean – the subjects that were at or near the centre of *Capitalism and Slavery*. These subjects still engage us today, not least of all because of the ongoing vitality of that book.

Additionally, in his book *The American Crucible: Slavery, Emancipation and Human Rights*, Robin Blackburn cites Hugh Thomas's jibe in his 1997 volume *The Slave Trade: The History of the Atlantic Slave Trade 1440–1870* to the effect that while "the memory of Dr Eric Williams may haunt the modern study of the Atlantic slave trade", Williams's argument that capital accumulated through the trade financed the Industrial Revolution "now appears no more than a brilliant *jeu d'esprit*".[4] Not so fast, Blackburn writes. "The 'Williams thesis' has made a come-back", he insists, a point he develops as part of his fourth chapter, "Slavery and Industrialization".[5]

And so it goes. That this gathering will do justice to *Capitalism and Slavery* I am sure. This is the main reason, perhaps, that I would like to stray from that focus to the larger question implied in a conference called "New Perspectives on the Life and Work of Eric Williams". After all, the other major conferences were motivated principally by *Capitalism and Slavery* – forty years later, or fifty years later. Our conference is driven by the fact of the centenary of Williams's birth. Therefore, it seems to me that I might be forgiven if I touch on other aspects of Williams's life and work. These aspects are perhaps no less important than the most remarkable book he published.

I mean in particular Williams's reputation and legacy today in Trinidad and Tobago. This must be, surely, an essential part of any centenary discussion of his "Life and Work". He was a scholar who published with distinction in *Capitalism and Slavery*, but, for many people, his true life's work was the founding and nurturing of a nation into such maturity as is possible for any country to attain in its first twenty-five years of political independence. And thus, if not here and now, at this conference, then surely, in this centenary year, *somewhere* must and will come the kind of appraisal that the occasion demands.

I know that this is a touchy business. A leading West Indian academic and intellectual assured me privately that a conference of this kind could not be held in Trinidad and Tobago at this time, so compromised is Williams's reputation there. I am not sure that this is true, but that man is hardly alone in his view of what must be considered the ultimate Williams controversy. In his invaluable book *Eric Williams and the Making of the Modern Caribbean*, for example, Colin Palmer explains his decision not to interview Williams's contemporaries for the study. He refrained because Williams "remains such a dominant, haunting, and polarizing presence in the life of Trinidad and Tobago that my search for the proverbial 'truth' would have been made much more difficult by highly partisan accounts of his career".[6]

For many people, of course, Eric Williams is forever the father of the nation of Trinidad and Tobago, forever the brave and brilliant son of the soil who returned from his study and service abroad with a depth and breadth of expertise, but also with a burning desire to bring new standards of social justice to his native land. He also sought to set in place a new legislative, moral and economic order that would transform the islands and their people. To others, however, Williams is the original problem. As we celebrate his centenary, his political legacy is, in some respects, in shambles. The People's National Movement, the political party that he created and kept in power from 1956 to his death in 1981, was resoundingly rejected in the last national elections in Trinidad – just as it was rejected in 1986, five years after Williams's death. (In 2015, the PNM returned to power.)

Of course, losing political power does not inevitably mean deserving to lose political power. Nevertheless, there appears to be in Trinidad and Tobago an almost metastasized sense of internal decay in the nation that cannot be divorced from attitudes and practices born – or so many people would insist – during those years when Eric Williams was its leader. Accomplished Trinidadian intellectuals and writers such as Sunity Maharaj and Raymond Ramcharitar have addressed the matter with vehemence born of a profound sense of frustration.

Ramcharitar, editorializing in the *Trinidad Guardian* newspaper, has even questioned whether independence from Great Britain in 1962 was not ill-advised. The central idea of Eric Williams's independence agenda, according to Ramcharitar, was not to end oppression but to become the new oppressor. Williams is said to have perverted the ideal of independence, political maturity and education. Under him, a series of compromised cultural institutions and activities replaced genuine education. "Black Power", according to this writer, "became, post-1970 [the year of an army mutiny and a possible attempt at a coup d'état], an arm of the PNM. This was Williams's idea of 'educating the masses': implanting narratives of ethnic ownership, entitlement, and, most insidiously, a logic that justified it."[7] The result was an exodus from Trinidad and Tobago of 250,000 people between 1962 and 1990, an exodus that has not stopped. "But the most odious and enduring legacy of Williams and the PNM", Ramcharitar continues, "has been the linking of ethnicity, nationalism, and culture, which dominates the national discourse to the present".

To another veteran writer, Gérard Besson, *Capitalism and Slavery* is almost foundational in the disaster that Trinidad and Tobago is seen to have become. This writer builds on Gordon Rohlehr's dazzling, oft-cited attempt early in the 1970s (in his essay "History as Absurdity") to demolish Williams's standing as a historian. Assessing the volume of Caribbean history *From Columbus to Castro* by Williams, Rohlehr had declared that "Dr Williams' notion of writing history has hardly developed since *Capitalism and Slavery*. . . . He still conceives of history-writing as the gathering together of a stockpile of facts to be hurled like bricks against living and dead imperialists."[8] Besson identifies *Capitalism and Slavery* and its denial of the major role of moral idealism in the ending of slavery as fundamental to the construction of what he calls Williams's "narrative". From this narrative would come nothing less than the encouragement of a cult of black victimhood that would have a devastating effect not only on the political ways of Trinidad and Tobago but on the very fibre of its moral being. Besson writes: "Was it a narrative that produced a political culture that successfully evades moral responsibility and commitment to the rule of law? . . . I believe that it was. Did it have any lasting relevance at all in a multi-ethnic society like Trinidad [and Tobago]? And is the political culture created by it of use to us today? I think not."[9]

Whether these negative assessments are deserved or not, I hope you find intriguing this attempt to link an act of historiography, or acts of habitual historiography, to the lifeblood of an emerging nation. While we question here this or that approach to matters such as mercantilism, capitalism, the abolitionists, and the slaves and their revolts, it might profit us to reflect on the idea that a train of historical, cultural and political reality was set in motion by the act of writing a book of history and to consider the contrast between the pristine-seeming rhetoric of books of scholarship, on the one hand, and the complicated, convoluted narrative of life itself,on the other.

Four questions seem pertinent to me here. The first concerns the quality of Williams's mind, his psychology, including those inevitable changes that overtook him during his twenty-five years in power, as he aged from forty-five to seventy. The second question involves Trinidad and Tobago as he found it in 1955 and 1956, when he first achieved power. The third is about the history that Williams himself made – not simply or even principally the books he wrote but the decisions he executed as a national leader. Last of all is the matter of his guiding principles, insofar as we can authenticate them.

Now, no one who did not serve Williams directly as a psychiatrist or psychologist – and no one, as far as we know, had that Hippocratic honour or responsibility – can do anything other than speculate about the relative quality of his mind, its health or degree of distress. I think of what a certain multiple biographer, Sigmund Freud, wrote about biography, by which he meant psychiatric biography: "Anyone turning biographer commits himself to lies, to concealment, to hypocrisy, to flattery, and even to hiding his own lack of understanding, for biographical truth is not to be had."[10] Few biographers can hear these words without wincing. And yet it would be unbecomingly timid to ignore Williams's signs and signals of distinct psychological turmoil and pretend that he was not touched by certain demons.

My second question: what did Williams inherit when he galvanized the electorate and virtually seized power in 1956? At one level, Trinidad and Tobago was yet another sleepy outpost of the British Empire, except for its oil and asphalt, its enchanting calypso and steel-band music, and its almost unrelenting insistence on its status as a paradise of race relations. At a deeper level, however, it was a kind of Gordian knot that would resist all efforts to unravel it seamlessly. It would require a braver man than I am to try to historicize the matter of the Trinidadian and Tobagonian personality (if one such personality exists), but there can be no plumbing of the essential mystery and challenge of the islands, and the difficulties facing Williams, without totalling up some of the more provocative elements of its history.

These include the fact of three hundred years of Spanish rule followed by 165 or so more years of British rule, modulated or muddled by the effects of the Cedula of Population. They also include as factors the resulting tensions and conflicts among the white leadership groups; the cultural irresistibility of Africans and their gifts despite the racist urge to suppress them; the multiplicity over the years of other ethnicities, but most especially the admission of indentured Indians starting around the middle of the nineteenth century; the sheer variety of gods and religions in the nation; the blessings and conflicts of sugar and oil; the role of labour and the left; the dramatic impact of American culture, first as theatre, then as military and occupying reality; the resulting distorted sense of modernity in a culture defined as heavily as it is by Carnival – although one must also remember that there are Trinidadians and Tobagonians enough to whom Carnival was and is folly, even wicked, tasteless folly. That sterner, more puritanical gaze only further complicated and complicates the character of the nation.

These are some of the strands in the Gordian knot facing Williams of which I spoke. By 1955, the country was in some ways already in a state of crisis, so that Williams was on solid ground when he said that year that "the dishonesty and immorality of life in Trinidad and Tobago are now a byword. . . . The poison is seeping through the entire body politic."[11] A distinguished professor of Caribbean affairs, Gordon Lewis, called Trinidad the "Sodom and Gomorrah of West Indian politics".[12] The Mudie Commission, appointed by the British government in 1956 to seek a capital for the proposed West Indies federation, rejected Trinidad and Tobago as the site because of "the corruptibility of its political life".[13] V.S. Naipaul would note "the squalor of the politics that came to Trinidad in 1946 when, after no popular agitation, universal adult suffrage was declared. . . . Corruption . . . aroused only amusement and even mild approval: Trinidad has always admired the 'sharp character' who . . . survives and triumphs by his wits in a place where it is felt that all eminence is arrived at by crookedness."[14]

This was the situation that obtained when Williams intervened. As for the highlights or flashpoints of his stewardship, I am thinking, first, of matters such as the basic stratagem by which he rose to power in 1956; his swift construction of the PNM; his mobilization of Afro-Trinidadians and Tobagonians especially in overwhelming numbers; his controversial response to his rejection by the Indian electorate, when he characterized it in 1958 as "a recalcitrant and hostile minority masquerading as the Indian nation, and prostituting the name of India for its selfish, reactionary political ends"; his confrontation and eventual compromise with the Roman Catholic Church in particular; his clashes with the local French Creole whites and their allies and sympathizers that reached its apogee, or perhaps its nadir, in the celebrated or infamous "Massa Day Done" address of 1961; his leadership during the brief life of the West Indies Federation, and his extinction of any hope that the federation would outlive its rejection by Jamaica; his campaign to win back for local control the US naval base at Chaguaramas, ceded or leased out by the British government in 1940; his protracted encounter with Black Power; his actions during the failed mutiny or coup d'état of 1970; and so on.[15] Then there is the encompassing matter of Trinidad and Tobago's economy and Williams's ventures in state capitalism, as well as a foreign policy that found him placing Trinidad firmly with the West against the Soviet Union and especially its arch-ally in the Caribbean, Cuba.

There is also the subject of civil rights in Trinidad and Tobago, especially when, believing the state to be threatened, Williams put in place mechanisms for the restriction of freedoms that many people found a gross betrayal of trust. The house arrest of C.L.R. James appeared to the poet Derek Walcott, for example, to be an ultimate act of treachery. And yet it has to be noted here – although it might be poor consolation to many observers – that Williams fought with elements of the national society without coming even remotely close to resorting to the abuses and even atrocities that other members of his generation of independence leaders around the world seemed to take easily in their crooked stride. No newspaper was shut down, no journalist dispatched to jail, no acts of ethnic cleansing perpetrated.

What of Williams's principles? Despite the buffeting they took at times because of political expediency, his psychological volatility, and other factors that make men and women stray from their more elevated beliefs, those principles existed. It might be argued plausibly that he had a conception of national unity and obligation no less defensible that that of, say, Abraham Lincoln in the American Civil War when he took controversial steps in his determination to save the Union. In his autobiography *Inward Hunger*, Williams dwells convincingly on his desire for interracial harmony with whites and certainly with the Indian population. As for whites and "Massa Day Done": "If Massa was generally white, but not all whites were Massa, at the same time not all Massas were white. That was the theme I constantly harped on – interracial solidarity, the national community."[16] He recounted his efforts to achieve reconciliation with the Indian community: at the Fifth Annual Convention of the PNM, "I call[ed] upon all party members to stop once and for all this infuriating nonsense that every Indian is anti-PNM. Every Indian is not anti-PNM, nor is every white. Some of the worst enemies of PNM are black as the ace of spades. Reaction knows no colour."[17] At independence, in 1962, he declared: "There is no mother Africa, no mother India, and no mother China. There is only mother Trinidad and Tobago, and a mother must never distinguish between her children."[18]

Pressed to enshrine in the independence constitution explicit quotas that would reflect the nation's racial diversity, he flatly refused to do so:

> I would far prefer to have the Government of Trinidad and Tobago accused of not dividing up the community into racial groups rather than have it accused of constitutional provisions that would establish a Negro President and an Indian Vice President or a Republic with a fixed proportion of seats or places to the various racial groups in the Cabinet, in Parliament, in the Judiciary, in the Police Service and in the Civil Service. As far as I am concerned that way madness lies.[19]

Accused, not without cause, of having so intimidated his own party that it became a cave of echoes of his own wishes and pronouncements, Williams was nevertheless capable of seeing the dangers of such intimidation. A visit to Ghana in 1963, seven years into his rule, left him dismayed at precisely this kind of abuse of leadership. Reporting home to his colleagues, he noted with disapproval how "the dominant note in Ghana is the domination of Nkrumah and the Convention People's Party. Nkrumah is everywhere – it is Nkrumah Market, Nkrumah University, Nkrumah House." Most remarkable to him was the standing of the party. "The Government is merely an arm of the Party", Williams noted disapprovingly. "The Party is the State, and Nkrumah is the Party. That is to say, one gets the impression that he is a prisoner of the Party machinery he has created."[20]

Williams was a proud nationalist, but he showed scant personal allegiance to what he called "narrow" nationalist bias. "Our one world is made up of diverse cultures", he argued, concerning the ideal scope of literary training for local students. "European literature is European, but there is the French school, the English school, the Russian school, each with its own distinctive characteristics. In seeking to develop an indigenous West Indian culture, the West Indian dependencies will have to seek inspiration and stimulus abroad. But the process is not one sided."[21] Fervently a Caribbean person, he neverthe-less saw an ideal Caribbean education as not only "a distinctive contribution to the lives of the West Indian people, but also a genuine contribution to the stream of that broad intellectual culture which, the more diversified it is, yet expresses the common humanity of our one world".

Diminutive in physical stature, Eric Williams loomed large to the people he governed. Opponents and supporters alike appealed to epic or quasi-epic names to find models appropriate to his standing. He was Prometheus and Pericles, Hitler and Goebbels, Caesar and Sawdust Caesar, Caligula ("Let them hate so long as they fear")[22] and, of course, Christ, in scathing fashion ("the apotheosis of the Messiah, man made God").[23] But in his one public act of self-identification with the immortals, as far as I know, he chose to link his name to that of Ulysses. At the conclusion of his autobiography *Inward Hunger,* he writes about his determination to prove that, like Dante's Ulysses, I

> Could conquer the inward hunger that I had
> To master earth's experience, and to attain
> Knowledge of man's mind, both good and bad.[24]

It is perhaps telling to note that Williams here chose an allusion to the Ulysses of Dante rather than to the somewhat more famous (in Williams's time) Ulysses of Alfred, Lord Tennyson, to ground his self-identification with the Greek hero. Tennyson's Ulysses, who is finally determined "to strive, to seek, to find, and not to yield", at first bemoans the fact that instead, ruling in the "barren crags" of Ithaca, he must "mete and dole unequal laws unto a savage race, / That hoard, and feed, and sleep, and know not me."[25] As much as he loved Trinidad and Tobago, Williams seems to have lived with a debilitating sense of a gulf between himself and most of the people of his own version of Ithaca.

"The entire West Indian tradition", Williams complained,

> is anti-intellectual. People's lives are bounded by the narrow materialistic considerations of the price of produce or the cost of living or the laziness of the workers or the growth of crime and delinquency or gambling or chasing after women (or men as the case may be) or just plain gluttony and imbibing. Add to that the movies and radio and . . . the equally pernicious television, and fit in somewhere in this schedule sleeping and working or making pretence of working, and the normal individual's day is complete. A Head of Government cannot be limited to such narrow and materialistic considerations. So I read deliberately, in silent protest against the bastardization of so-called West Indian intellectualism.[26]

As Williams doubtless knew, Dante's Ulysses speaks his words in a place deep in Hell, specifically in the eighth ditch of the eighth circle of Hell. Why Dante condemns Ulysses is a matter of some debate, but what was the source of Williams's sombre self-evaluation? I think that as much as he was a man capable of gaiety, wit and charm, he was also a man constantly and increasingly in pain. His choice of Ulysses as his model and mentor, his alter ego out of the classical world, speaks, I think, to his ambivalence about home, his knowledge of the necessity of power but also of its corrosive dangers, and his sense of personal frustration and recrimination despite the grand achievements of his life.

In conclusion, I can only agree with the last words of Selwyn Ryan in *Eric Williams: The Myth and the Man*:

> Whatever the lens through which we choose to view him – whether straight, prismatic or crooked – he left Trinidad and Tobago better than he found it in 1956, leaving indelible footprints on our landscape. The "hero" had many-splendoured visions, but could not complete all the tasks he assigned himself. And so, Williams was not Plato's mythical, unblemished philosopher-king. He was challenged in many ways. On balance, however, his performance was worthy of History's applause.[27]

Erica Williams Connell (Williams's daughter) has movingly said that "great men are doomed to die feeling they have failed".[28] But I do not think that history – that is, we – can with justification judge Williams to have failed. Trinidad and Tobago was fortunate to have him, for all his flaws, as one of its children in the early days of the century, just as the history profession was fortunate to have him join its ranks when, as a young, brown-skinned man from a distant tropical island, he first appeared at the gates of Oxford University in 1932 and sought admission to its treasures.

The fact that, a century after his birth and three decades after his death, we have come to the same place to evaluate the man and his work is eloquent testimony to the fact that Williams's considerable intellectual powers, his amazing level of energy, his achievements as a scholar, his dedication to serving the people of the Caribbean – all mark him as one of the extraordinary men of the twentieth century.

NOTES

1. Selwyn R. Cudjoe, ed., *Eric E. Williams Speaks: Essays on Colonialism and Independence* (Wellesley, MA: Calaloux Publications, 1993), n.p.

2. Heather Cateau and S.H.H. Carrington, eds., *Capitalism and Slavery Fifty Years Later: Eric Eustace Williams – A Reassessment of the Man and His Work* (New York: Peter Lang, 2000), 1.

3. Seymour Drescher, "Civilizing Insurgency: Two Variants of Slave Revolts in the Age of Revolution", in *Who Abolished Slavery? Slave Revolts and Abolitionism: A Debate with João Pedro Marques*, ed. Seymour Drescher and Pieter C. Emmer (New York: Berghahn Books, 2010), 120–21.

4. Cited in Robin Blackburn, *The American Crucible: Slavery, Emancipation and Human Rights* (New York: Verso, 2011), 87.

5. Ibid.

6. Colin Palmer, *Eric Williams and the Making of the Modern Caribbean* (Kingston: Ian Randle, 2006), 13.

7. Raymond Ramcharitar, "This State of Independence", *Trinidad Guardian*, 31 August 2011.

8. Gordon Rohlehr, "History as Absurdity", in *My Strangled City and Other Essays* (Port of Spain: Longman Trinidad, 1992), 21.

9. Gérard Besson, "Some Remarks on the Historical Narratives of Trinidad and Tobago. And Some Comments on the Personality and Background of the Man Who Reconstructed Them, Dr Eric Williams" (manuscript, n.d.), 119.

10. Letter from Sigmund Freud to Arnold Zweig, 31 May 1936, in *Letters of Sigmund Freud* (New York: Basic Books, 1960), 430.

11. Cited in Cudjoe, *Eric E. Williams Speaks*, 188.

12. Cited in Selwyn Ryan, *Eric Williams: The Myth and the Man* (Kingston: University of the West Indies Press, 2008), 137.

13. Ibid., 137.

14. V.S. Naipaul, *The Middle Passage* (London: Penguin, 1962), 72.

15. Ryan, *Eric Williams*, 178.

16. Cudjoe, *Eric E. Williams Speaks*, 363.

17. Eric E. Williams, *Inward Hunger: The Education of a Prime Minister* (London: Andre Deutsch, 1969), 265.

18. Cudjoe, *Eric E. Williams Speaks*, 363.

19. Williams, *Inward Hunger*, 304–5.

20. Ibid., 291–92.

21. Ibid., 75.

22.   Ryan, *Eric Williams*, 332.

23.   Ibid., 466.

24.   Williams, *Inward Hunger*, 343.

25.   Alfred, Lord Tennyson, *Selected Poems*, ed. Christopher Ricks (New York: Penguin Classics, 2008), 49–50.

26.   Williams, *Inward Hunger*, 327.

27.   Ryan, *Eric Williams*, 755.

28.   Ken Boodhoo, "My Father: Interviews with Erica Williams-Connell", in *Eric Williams: The Man and the Leader*, by Ken Boodhoo (New York: University Press of America, 1986), 10. Erica Williams Connell is the daughter of Eric Williams.

Chapter 2

Eric Williams, His Associates and the Imagination of an Anti-colonial Society

LYDIA LINDSEY

At no time since Chartism in the 1840s was Britain in such intellectual turmoil as between 1933 and 1939. The seething cauldron of political and social
ideas was generated by the Great Depression, the success of the first Russian
five-year plan, the rise of Nazism, the real threat of a fascist movement in
England, the spread of Marxism and the anti-imperialism struggle.[1] During
the 1930s, African and West Indian scholars, professionals, university students, artists, workers and political activists in London imagined conceptions
of anti-colonialism that reshaped the public debate on imperialism. An objective of this chapter is to position historian Eric Eustace Williams, the first
prime minister of the independent Trinidad and Tobago, within the milieu
of West Indians who were living in London during the 1930s and imagining
anti-colonial societies, particularly George Padmore[2] and C.L.R. James.[3] Padmore and James have been singled out because they, too, were Trinidadian,
political theoreticians, writers and activists in London during the 1930s and
were friends of Eric Williams.

The 1930s witnessed a dramatic surge in black political organizing and
activism in London due to the developments in Africa and the Caribbean as
well as the work of Padmore and James. They generated a sense of mission
which allowed black intellectuals to believe that their actions in the metropole
could have far-reaching consequences in the colonies. Through their organizations, publications and personalities, they formed new alliances around
race and stimulated dialogues on colonial reforms. The London duo was a

stylish set, each in a different way. James was very tall, "noticeably good look-ing", and his memory was extraordinary. He could quote Marxist classics as well as Shakespeare in a soft, lilting English that was a delight to the ear. He was an elegant writer and a dynamic speaker. Then, Padmore was a "very handsome man . . . he was just under medium height, slender, quick in his movement . . . naturally graceful".[4] Most striking was Padmore's neatness in his dress: "His shoes shone so you could see your face in them; his trouser creases could shave you." He was known to have been "immensely kind and generous". Padmore was a journalist, but foremost he was an activist and organizer. Padmore and James provided a space for the young Eric Williams to imagine an anti-colonial nationalist society within the context of a political federation in the anglophone Caribbean.[5]

Williams's interactions in the heart of the British Empire allowed him to think about difference and impelled him to act as a voice of a multinational racial community, transcending its differences. With each racial conflict or international crisis, moments of cooperation accelerated and produced a black nationalist political imaginary that constituted elements of a transformative political vision. London gave Williams a privileged vantage point from which to develop a sense of history that drew upon the constituent elements of humanity, internationalism, nationalism, economics and self-determination. He learned the language of internationalism in order to articulate a vision of black self-determination and unity.

On 7 November 1932, Williams arrived in England with his father, Thomas Henry Williams, and his friends.[6] He soon settled into university life at Oxford while remaining close to his Trinidadian friends. He found time to read novels and poetry, attend plays and visit art galleries. He had been an excellent sportsman in high school and distinguished himself in both cricket and football. He formed a team with other colonial students – West Indians, Africans and Indians – and played cricket against various colleges and other friendly teams. This informal experience provided an opportunity for Wil-liams to get to know and work with colonial peoples from different islands and regions of the world.[7]

From 1932 to 1938, Williams undertook and completed his undergraduate and postgraduate studies at Oxford. Upon his arrival in England, he rekindled his friendship with James, who had been his teacher at Queen's Royal College and who had prepared him for his Oxbridge entrance exam. Queen's Royal College was modelled on an English public school. There was an emphasis on the classics, European history, literature and sports. Williams, in his autobiography, *Inward Hunger*, wrote that " 'Be British' was the slogan not only of the Legislature but also of the school . . . instead of the school helping to obliterate the differences of race, religion and nationality inherent in the demographic structure of Trinidad, it helped to accentuate them".[8] While education was the primary means of mobility for the "coloured" and black middle class, it remained the preserve of a select few. Less than one per cent of West Indian children attended secondary school, and Williams was in that group.

On 18 March 1932, a few months before Williams's arrival, James had arrived in London aboard the *Colombia* – and much to his surprise, he later met Padmore at a meeting. James had gone to a meeting at Gray's Inn Road because he had heard "a great Negro Communist" from Europe was coming to speak. There were about fifty people in the room, mostly black, and in walked Padmore with one or two associates. Padmore spoke "about the struggles of the Negro the world over". He exuded authority. James recalled that he "was struck by the admiration and the awe with which the whole audience listened to him and looked at him". Between 1930 and 1935, Padmore organized and educated "the Negro masses on a world scale in the theory and practice of modern political parties and modern trade unionism".[9] That night after the meeting, James had a reunion with Padmore, his old school chum. During their conversation, Padmore spoke a great deal about self-government for the West Indies and similar matters, but James had not yet entered politics; he was wrapped up in English literature and cricket.[10]

James often said that he took Williams in while he was "still in knee pants". Their relationship was personal as well as scholarly. In James's unfinished autobiography, he described how, on quite a few evenings, he went pub crawling in London with Williams and his friends. James would put in his pocket books on Marx, Jane Austen or H.G. Wells, which he faithfully read during breaks.[11] Williams also had a group of Trinidadian friends in London whom he had known since high school. They included Ray Dolly, Halsey McShine, John Pillai and Joey Ribeiro, who had been his high school cricket captain and became his brother-in-law after Williams married Elsie Ribeiro in March 1937.[12] While at Oxford, Williams spent holidays with James. The two of them, along with McShine, spent fabulous holidays in Lancashire with Learie and Norma Constantine, the West Indian cricketer and his wife.[13]

To be sure, Williams kept his nose to the academic grindstone, but his writings suggest that his stay at Oxford contributed to his intellectual development in more than one way. He explained that his general education came not merely from living in an advanced metropolitan country but from the bonds he formed with others in nationalist movements.[14] His exposure to racial prejudice forced him to make alliances across boundaries that would have been unthinkable in Trinidad. Eric Williams's biographer, Colin Palmer, contends that Williams's ferocious anti-colonialism was honed during these years. Williams, however, never openly acknowledged the influence of Padmore, James and others on the evolution of his political consciousness. Besides being an independent thinker, Williams's "chronic intellectual arrogance" would not permit him to publicly identify any ideological godfathers.[15]

When Williams arrived in Britain, there were several black organizations to advise and guide coloured people on anti-colonial matters. They included the League of Coloured Peoples (LCP), the Negro Welfare Association (NWA) and the West African Student's Union (WASU).[16] Later, the International African Friends of Ethiopia (IAFE) and the International African Service Bureau (IASB) were founded. Blacks in London organized conferences, held demonstrations and adopted resolutions that supported militant trade unionism in the West Indies. Unlike the reports from the Colonial Office that claimed that these groups were stirring up unrest in the West Indies, Williams thought that they were largely ineffective.[17] There is no clear evidence that Williams was an active member of any of these organizations, but there are writings of his that appear in *International African Opinion*, the organ of the IASB, and the *Keys*, the organ of the LCP. Williams spoke at IASB and WASU gatherings as well as attending meetings with C.L.R. James and Padmore.[18] Years later, Tomasi R. Makonnen, the Guyanese activist, described Eric Williams as the type of student from the 1930s generation that one would expect to be rebellious.[19]

Padmore served as the conduit in Williams's relationships with Alain Locke, Abram Harris and Ralph Bunche, who were a part of the radical intellectual circle of Howard University's scholars. These relations were significant in shaping Williams's academic career as well as aspects of his intellectual development. On 20 May 1936, in the midst of the Abyssinian crisis, Padmore wrote from London to Locke explaining that he had discussed his letter with Williams and that Williams was glad to learn of his "fraternal interest in young scholars".[20]

In May 1937, Bunche read Williams's dissertation and wrote a strong letter recommending him for a position at Howard University. Bunche thought that the dissertation was a "scholarly and well written piece of work", and that Williams displayed a "thorough understanding of the historical background and . . . administration of the West Indies". He could deliver "special lectures on the government of India, the administration of the Crown Colonies, the history of Imperialism and Political and Economic Implications of the Slave trade". He had a grasp of the "difficult area of comparative government, and particularly so in regard to the government of the British Empire". Finally, Bunche thought that Williams "exhibited a fine ability toward intelligent analysis of the states and problems of minority peoples under modern institutions".[21] Harris and Locke also wrote a joint letter of recommendation on Williams's behalf. Williams was grateful for the recommendations; he wrote to Bunche and Harris to thank them, and he sincerely believed that their letters would work to secure him a position at Howard University.[22]

In Locke and Harris's letter, they proposed offering Williams a joint appointment in the Departments of Philosophy and Economics, with his salary divided between the two respective budgets and a concomitant division of teaching time by mutual agreement. They stressed that Williams, as a student at Oxford, "had the broadest of training in institutions having this policy of the close correlation of several social studies". They suggested that he could teach courses in social philosophy and institutional economics. They pointed out that he was known to both of them "as a man eminently suited to the task they had outlined", and he held honours degrees from Oxford University. By the fall of 1936, Williams had an application on file in the dean's office.[23]

Edward P. Davis, the dean at Howard University, was impressed. He wrote to Bunche in London saying that Williams "must be a man with ability bordering on genius to have made an impression on three specialists in three different fields". Regrettably, Williams did not get the position. Davis wrote to Bunche explaining that the board of trustees could not sanction his employment, but Davis hoped that they could use his services later.[24] Williams was disappointed about being turned down for the position. He had already been stressed trying to get his dissertation typed, since Elsie, his wife and typist, had bronchitis. After the news from Howard University, Williams described himself as being in "a hell of a mess".[25]

Williams knew that racial considerations would keep him from ever getting a fellowship at All Souls College, Oxford. Years later, he would say that the race question was very much in evidence at Oxford. It was much less overt and much less vulgar than in the United States – to be sure, Oxford, England, should not be confused with Oxford, Mississippi – but he felt racial prejudice everywhere, from the cricket field to the dining hall. The year 1936 was proving to be a difficult year for Williams. In order to meet his financial obligations, he had to take a job teaching English to Burmese students at Oxford.[26] In late 1936, after a year of pursing a second undergraduate degree, Williams abandoned his philosophy, economics and politics studies and switched to research for a doctoral degree. Williams read history because it was the best preparation for politics. This decision turned out to be the most critical one in Williams's academic career and helped to inform his anti-colonial thinking. He later regarded it as the most important decision that he made in his life.[27]

From 1936 to 1938, while the West Indian worker unrest was unfolding, Williams was busy conducting his research at the Public Record Office, the British Museum and the Rhodes Library – however, he found time to attend James's and Padmore's anti-colonial meetings, read their magazines and pamphlets, and take part in their discussions.[28] Williams also attended lectures with a radical perspective at the WASU.[29] This organization was founded in August 1925 to establish a hostel for and forge unity among West African students, but, in succeeding years, it came to embrace all African students. It joined with other black organizations to confront the common problems of racism and colour prejudice. Lapido Solanke, a Nigerian, became the secretary-general and editor of the organization's journal, *Wasu*. The magazine began publication in 1926 and included articles by prominent supporters from the United States, including Alain Locke. Locke and Padmore had always shared an interest "in starting a youth movement among Negro Students – Africans, West Indians + Afro-Americans – for the purpose of developing a spirit of brotherhood & better understanding".[30]

In the summer of 1928, Locke delivered an address at WASU entitled "Afro

Americans and West Africans: A New Understanding".[31] WASU had become a training ground for future political leaders, as well as an important anti-colonial organization engaging in a wide range of anti-colonial activities.[32] At WASU's gatherings, Williams met and often mingled with African and Caribbean activists and intellectuals such as W. Arthur Lewis, Johnstone Kenyatta, Isaac Theophilus Akunna Wallace-Johnson, Benjamin Nnamdi Azikiwe, T.R. Makonnen and Amy Ashwood Garvey. The discussions that took place among these people were important in creating international anti-colonial networks and liberation groups on both sides of the Atlantic. Many of them would lead movements in their native countries and become leaders in their independent nations. These men and women gave Williams insights into their pan-African ideology.[33]

To be sure, Padmore was a person "to whom the political-inclined among the blacks gravitated".[34] The summer before Williams arrived in Britain, Padmore wrote to him and sent him a copy of the *Negro Worker*. Padmore had been motivated to do this after talking in London with Ivan Stewart Lloyd, who was a medical student at Edinburgh University and a future People's National Party leader in Jamaica. Lloyd told Padmore that Williams had "more interest in socio-economic matters than" he previously had. Padmore was pleased to learn of Williams's newfound interest. He laughingly wrote to Cyril C. Ollivierre, an old Trinidadian friend, "Well, everybody grows up some day & the crisis is accelerating this growth in many cases."[35] Throughout Williams's stay in Britain, he was "in constant touch" with Padmore, who emerged as the key "Negro" revolutionary in London. James contended that "the foundations of the approach to politics of all budding leaders in the African and other Negro colonial territories between 1930 and 1938 were laid by George Padmore".[36] By 1942, Padmore saw himself "as a sort of 'Elder Statesman' & 'Father Adviser' to the Leftward elements among the West African Student Union".[37] Williams attended informal evening classes at Padmore's flat where he, Prince Hosea Akiiki Nyabongo, W. Arthur Lewis and others would discuss the struggles of colonial societies.[38] Nyabongo was studying for his doctorate at Oxford, and Lewis was pursing his degree at the London School of Economics;[39] Nyabongo lived intermittently with Padmore.[40] But Williams "avoided all the wishy-washy political movements of the day, whatever their label".[41] He was not a joiner – but, like Bunche, he was occasionally an outsider on the inside within leftist circles.[42] By attending these meetings, Williams's anti-colonial views were informed and enlarged, against the backdrop of the Italo-Ethiopian War and the labour unrest in Trinidad. Williams wrote about his long conversations with Padmore. He was his political sparring partner, friend and confidant. When Elsie could not complete the typing of his dissertation, Padmore came to his aid, recommending a typist, whom Williams hired and whom he called "a bloody old cow from Underwood's who couldn't spell damn, was impudent etc.". The woman eventually walked out.[43]

The organizations that existed when Williams arrived in Britain were small but interconnected.[44] The black population was also small: according to the 1930s census, there were 5,232 African natives and 8,595 West Indians living in England. The LCP and other organizations had always pooled their resources; they would not have been able to accomplish anything otherwise.[45] Padmore had complained to W.E.B. Du Bois, the prominent African American intellectual and activist, that "our difficultly is that we have not enough cadres in England who can afford sufficient time to carrying out the work".[46] Padmore understood that the LCP gave the illusion of being a mass organization. While not undermining its importance, he understood its limitations.[47]

Founded in March 1931 at the YMCA, the LCP sought to promote an understanding between the white and coloured peoples in Britain. It advanced the economic, educational, political and social interests of black people and advocated self-government for the West Indian and African colonies. The LCP aspired to be a vehicle for transnational black unity and interracial harmony and cooperation. It claimed the rights of citizenship for blacks in the metropole as well as in the colonies. It demanded equal opportunity for all peoples.[48] The founder was Harold Moody, a Jamaican physician. Moody and his organization were "conservative, especially when it came to trade unions and communism".[49] The LCP had a membership chiefly comprised of students, but it also focused on the concerns of black professionals. Its journal was called the *Keys*.[50]

The LCP had close ties with African American historians. Charles H. Wesley, professor of history at Howard University, was one of its founders, and Carter G. Woodson, founder of the Association for the Study of Negro Life and History, addressed the organization and later wrote a review of Williams's *Capitalism and Slavery*, where he identified the work as representing "the beginning of the scientific study of slavery from the international point of view".[51] Woodson argued that, in most cases, authors who wrote on slavery did not have "the mental grasp of the meaning of the social, commercial and industrial factors involved; and they have been too near to the age discussed or too closely connected by ties of blood with the participants in the slave trade and slavery". He felt that, based on his Oxford studies, Williams had a unique advantage in undertaking the task to write a scholarly and scientific account of the subject.[52] Woodson's review also explicitly treated *Capitalism and Slavery* as an anti-colonialist study.

The *Keys* provided an outlet for Williams to get his ideas into print. More importantly, it was his first opportunity to express the perspective advanced in his dissertation without having to adjust to his thesis committee's preferences. In the October–December 1938 issue, an article appeared titled "That Emancipation Complex", signed by "E.W.". Labelling the "emancipation complex" as "the spread of persistent propaganda to the effect that abolition was a gift from heaven by a few reformers", his objective was "to prick that 'emancipation bubble' – both in terms of the conventional wisdom that British humanitarianism produced emancipation and that emancipation had brought freedom for the ex-slaves".[53] In its similar treatment of the subject, Woodson saw Williams's *Capitalism and Slavery* as a weapon in the struggle against colonialism.[54] Years later, Williams used his thesis "that Britain had exploited black labour and despoiled the West Indies to promote its own economic well-being as a weapon to demand more British aid when he became the prime minister of Trinidad and Tobago".[55]

In 1964, Claudia Jones, editor of the *West Indian Gazette* and Trinidadian-born activist, wrote a critique of *Capitalism and Slavery*.[56] Her review came upon the book's first publication in England, even though it had appeared twenty years before in the United States.[57] Jones connected the significance of the twenty-year-old work to the present-day conditions of her readers. She argued that black leaders should acquaint West Indians, Africans and Asians with their respective histories and cultural heritages. She was critical of "pseudo-intellectuals" who ignored or were unaware of the significance of cultural heritage in the search for a usable racial identity for black people. Indeed, she argued that black people had equated the history of English imperialism with their history. This lack of historical perspective was at the root, as Eric Williams correctly noted, of a society that eulogized the colonialists and whose knowledge of West Indian history was limited to that of the Anglo-Saxon conquests. Jones noted that the task before them was to learn the authentic history of the Caribbean, of the Morant Bay Rebellion, of the maroons, of the early labour struggles of Captain Andrew Arthur Cipriani, of trade unionism, of West Indian patriots and all the struggles that created the preconditions that led to the contemporary struggles for nationhood.[58]

As Jones saw it, black people's history should centre on some under-standing of *Capitalism and Slavery*. She concurred with Williams's thesis that slavery was abolished because of capitalist imperatives and "not as traditionally claimed, for humanitarian measures". Jones noted Williams's observation that the "British humanitarians were a brilliant band", but they "seriously misunderstood, sacrificed scholarship to sentimentality", and "placed faith before reason". She felt that he correctly argued that "British abolitionists confined their condemnation of slavery 'only to Negroes . . . in the British West Indies' and not the system as a whole". Williams further argued that "wage labour had become more profitable than slave labour" – but slave labour was intricately intertwined with the sugar preferences of West Indian planters. "The abolitionists supported the view that the West Indian sugar monopoly was unsound in theory: It was unprofitable in practice. Slavery had to be destroyed in order to destroy the West Indian sugar monopoly."[59]

Within their mentor-student relationship, Williams and C.L.R. James shared and promoted many ideas. Together, they spent countless hours reading Aristotle, Hobbes and Rousseau as well as discussing West Indian history and history in general. James recalled Williams sending his papers from Oxford on Rousseau, Plato and Aristotle for James's comment. It is likely that James influenced Williams's appreciation of literature, art and drama as well as his views on Britain's response to the Haitian slave revolt. Years later, James insisted that Williams did nothing without consulting him.[60]

As the study of literature began vanishing from the centrality of James's consciousness, it was replaced by political philosophy. James's politics were being radicalized at the same time that he was playing an increasing role in influencing and shaping Williams's political ideology. Between 1936 and 1938, as Williams conducted his research for his dissertation, he was assisting James with his research on *The Black Jacobins*. In 1936, Williams accompanied James to the Bibliothéque Nationale in Paris, where they also met Tiemoko Garan Kouyaté, "a prominent French Negro Communist". James spent three to four months in the archives in Paris in the second half of 1936. By aiding James in his research, Williams was exposed to manuscript sources, Marxist theory and a number of black African radicals.[61] Some of the fruits of this research would be published by Makonnen, who had created a space for black writers in Britain. Makonnen raised the capital to set up the Pan-African Publishing Company, specializing in anti-colonial materials, all of which served as part of the bases for the modern black anti-colonial movement. Eventually, he published Eric Williams's *The Negro in the Caribbean*.[62]

Williams's *The Negro in the Caribbean* was an assault on colonial rule in the Caribbean.[63] It began with a discussion on the early economic system of the West Indies and its historical relation to slavery, showing the effects of sugar cane production upon the social and political structures in the islands. He had developed much of his argument in *Capitalism and Slavery*. Williams advocated for the formation of a coalition of the working class, the anti-imperialist classes and the national bourgeoisie to contest the imperial presence in the islands. He maintained that this anti-colonial national liberation movement was necessary to develop a strong national bourgeoisie that would be capable of protecting the people's interests for as long as possible, even after independence. He understood that the old colour-class social order was being undermined by the emergence of a new class-based militancy spawned by the Maritime Union and Oilfields Workers' Trade Union in Trinidad. The mostly brown-skinned middle class had to join forces with the workers. The labour and nationalist movements were on the march and could not be contained.[64] Politically, however, Williams disclaimed any socialist leanings. Yet *The Negro in the Caribbean* did not endear him to the colonial authorities or to the Anglo-American Caribbean Commission where he was working. His superiors were affronted by his opposition to racialism and colonialism.[65]

For a brief period, it seems as though Eric Williams became the advisory editor to the *International African Opinion* after C.L.R. James left for the

United States.[66] James was the editor of the *IAO* until October 1938, when he sailed to the United States "to recuperate from a serious illness and to undertake certain literary work". In James's absence, Makonnen was to act as editor-in-chief, Babalola Wilkey of Nigeria would be the business editor and Jomo Kenyatta would be in charge of the IASB. But problems soon arose: Makonnen resigned his position and Wilkey was expelled "from its ranks for political unreliability".[67] William Harrison, a black American who was engaged in postgraduate studies at the London School of Economics, stepped into the breach and helped with editing.[68]

The IASB was facing other difficulties as well. As the threat of World War II grew, the IASB was placed under rigid surveillance by the authorities, and every obstacle was put in its path to prevent normal functioning. Friends in influential circles advised Padmore to flee because it was expected that, as soon as war was declared, the IASB would be completely suppressed and its members placed in internment. Padmore's political work and his pronounced anti-imperialist views made him an official target. It was natural that, as the threat of war increased, Padmore and his organization would be the first to feel the effects of repression which were invariably associated with war fever. Williams, too, was concerned about the situation, but he did not express the same level of anxiety as Padmore;[69] unlike Padmore, Williams did not take any precautionary measures to protect essential documents or himself.

Padmore was advised to leave England "before the frontiers were closed" and to safeguard his own freedom so that he could continue to be of some service to black "people in precisely the circumstances where they most need aid and advice". However, in doing so, Padmore confronted a variety of obstacles. He was barred from entering the United States, but had managed to secure a visa for Haiti; "the consul was a very race-conscious fellow, a great admirer of what" the IASB was doing for the race. Padmore cabled Locke for help, and he and other Howard faculty members responded immediately. But by 3 October 1938, the storm had abated, at least temporarily. Padmore put off going to Haiti, opting instead to journey to America as soon as he could get somebody to post a bond for him. Writing to Locke, he said that he was still carrying on his "shoulders the responsibilities of a great cause".[70] In his reply, Locke wrote that he did not have any assets and was unable to post a bond for Padmore. He informed Padmore that there was a wave of suspicion of all foreign agents in the United States, advising him instead to proceed with his work in London as long as there was "a clear international sky". For money, Locke suggested that Padmore and Eric Williams collaborate on writing a pamphlet about West Indian affairs.[71]

Williams soon wrote to Locke, telling him that he and Padmore had agreed to write the pamphlet.[72] By March 1939, Williams, like Padmore, was trying to avoid the disruptions occasioned by war or the threat of it.[73] The IASB's operations were moved to the same address as the headquarters of the Independent Labour Party under the auspices of Padmore. He remained in command of the IASB but was being drawn closer into the ranks of the ILP, and soon he became virtually in charge of the ILP's activities dealing with the peoples of African descent.[74] It was during this period that Padmore was short of assistance; Williams probably stepped in to help Padmore with the affairs of the *IAO* while working on the pamphlet. He was available because he had finished his graduate studies and did not have a university position.

During this period, Williams travelled and did research on current issues in the West Indies, which he published in the *Keys* under his name, in addition to some pieces in the *IAO* under the pseudonym E.E.[75] Writing for the *IAO* fulfilled Williams's political desire to use historical evidence to draw conclusions that showed the capacity of the black West Indians for "advancement and estimate to what extent his white master has fulfilled his self-imposed mission of civilization and trusteeship".[76] Using the initials E.E., Williams wrote a review of journalist Arthur Calder-Marshall's *Glory Dead* that discussed the 1937 strikes in Trinidad. He began his review by quoting Lloyd George's "description of the West Indies as the slums of the Empire". Williams wrote that Calder-Marshall's book described the slums of Trinidad as "a timely exposure of the foulness of democracy's nest",[77] and he concluded that the book was "no Cook's tour on which this shrewd observer and racy writer" took him. The book dealt with the protest of the workers, led by Tubal Uriah "Buzz" Butler, who had inspired it, and the East Indian Adrian Cola Rienzi, who had called attention to the social conditions in the island.[78]

Williams found that the weakest part of the book was the discussion of the vital questions of politics. While the author did call for an "extension of the franchise", Williams was insistent on the principle that "there must be full adult suffrage and payment of councillors". He argued that "only full self government will remedy the gross anomaly. . . . [T]hat is the only solution". Undoubtedly, the achievement of self-government was the foundation upon which Williams placed the development of an anti-colonial society. But Williams did agree with Calder-Marshall's point in *Glory Dead* that the 1937 Trinidadian strikes were caused by the increasing cost of living as well as the "British betrayal of Abyssinia".[79]

Continuing to use the pseudonym "E.E.", Williams wrote about the relationship between compulsory education and self-determination. Williams wrote that the British West Indies, like other colonies, were an employer's paradise, where the defenceless working classes were exposed to the worst forms of exploitation. He thought one of the most crying evils in the society was child labour. Child labour persisted and compulsory education remained unenforced because employers wanted to maintain exploitative conditions. There was a fear that an improvement in educational levels would raise wages and reduce the supply of labour. Williams saw compulsory education as a fundamental tenet of a democracy. Self-government and national independence were central themes in his early writings. Introducing compulsory education was one of Williams's first policy measures when he assumed the mantle of prime minister of Trinidad and Tobago.[80]

In 1939, the IASB published a pamphlet, *The West Indies To-day*, written by Williams. In the pamphlet, Williams not only informed the British public about conditions in the colonies but also laid out a strategy for creating an anti-colonial society.[81] The pamphlet provided an invaluable glimpse into the genesis of Williams's anti-colonial thinking. As in *The Negro in the Caribbean*, the pamphlet opened with a discussion of the early economic system of the West Indies in its historical relation to slavery. Williams repeated the argument laid out in *Capitalism and Slavery* that the mother country owed these colonies a huge debt. He explained that vast wealth was raised in the West Indies but was not used to develop the islands culturally or economically. Most of it went to Britain, where it helped to finance the Industrial Revolution, to build beautiful homes and country houses, and to fill the pockets of the famous West Indian planters who dominated Westminster in the eighteenth century. Then, "when depression set in nothing was left of their former greatness to save the islands from poverty". He concluded that trade unionism was the primary weapon in the fight for economic emancipation but reminded workers that "their economic struggle cannot be divorced from their political aspirations".[82]

Williams sought to address racial and class prejudices within the context of an anti-colonial epistemology. He wrote that it was "indeed safe to say that race would not play much part in West Indian affairs if whites did not rule". In this regard, Williams echoed his argument in *Capitalism and Slavery* that anti-black or anti-African racism was a consequence of the Atlantic slave trade rather than its cause. He expanded upon this point in *The West Indies To-day* by illustrating that whites openly practised colour prejudice and sought special preserves for themselves, and thus he asserted that the racial factor could not be excluded from any study of West Indian life. Then he introduced a class analysis by identifying whites as an aristocracy that dominated everything – agriculture, commerce, industry, government, religion and social life. They were not merely birds of passage, since many of them descended from families that had lived in the islands for more than a century.[83]

The Ethiopian question marked a significant stage in Williams's development of an anti-colonial political consciousness.[84] Ethiopia was an African nation, and its defeat symbolized the final victory of whites over blacks. In 1937, after the Addis Ababa massacre in which over six thousand men, women and children were slaughtered by Italians, Williams spoke at several protest meetings in London. He was at the centre of the struggle against imperialism at the Aggrey House, and he advocated for the League of Nations to support Ethiopia.[85] Mussolini's attack on Ethiopia had drawn Williams into overt political activity; it has been claimed that this accounted for his initial entry into the political arena.[86] In the *IAO*, Williams wrote that the "British's betrayal of Abyssinia", the agitation for freedom and the increasing cost of living as well as the expressed desire for more militant trade unions caused the 1937 Trinidadian strikes.[87] He began to imagine anti-imperialist mass movements arising among "coloured" peoples in Trinidad connected with the Abyssinian crisis, creating a firm alliance between the international working-class movement and suppressed peoples everywhere.[88]

Using the Italo-Ethiopian crisis as his example, Williams argued that a black nation-state would retain, at best, an illusion of independence and its future would remain in doubt as long as the alleged racial inferiority of non-Europeans could be used to legitimize the violation of another nation's sovereignty. Consequently, the anti-colonial struggle must include attacks on capitalism, imperialism, fascism and racism. Mussolini's aggression in Ethiopia, the only independent African state to avoid European penetration, was equated by Williams with racism and a violation of African sovereignty. He maintained that anti-colonialism could not be separated from racial justice. Williams concluded that the major powers' approach to the Abyssinian crisis demonstrated that the position of the sovereign African state within the global family of nations was analogous to that of colonial subjects in the British Empire.[89]

Williams, the British left and the black community were enraged with Britain's non-interventionist position and with its arrogant attitude about the empire while proclaiming the virtues of indirect rule and strong opposition to independent movements.[90] Williams "pooh-poohed" Reginald Coupland's lecture at Oxford where he maintained that "the British would do justice to Africa because they are heirs and guardians of a great tradition". Coupland's assertion forced Williams to rethink that great tradition. He concluded that Britain was not going to do justice to the West Indians, because the Hoare-Laval peace plan was irreconcilable with justice for Ethiopia.[91]

The Italian invasion of Abyssinia galvanized black anti-colonial intellectuals and activists in England into forming the International African Friends of Ethiopia, thereby continuing a trend in pan-Africanism. James started the organization along with Amy Ashwood Garvey, Ras T. Makonnen and others. W. Arthur Lewis and other students like Williams joined IAFE in their activities.[92] The group was founded in the summer of 1935 after Padmore's article "Ethiopia and World Politics" was published in the *Crisis*, the organ of the National Association for the Advancement of Colored People.[93]

"Ethiopia and World Politics" was the first article of Padmore's to appear in the *Crisis* after his expulsion from the Communist Party. Padmore's concern over Ethiopia was clearly evident in the article. He condemned the cynicism of the Western powers and their failure to help Ethiopia. He called for support for Ethiopia, stressing that it was "the duty of every black man and woman to render the maximum moral and material support to" Ethiopia. In response to his call, the IAFE was formed, and, by August, there were large demonstrations in Trafalgar Square as well as in Harlem. Arnold Ward of the NWA said that Padmore's article was widely read by blacks in London and was directly connected with the political activism against Italian aggression in Abyssinia.[94] In this way, Padmore was the spiritual sponsor of the IAFE. The IAFE was viewed initially as having only slightly anti-imperialist tendencies, but it moved considerably left.[95]

Amy Ashwood Garvey, who was the first wife of Marcus Garvey, was intensively involved in the activities promoted by the IAFE. Her path crossed with Williams; they were well known to each other.[96] She was the sole proprietor of a fashionable little restaurant on New Oxford Street called the International Afro Restaurant, where race intellectuals, students and theatrical people from all parts of the world could rendezvous and enjoy home-cooked dishes. It was a restaurant by day and a think tank by night. Then, in the summer of 1936, it became a full-fledged nightclub with the same mission. It was reorganized with the help of Rudolph Dunbar and Sam Manning, took on the name the Florence Mills Social Club and was located on Carnaby Street.[97] Amy Ashwood provided a milieu where young people and seasoned veterans could prepare for a future of struggle against imperialism. She understood that the struggle "would demand the highest sacrifices of leadership and statesmanship".[98] Amy Ashwood was "an integral part of all the political happenings swirling around the restaurant". The IAFE was founded by James at the International Afro Restaurant from an ad hoc committee convened by Padmore. Meetings were held at the restaurant, and Amy Ashwood organized meetings throughout the country on behalf of the IAFE. When peace was mentioned to her while she was on a train from Liverpool, she retorted with a shade more scorn than sorrow in her voice: "It is too late. Now we will fight, Ethiopia will triumph."[99]

The International Afro Restaurant and the Florence Mills Social Club represented a new era in black nationalism. It was more than a nightclub and restaurant; it was a place that provided "tribal fellowship", love and support to "black people who needed shelter from the stress and strain of living" in the mother country. "It was an economic turnstile that earned from the rich and fed the poor." It was commonplace "to see prominent race leaders hotly engaged in ideological disputes while sipping a pot of tea". Padmore attended London's "coloured" nightclubs, but used these occasions as sources for his "bread-and-butter" journalism. Padmore, like Williams and others, found time for socializing, but the content of the discussion or the purpose of an evening of entertainment often returned to political subjects.[100] These various encounters stimulated political thinking and imagination about the future of colonial societies. They were the "junction box".[101]

Williams acknowledged the role of Amy Ashwood in the rise of Garveyism when he wrote about Marcus Garvey in *The Negro in the Caribbean*. He credited Marcus and Amy with the energy and ability to use the upheavals in the world as a basis for the creation of significant mass movements. Amy's dedication to the international mission of Garveyism was not missed by Williams. Garveyism had helped to bring black people to a new level of racial and cultural consciousness.[102] Williams and many other starved "students sated their sagging" stomachs because of the generosity of Amy Ashwood, Sam Manning and Rudolph Dunbar.[103]

The IAFE meeting held at Farrington Memorial Hall on 28 July 1935 was described as a "gigantic meeting".[104] It was presided over by Amy Ashwood. The speakers were all black, and they represented several African and West Indian territories. The content of the speeches fell into two categories. First, there were those aspects of the speeches stressing that the "eyes of the colored races all over the world were watching Abyssinia, and the results of any attack, whether successful or not, might easily be to awaken at last an active desire to combine against European domination". Second, there were those speeches suggesting that the Italian-Abyssinia dispute had graver issues embedded in "such matters as the sanctity of treaties and the rights of an independent people to defend themselves against aggression".[105]

Williams "regularly attended these meetings, even appeared on the speaker's platform".[106] It is reasonable to assume that he was one of the speakers or at least that he was present in the audience, since his godfather, an acknowledged founder of the West Indies Federation, T. Albert Marryshow, was among the speakers.[107] Marryshow was a member of the legislative council of Grenada and vice-president of the IAFE. He warned that if the League of Nations remained silent in the face of the attack on Abyssinia, "coloured races would be under no illusion as to the cruel destiny mapped out for them by others". He reminded the audience that "the British Empire was in racial make-up mainly a 'coloured' empire". And for this reason, "the Empire was safe and secure only in so far as 'coloured' people were safe and secure, prosperous and progressive".[108]

Williams would have also heard Samuel R. Wood and Chief George E. Moore of the Gold Coast Aborigines' Rights Protection Society on their deputation to England, because they, too, spoke at the meeting.[109] Wood and Moore had come to protest against certain laws, especially the right of the government to confiscate literature that it deemed seditious, as well as to demand constitutional reform.[110] On Sunday, 25 August 1935, at Trafalgar Square, the IAFE held its first open-air meeting.[111] The *Chicago Defender* reported that the meeting "drew heavily on London's Race population which found itself fortified by its white citizens" and that it was one of the largest open-air mass meetings held in England since World War I.[112] The *Guardian* reported that there were about seventy black speakers.[113]

Amy Ashwood also spoke at this meeting. She used her "oratorical skills to dramatize the moral failure of Britain and her Western allies who preferred a policy of appeasement and delay rather than to attack the unjust fascist territorial expansion in Africa when people everywhere were seeking freedom".[114] Amy Ashwood shared the same position as Williams when she urged the League of Nations to take measures to restrain Italy from breaking international law.[115] She "electrified the mammoth gathering of protesters and solicited their support to stand behind Ethiopia's demand for international justice".[116] Her voice was loud and powerful – as it needed to be, because regardless of the size of the group, police regulations did not allow the use of amplifiers, so the speakers were actually limited by the range of their voices. It took a powerful voice to reach the crowd "amidst the noise of traffic, the buzzy talk, the cries of sellers of ice cream and a score of different Socialist, Communist, and fascist Magazines".[117] Williams was exposed to an array of open-air oratory at Trafalgar Square and Hyde Park – a practice that he would later emulate in Woodford Square, Port of Spain, to educate the Trinidadian citizenry. At times, Williams would speak to over twenty thousand people as they stood in silence. Claudia Jones described Williams as an able speaker, a debater who could evoke and provoke new ideas. He was quick at repartee and quick to deflect questions.[118]

In the spring or summer of 1935, Padmore unexpectedly came to James's flat and told him that he had broken with the Kremlin and would henceforth be living permanently in England.[119] With Padmore's involvement with the "junction box", there was a dramatic increase in political organizing and agitation.[120] He emphasized that political liberation was not a gift from London or other colonial powers, insisting that the black masses were the agents of their own liberation.[121] He said that he left the Communist Party because the party would betray black interests when they conflicted with Soviet policy. He maintained that independence should be immediate, regardless of a colony's social and cultural development.[122] The party line, however, was that the Comintern expelled Padmore for his connections with agents provocateurs, for his ties with bourgeois organizations on the question of Liberia and for "false" positions on the national question; instead of class unity, he promoted race unity.[123] Padmore, despite these criticisms, retained the support of Africans and West Indians. By no means did it weaken the relationship that he had with Williams; if anything, it might have strengthened their friendship.[124]

Padmore and James, like Williams, sought to transform colonial states into independent national states.[125] In *The Negro in the Caribbean* and his review of Calder-Marshall's *Glory Dead*, Williams argued that only full self-government with a rational economy would remedy the gross injustice that existed in colonial areas.[126] Williams and Padmore agreed that self-determination was not simply a matter of guaranteeing democratic rights or removing the barriers to black political power, nor was it a matter of creating a nation-state wherever black people found themselves to be an oppressed majority. These were partial demands. The struggle was about promoting and supporting a people's movement that could lead to constructing anti-colonial societies rather than decolonized units.[127]

Against the backdrop of the Abyssinia War and the renewed expression of political and economic discontent in the British West Indies and Africa, disparate black intellectuals and workers came together to form a new alliance – the International African Service Bureau. As interest in Ethiopia continued, the International African Friends of Ethiopia helped to spawn a broader movement that was housed in the IASB. The IASB became a "regular mecca for all revolutionaries from all the colonies and a rendezvous for the Left".[128] Williams characterized the group as an anti-imperialist group that was well known in the city.[129] The new organization was an advocate for democratic rights, liberties and self-determination. It linked protest to the aggressive dissemination of news. This was predicated on the belief that information empowered people.[130]

The consensus at the time was that "London was the critical point of contact where Pan African, socialist and anti-colonial ideas were shared and enlarged".[131] The IASB was an organization that sought "to gain the support of all Britons, regardless of party affiliation, in agitating for constitutional reforms, such as granting of freedom of speech, press, assembly and movement, and other democratic rights" which were denied to millions of loyal black subjects all over the world.[132] The Colonial Office believed that the IASB was guided by Trotskyite and Marxist principles because of its association with Padmore and James. It was, however, an organization which represented the democratic rights of colonial peoples and their struggle for autonomy.[133]

After Williams secured his position with the Anglo-American Caribbean Commission, he began blurring his affiliation with the IASB because of its anti-imperialist stance. This began with denying that he had authored *The West Indies To-day* and the circumstances surrounding the publication of *The Negro in the Caribbean*. By the mid-1940s, Williams believed that the publication of his work under the auspices of the IASB "might give rise to embarrassment".[134]

He told the Anglo-American Commission that he had merely read the IASB's *The West Indies To-day* booklet. He understated the weight of his editorial pen. Williams and Padmore had collaborated on the pamphlet. Williams was paid by Howard University and did most of the work – he provided the historical material that he had derived from the research for his thesis, while Padmore gave the contemporary, economic and political perspectives. Padmore had preferred that Williams assume the whole job and gain the requisite experience.[135] Williams hoped that the booklet would "fill a great void" and thought that "a larger study of these interesting colonies was needed". He wrote to Locke saying that he was trying to persuade the International Labour Office to give him a commission to do a report on the islands for them. He lamented that the only difficulty was that such a report must be purely factual and unbiased.[136]

When Williams took the part-time position at the Anglo-American Caribbean Commission, he had volunteered to show the commission anything he intended to publish or say in a lecture. He said that he did this in order to protect himself from inaccurate accounts of his writings. Williams wanted his book published, but felt that, in his present position with the commission, the publication of his book under the auspices of the IASB might prove embarrassing. To protect himself, he maintained that the manuscript was out of his control. Williams wrote a letter to the commission that implied that the Pan-African Publishing Company, affiliated with the IASB, had practically begged him to publish his study with them. He wrote that, before he was fully connected with the commission, he had been approached by the IASB for permission to publish an English edition of *The Negro in the Caribbean*. He gave his consent when he was a private citizen, but then the publication of the book was delayed due to a shortage of paper. He was eventually notified that the IASB was going ahead and wanted his "consent for the necessary changes in statistics that would be appropriate for an English public".[137]

At the commission's request, Williams wrote a letter to Padmore requesting that a prefatory note be inserted in the book to the effect that he had never been a member of the IASB, nor did he subscribe to its views and policies. Padmore, too, was concerned about having Williams's name being directly linked with the IASB since a red-phobia loomed over the Western political hemisphere. Padmore complied with Williams's request. He carefully wrote in the foreword of *The Negro in the Caribbean* that Williams had never been a member of the IASB and did not "necessarily endorse its aims and objects". On the inside back cover of the book, there was an advertisement for the IASB that asked: "What is the International African Service Bureau?"[138] As Williams distanced himself from the leftist groups, he made no mention of this advertisement. He was primarily concerned about avoiding association with communism.[139]

Nonetheless, in December 1948, Williams was accused of being a communist. The Federal Bureau of Investigation soon privately cleared him of any suspicion, but he felt compelled to state his case publicly. In his famous "Let Down My Bucket" speech that he delivered after leaving the Anglo-American Commission in June 1955, he told the crowd in Port of Spain that he had never been connected with any political organization at all, except that, when he was at Oxford, he had regularly attended meetings held by the Indian nationalist students.[140] On the face of it, Padmore's words in the foreword to *The Negro in the Caribbean* were intended to place some distance between Williams and the political activities and positions of the IASB. But it was common knowledge that an informal relationship between James, Padmore and Williams continued to flourish. They constantly exchanged facts and ideas about all sorts of political subjects.[141]

The Colonial Office agreed with the sentiment among blacks in London that the IASB was the most active organization working for the "rights of coloured people" and particularly West Indian affairs.[142] The IASB continued the tradition of one of its parent organizations, the IAFE, by endeavouring "to make known to the British people the real wishes, needs and problems of Africans and people of African descent within the Empire".[143] By 1937, the IASB and outsiders/insiders like Williams began to formulate a new ideology of colonial liberation and racial equality designed to challenge existing ideological constructs, including communism.[144] In *The West Indies To-day,* Williams wrote that one could not say how long it would take before "black humanity" would come to the shores of the Caribbean, "but the prospect is a challenge which West Indians, at home and abroad will not leave unanswered".[145] Williams and others in this group were constructing an ideology of colonial liberation and racial equality that was turning increasingly towards self-reliance and non-alignment.[146]

The colonial event that aroused the most publicity and concern in the late 1930s was the workers' unrest in the Caribbean.[147] The turmoil informed Williams's thinking on the role of intellectuals in the labour movement and the future of the West Indies. In *The West Indies To-day,* Williams was critical of the overwhelming majority of coloured intellectuals for neglecting and deserting the masses of their fellow countrymen: "The common people have taken the situation into their own hands and have indicated that they are no longer prepared to acquiesce silently in their present intolerable conditions." Williams wrote that the labour disturbances, strikes and riots had forced intellectuals to think about their role in the struggle to gain economic and social emancipation and political self-determination.[148]

In an editorial in the *IAO,* Williams wrote that West Indian intellectuals owed it to themselves and their people to become conscious of the true destiny of their countries. He suggested that West Indian intellectuals approach the workers' movement with a true recognition of the collective strength, dignity and worth of the masses. But he cautioned intellectuals not to approach the movement to guide it as horses between the shafts. He pointed out that "the masses are the raw material for the political activity of the few" and that "the struggle for democratic rights must lead to the political struggle for com-plete West Indian independence leading to the socialist commonwealth".[149]

The Colonial Office suspected that there was a direct relationship between the IASB and the strike leaders in Trinidad. The IASB and those associated with it, such as Williams, were not considered to be independent agents; the Colonial Office thought that the IASB had communist leanings of some sort and that it was a stalking horse for the communists whose aim was "to discredit all 'reformist' and welfare work by employers and oppose any col-laboration with capitalists".[150] The IASB pushed back against this accusation, arguing that, because British imperialists were faced with a wide spread revolt from colonial workers, they took refuge behind their old battle cry of "Bolshe-vik agitators", "Moscow gold", and so on.[151]

The Colonial Office believed that the IASB had also been formed to launch new anti-colonial campaigns. The existence of communism in Britain was one thing, but, in the colonies, it was quite another. Coloured workers were regarded as being more impressionable than other peoples, and there might be a tendency in them towards chronic instability that could make the pot boil over. Trinidad received a fair share of attention from the IASB, because Adrian Cola Rienzi, who was promoting the trade union movement, was seen as working for the organization. The Colonial Office believed that it was no accident that Padmore and James were Trinidadians and that there was a trained party man in Trinidad in the person of Rienzi. Some in the Colonial Office were convinced that the basis for the troubles in June 1937 had been in the making for a number of years through the work of Rienzi, Padmore, James and others.[152] The Colonial Office recognized Padmore as a well-known and able intellectual exponent of anti-imperialism, and they were aware of his influence on those in his circle, like Williams.[153]

Williams identified Rienzi as the most respected trade union leader in Trinidad.[154] Rienzi was affiliated with the NWA. In the *Negro Worker,* he had written that the leaders of the Trinidad Working Man's Association (the only organized workers' movement in Trinidad) had been misled by all kinds of promises from the British reformist politicians. They were now realizing that "the Labour Party, despite its name labour . . . [was] as imperialistic as Tories" and would never support the struggles of the colonial peoples for self-determination.[155]

The Colonial Office agreed with Williams's assessment that Rienzi exercised great influence among the labouring classes, but it did not have any confidence in his leadership. It thought that Rienzi was a dishonest knave who would fall in the near future but who would cause considerable trouble before that occurred.[156] The movement was fighting against powerful obstacles. Employers had the great weapon of victimizing workers, and they had not hesitated to use it. And, as Williams pointed out, labour leaders were shadowed by the police, while sedition laws were applied loosely.[157]

Williams argued that the climax of the labour movement was reached in November 1938 with the convening of the Labour Congress of the West Indies and British Guiana. He concluded that the labour movement was on the march towards making the "West Indies of the future a country where the common man may lead a cultured life in freedom and prosperity".[158] In his review of Calder-Marshall's *Glory Dead,* Williams maintained that the 1937 Trinidadian strikes were also caused by the "British's betrayal of Abyssinia".[159]

The Colonial Office was especially concerned about the meetings the IASB was organizing in connection with the current Trinidadian and Barbadian strikes. Williams's historical analysis of the abolition of the slave system was cited in the speeches at these demonstrations; his ideas had become the language of change.[160] At the 1938 gathering in London, Padmore gave a long discourse on the "conditions existing in the West Indies and appealed to the workers of Great Britain to unite in bringing pressure to bear upon the Government to alleviate the hardships prevalent amongst the negroes in the West Indies and to allow them to have trade unions to fight for them and to safeguard their interests". He concluded by reading a resolution pledging the support and solidarity of the coloured people in London with their brethren in the West Indies.[161] Padmore's resolution was "enthusiastically and unanimously passed". It echoed many of the same sentiments expressed in Williams's review of Calder-Marshall's *Glory Dead.*[162]

Ben Bradley of the Communist Party of Great Britain, who was in charge of colonial affairs, probably understood the political position of the IASB and the mindsets of Padmore and James better than the Colonial Office did. Bradley identified the men of the IASB as Left Socialists. They, like Williams, were "students not of the lying piffle usually taught in schools about the glories of Empire, but of the true facts showing how Empire has been used to destroy independence of weak countries so as to rob the inhabitants of their land" and wealth. Bradley characterized Padmore and James as being "veritable thorns" in the side of Britain because they had established the ideological paradigm that Williams would follow. They were "using their education and ability not to slavishly hymn the praises of England", like so many educated West Indian people, but to expose the empire for what it really was.[163]

However, Bradley was critical of Padmore and James because they had put forward racialist positions that set white against black, which he felt was akin to a fascist ideology. They had opposed the struggle for a united front of all democratic peoples against fascism. For this reason, Bradley believed that Padmore and James had done more harm than good to working-class movements, particularly in the colonies. Their disruptive activities consistently sabotaged the unity between whites and blacks. Bradley was trying to dissuade communist affiliates from adopting the strategy being promoted by Padmore, James and the IASB.[164] For his part, Williams embraced Padmore's and James's radical ideas when it suited him. Williams sometimes indulged in militant and racialist rhetoric but eschewed the socialist label. Residing at the intellectual centre of British imperialism, he believed in an expansive anti-colonial nationalism embedded in liberalism.

The British government appointed a royal commission under the chairmanship of Lord Moyne to investigate conditions in the West Indies after the 1937–38 riots. Williams wrote, in *The West Indian To-day,* that the direct action of the masses forced the secretary of state for the colonies to appoint a royal commission that would inquire into their intolerable conditions and grievances. But Williams did not think that the masses had any illusions that they would "obtain anything positive from the Commission".[165] In early September 1938, a select committee of the IASB, with the aid of West Indian black experts from the LCP and NWA, prepared a memorandum putting the case for workers and peasants before the Royal Commission. The memorandum was approved and presented on behalf of other black organizations in London.[166] The rhetoric of the memorandum linked independence to the Italian invasion of Abyssinia and to the disturbances in the British West Indies, and it declared that West Indian progress depended on "the establishment of democratic government fully representative of people of these territories".[167]

The IASB participated in the writing of the memorandum, but it was critical of the Royal Commission from its inception. On the cover of the August issue of the *IAO*, an article questioned the make-up of the commission. It was emphasized that there was an "overweight of Conservatives" on the commission and that it did not include any "African or person of African descent". The IASB argued, for this reason, that the commission could not inspire any "initial confidence in the success of its efforts". The article pointed out that W. Arthur Lewis would certainly have been qualified as a person of African descent to serve on the commission. He was the first "coloured West Indian" appointed as a lecturer at the London School of Economics and Political Science.[168]

Another article in the *IAO* on the Royal Commission stated that the commission was "a bluff". It pointed out that the government already knew the conditions of people in the West Indies. The *IAO* echoed the demands voiced by Williams in his review of *Glory Dead*, such as that "West Indians must organize themselves and demand (1) a democratic Constitution, and (2) manhood suffrage". It also demanded that the "labour Movement and other friends in England must support them without reservation". The article acknowledged that "a democratic constitution would not solve all the difficulties, but it would put the people on the way to making whoever rules listen to them". It predicted that as long as power rested with the Colonial Office, commissions would conclude that "local whites would cheat" the West Indian people.[169] Williams's fingerprints were all over the *IAO's* article. Evidently, the commissioners did learn something quite devastating; their report contained such severe criticism of the colonial system in the West Indies that it was not made public until after World War II.[170] Lord Moyne's commission was strident in its condemnation of the social and economic policies of the British government. Its findings revealed that a system existed that had taken the wealth of the colonial territories away from their shores and did little to promote the welfare and prosperity of the subject peoples. This conclusion was clearly in line with Williams's anti-colonial propositions.[171]

Williams later wrote that the commission led to a conference, held in Dominica, that called for a constitution based on a federation of the islands and full, elective control of the legislative assemblies. The moving spirits of the conference were Cipriani of Trinidad and Cecil Rawle, a political activist in Dominica. In 1938, a Labour Congress of the West Indies and British

Guiana met in British Guiana and demanded a federation of the territories. The argument was that federation was the indispensable precursor to the attainment of independence.[172]

The Abyssinian crisis and the labour unrest became the lens through which Eric Williams, as a student at Oxford, viewed the empire, colonial violence, conquest and domination. Collectively, the issues of the *Keys, IOA, African Sentinel, Africa and the World, Negro Worker* and *Wasu* – and their numerous articles on of the "rape" of Abyssinia that regularly appeared alongside pieces on the disturbances in the West Indies and West Africa – produced a range of black international activity in London. Their respective organizations, LCP, IAFE, WASU, IASB and NWA, influenced Williams's anticolonial epistemology and provided an outlet for some of his early writings on slavery, the role of West Indian intellectuals and Caribbean conditions. He used the lessons of history to critique the contemporary problems that had been created by colonialism. James pointed out that Williams connected West Indian history with a "surging stream of modern history and political theory" that heretofore was absent; and this marked the genesis of his West Indian nationalism, anti-colonialism and independence.[173] Williams's study of slavery addressed the role of the slave system in the construction of European economies. Variations of Williams's historical analysis of the abolition of the slave system formed the core of the message delivered by James in his speeches at protest rallies. In promoting the well-being of Trinidad and Tobago as head of its government, Williams used his slavery thesis as a weapon to extract concessions from the Colonial Office.

The Williams thesis was a rhetorical voice that fed the demands for self-government and the independence of the colonies. As Carter G. Woodson has suggested, Williams's work was invaluable in imagining what democratic forces were to be devised to replace an imperialism that was mainly concerned with the production of wealth.[174] Williams's academic training influenced his anti-colonialist thinking and his nationalistic outlook.

The 1930s witnessed a dramatic surge in black political organizing and activism in London due to the events in Africa and the Caribbean and to the activities of Padmore and James, who created the space in which Williams could propose, construct and design a reconstituted British Commonwealth of nations as an association of independent and interdependent states. In this ferment seething like an African pot, Williams began to envision an anti-colonial world in terms of discrete, regional units, like the West Indies federation or a united West Africa, that would not obliterate local political identifications. Instead, they would constitute an alternative black sphere through which to confront persistent contradictions of the imperial order and create an alternative transnational politics. He drew connections between racism and colonial exploitation and sought to link attacks on capitalism, imperialism, fascism and racism to an anti-colonial struggle.

James contends that Williams's presence in Europe during the 1930s was an important "accident" in his intellectual development and political training. Williams was influenced by the great political debates that were taking place, and, like others, he sought to include the West Indies in them. James believed that Williams's tenure at Oxford gave him a thorough grounding in these ideas and introduced him to the fundamentals of British parliamentary democracy. He watched Williams as he matured and took West Indian history and political theory to spaces where they had never been intellectually. His nationalism did not begin in 1956 with the genesis of the PNM; it had existed since his days at Oxford – the ideas that animated independence and nationalism were at the very core of his being. James would later challenge Williams's credentials as an intellectual and as an original thinker, but at this point in Williams's life, he praised him fulsomely.[175] In the 1930s, London was a site of intense debate and remarkable collaboration among colonial peoples. Williams's experience with the anti-colonial networks operating in London was just one strand of a much larger story. His willingness to participate in events with those on a more leftist political spectrum was a mark of maturity and tolerance.

Williams made the case for an important role for West Indian intellectuals, like him, in the future leadership of the new independent societies that he imagined. He had absorbed European cultures and political ideologies. The consciousness of his personal equality with anyone "was fortified by his special experiences in England of the thirties". He had seen the anti-colonial case completely triumphant in exposition, debates and discussions. In his own particular field of history, he had overthrown the traditional view, propagated by British historians, on the causes of the abolition of the slave system.[176] Williams profited from his friendships with Padmore, James and others. He embraced their radical ideas when they were in sync with his imagination of an anti-colonial nationalism, and he took advantage of Padmore's Howard University connections. Williams lived at a time that was far removed from slavery, but he recognized its continuing significance for the contemporary societies of the Caribbean and elsewhere. With his PhD in hand, he showed that he was an intellectually gifted black man. When he left London, the "junction box", in 1939, he belonged to a new generation of West Indian intellectuals.

NOTES

1.   C.L.R. James, "A Convention Appraisal: Dr Eric Williams, First Premier of Trinidad and Tobago – A Biographical Sketch", 12 May 1960 (University of Florida, George A. Smathers Libraries, Gainesville, Florida, 2004–2011), 4.

2.   Malcolm Ivan Meredith Nurse (1902/1903–59), later known as George Padmore, was a reporter for the *Weekly Guardian* in Trinidad. He was the son of Hubert Alfonso Nurse a remarkable schoolmaster with a tremendous political mind. In 1924, he went to the United States to study sociology and political science at Fisk University in Nashville, Tennessee. In 1927, he enrolled at New York University but never attended classes. Later, he enrolled in Howard University to attend law school in Washington, DC. At Howard, he was an outspoken student who cultivated relationships with Ralph Bunche and Alain Locke. He became active in the Communist Party and took on the *nom de guerre* George Padmore. It was common for revolutionary figures to adopt false names to hide their identities from the government and to protect their families. In 1929, he went to Moscow, where he was appointed head of the Negro Bureau of the Red International of Labor Unions. Then he became the executive secretary of the International Trade Union Committee of Negro Workers. In this capacity, he wrote six pamphlets and edited the *Negro Worker*. In 1934, he was expelled from the Communist Party. Padmore was a revolutionary figure in the anti-colonial movement. Central to his advocacy was for black people to have political, economic, social and cultural self-determination. For this and related reasons, his conceptualization of pan-Africanism was predicated on a Marxist critique of capitalism. Padmore's political activism and revolutionary visions set the stage for many black states to emerge in the twentieth-century Caribbean and Africa, which is why C.L.R. James referred to him as the Father of African Emancipation.

Cyril Lionel Robert James, "Interview", *Gaither Reporter*, 31 December 2000, 8; James R. Hooker, *Black Revolutionary: George Padmore's Path from Communism To Pan-Africanism* (New York: Frederick A. Praeger, 1967), 6; *Communist and West Indian Labour Disturbances*, 1938, CO 295/606/4; "Hoover Wins H.U. Straw Vote", *Afro-American* (Baltimore, MD), 10 November 1928, 2; "Sir Esme Addresses Howard U. Meeting: Ignores Propaganda by 'Anti-Imperialistic' Youths Which Officials Repudiate", *Washington Post*, 6 December 1928, 24.

3.   *C.L.R. James Report Summary*, 30 January 1934, KV 2/1824; *Description of Cyril Lionel Robert James*, 12 July 1938, KV 2/1824. C.L.R. James (1901/1902–89) was a school friend of George Padmore and a secondary school teacher of Eric Williams. When James was a boy, he and his father used to listen to Padmore's father, H.A. Nurse, with great respect and consideration. Nurse lived in a room filled with books, and James looked upon him as a revolutionary. He was friendly with Padmore, but not as close as they later became in England. In 1929, James went to the United Kingdom. He divided his time between legal studies and journalism. He wrote on cricket for the *Manchester Guardian*. He became a strong advocate of self-determination for blacks in the British West Indies and a bitter enemy of imperialism. He studied law for a period and became an active member of the Independent Labour Party. In 1936, James became an ardent Trotskyist and took an active part in forming the Marxist Group of the Trotskyist Movement. To the dismay of Arnold Ward of the Negro Worker Association, James described himself as "middle-class negro intellectual". *Report on Investigating into the Political Influences with Trinidad Labour Troubles 1937 and Communist Activities Affecting Industrial Interests in British Colonies*, 22 March 1938, CO 295/606/4; C.L.R. James, "Notes on George Padmore" (London: Institute of Commonwealth Studies, 1959), 11–12; James, "Interview", 8.

4.   Carol Polsgrove, *Ending British Rule in Africa: Writers in a Common Cause* (Manchester: Manchester University Press, 2009), 5, 36.

5.   James, "Notes on George Padmore", 46.

6.   Williams sailed on 20 September 1932 to attend Oxford University. In 1931, he won the Island Scholarship and received the Jerningham Gold Medal of Queen's Royal College. His intentions were to study for a bachelor's degree with honours in modern history. Before Williams left Trinidad, he acted as an assistant master at Queen's Royal College from September to December 1931, and then from March to August 1932. He was also a lecturer in English and history at the Government Training College. See "Mr Eric E. Williams: Scholarship Winner in Trinidad off to UK", *Daily Gleaner*, 17 September 1932, 5.

7.   Ken Boodhoo, "Interview of Dr Halsey McShine, Port of Spain, 3 March 1998"; "Interview of Dr Halsey McShine, Port of Spain, 24 July 1997"; "Interview of

Dr and Mrs Dolly and Daughter Hilary by Ken Boodhoo, Pointe-à-Pierre, 27 July 1997", in *The Elusive Eric Williams* (Kingston: Ian Randle, 2001), 58–59; Selwyn D. Ryan, *Eric Williams: The Myth and the Man* (Kingston: University of the West Indies Press, 2009), 790f9.

8. Anna Grimshaw, ed., *Special Delivery: The Letters of C.L.R. James to Constance Webb, 1939–1948 by Constance Webb*, C.L.R. James (Oxford: Blackwell, 1995), 5; Eric Williams, *Inward Hunger: The Education of a Prime Minister* (Princeton, NJ: Markus Wiener, 2006), 22, 33.

9. James, "Notes on George Padmore", 9.

10. Letter from George Padmore to Alain Locke, 17 December 1936, 32 Russell Square, London, WC.1, Alain Locke Papers (ALP), Mooreland Spingarn Research Collection (MSRC), Howard University, Manuscript Division, Washington, DC, Box 164–76 Folder 16; James, "Interview", 8.

11. Kent Worcester, *C.L.R. James: A Political Biography* (Albany: State University of New York Press, 1996), 50.

12. Ken Boodhoo gives the date of Eric and Elsie's marriage as 30 January 1937, while ancestry.com gives it as March 1937 without providing the exact date. Both sources place the marriage in the early half of 1937 and not 1939, as some sources have suggested. Boodhoo, *Elusive Eric Williams*, 51; England and Wales, Marriage Index: 1916–2005 (Provo, UT: Ancestry.com Operations, 2010), accessed 14 July 2016 from ancestry.com.

13. *Nation*, 7 August 1959, n.p.

14. Williams, *Inward Hunger*, 53–54.

15. Colin A. Palmer, *Eric Williams and the Making of the Modern Caribbean* (Chapel Hill: University of North Carolina Press, 2006), 24.

16. Letter to Sir John Maffey, Permanent Under Secretary of State for the Colonies, from Ethel S. Fegan, 24 June 1937, CO 323/1521/2; West African Students' Union: African Hostel Committee, 1936, CO 847/7/2.

17. Eric Williams, *The Negro in the Caribbean* (Washington, DC: Associates in Negro Folk Education, Bronze Booklet Series, 1942; reprint, New York: A & B Book, 1994), 95; Communist Activity in the British West Indies: Report on Investigating, CO 295/606/4.

18. "International African Service Bureau (IASB)", *African Sentinel*, October–November 1937, 4, MEPO 38/91; Ras Makonnen, *Pan-Africanism from Within* (London: Oxford University Press, 1973), 117–19, 120; Kwame Nkrumah, *The Autobiography of Kwame Nkrumah* (London: Panaf, 1957), 37; Hooker, *Black Revolutionary*, 44, 132.

19. Makonnen, *Pan-Africanism from Within*, 128, 145. Tomasi R. Makonnen, or George or Thomas Nathaniel Griffith (1902–83), was born in British Guiana

and probably graduated from Queen's College in Georgetown. Later he went to Texas to study mineralogy, then in 1932 he went to Cornell University in New York. He spent his holidays in Harlem, where he participated in agitation against high rents. He and his West Indian and African friends, including Nnamdi Azikiwe, organized the Libyan Institute, where they presented papers on Africa. He arrived in Britain in January 1936 from Copenhagen and started living with George Padmore. In 1934, Griffiths assisted Padmore in Denmark after he had been sacked by the Comintern and deported from Germany to Denmark. After protesting the Danish exporting mustard to Italy that could have been used to make mustard gas to use on the Ethiopian people, both were deported to London. In 1935, Padmore organized the Pan-African Brotherhood – also known as the Pan-African Federation, Pan-Afro Federation and Pan-Afro League – and Makonnen was the secretary. Later, Makonnen was the publicity officer of the IASB. In the 1940s, he developed a flair for business, and he owned restaurants and a bakery in Manchester. His business connections were advantageous in planning the Pan-African Congress in 1945. See *Report on Investigating*, CO 295/606/4; J. Ayodele Langely, *Pan-Africanism and Nationalism in West Africa 1900–1945* (London: Oxford University Press, 1973), 337n34; Jonathan Derrick, *Africa's "Agitators": Militant Anti-Colonialism in Africa and the West, 1919–1939* (New York: Columbia University Press, 2008), 386; Kenyatta, Cross-Reference, 18 March 1938, KV 2 1797; Letter from T.R. Makonnen to W.E.B. Du Bois, 2 February 1949, William E.B. Du Bois (WEBD) Papers, Special Collections and University Archives, W.E.B. Du Bois Library, University of Massachusetts, Amherst, MA, Microfilm, Reel 64, 206; "Dr Williams in Africa Sees Sandys on BG", *West Indian Gazette*, March 1964, n.p.

20. Postcard from George Padmore to Alain Locke, 20 May 1936, 32 Russell Square, London, WC.1, ALP, Box 164–76 Folder 16; Letter from George Padmore to Alain Locke, 11 October 1938, ALP, Box 164/76 File 16; Letter from Alain Locke to Malcolm [Nurse], 11 October 1938, ALP, Box 164–96 Folder 27.

21. Letter from Ralph Bunche to E.P. Davis, 25 May 1937, Ralph Bunche Papers (RBP), Schomburg Center for Research in Black Culture, Manuscripts, Archives and Rare Books Division, New York Public Library, New York, Box 10 Folder 14.

22. Letter from Eric Williams to Ralph Bunche, 27 May 1937, RBP, Box 10 Folder 14. Williams may have also written Alain Locke thanking him for the letter of recommendation, but this letter has not been located, nor have any references to the letter been cited.

23. Letter from Alain Locke and Abram Harris to E.P. Davis, 17 November 1936, ALP, Box 164-3 Folder 13.

24. Letter from E.P. Davis to Ralph Bunche, 21 June 1937, RBP, Box 10 Folder 14.

25. Letter from Eric Williams to Ralph Bunche, Sunday (nap) 1937, RBP, Box 10 Folder 14.

26. Boodhoo, *Elusive Eric Williams*, 62–64.

27. Williams, *Inward Hunger*, 45–46; Ryan, *Eric Williams*, 25–27; James, *Convention Appraisal*, 4.

28. Boodhoo, *Elusive Eric Williams*, 62–64; C.L.R. James, *Party Politics in the West Indies* (Port of Spain: Vedic, 1962), 158.

29. Ibid., 59, 92.

30. Letter from Malcolm Nurse [George Padmore] to Alain Locke, 14 December 1927, 205 West 118th Street, New York City, ALP, Box 164/75 Folder 20.

31. Alain Locke, "Afro-Americans and West Africans: A New Understanding", *WASU*, 8 January 1929, 18–24.

32. Boodhoo, *Elusive Eric Williams*, 59, 63, 92, 157. In 1925, the WASU emerged out of several organizations. One of these organizations was the Nigerian Progress Union, which was cofounded in 1924 by a Nigerian law student, Ladipo Solanke, and a Jamaican, Amy Ashwood Garvey. See Gabriel O. Olusanya, *The West African Students' Union and the Politics of Decolonisation, 1925–1958* (Ibadan, Nigeria: Daystar Press, 1982), 6, 14, 19; Hakim Adi, "Pan-Africanism and West African Nationalism in Britain", *African Studies Review* 43, Special Issue on the Diaspora (April 2000): 81–82n2; Hakim Adi, *West Africans in Britain 1900–1960: Nationalism, Pan-Africanism and Communism* (London: Lawrence and Wishart, 1998), 52–88.

33. Letter from Isaac T.A. Wallace-Johnson, London, 6 April 1937, CO 323/1517/2. Isaac Theophilus Akunna Wallace-Johnson (1894/1895–1965) was born into a poor Krio family in Wilberforce Village in Sierra Leone. In July 1930, he attended the International Trade Union Conference of Negro Workers in Hamburg and was elected to its presidium. He served on the editorial board of the conference's publication, the *NW*, under an alias. During this time, he met many prominent black communists. After studying in Moscow in the early 1930s, Wallace went to London in February 1933, where he began his association with the NWA. Samuel K.B. Asante, "The Aborigines Society, Kwame Nkrumah and the 1945 Pan African Congress", *Institute of African Studies Research Review* 7 (1972): 50; Samuel K.B. Asante, "The Italo-Ethiopian Conflict: A Case Study in British West African Response to Crisis Diplomacy in the 1930s", *Journal of African History* 15 (1974): 293; "Gold Coast", *West Africa*, 3 April 1937, 423; "W.A. Youth League Notes", C.L. Lambert, 22 March 1937, CO 96/740/4; Benjamin Nnamdi Azikiwe, biographical data, n.d., KV 2/1817; Johnstone or Jomo Kenyatta, 3 July 1936, KV 2/1797; Benjamin Nnamdi Azikiwe, 2 July 1936, KV 2/1817.

34. Peter Abrahams, *The Black Experience in the 20th Century: An Autobiography and*

Meditation (Bloomington: Indiana University Press, 2000), 37; Letter from Eric Williams to Alain Locke, 1 January 1939, St Catherine's, Oxford, ALP, 164/93 Folder 23.

35.   Cyril C. Ollivierre (1903–75), Ivan S. Lloyd (1903–93) and Padmore's paths had crossed as students. Ollivierre was an old schoolmate of Padmore's from St Mary's College. At Howard University, he was president of the Garvey Club and helped Padmore to organize a protest attacking the British ambassador. Ollivierre was also the connection between Azikiwe and Padmore: when Azikiwe was broke, Ollivierre was instrumental in his securing him a job with Alain Locke, which enabled him to earn money to enrol at Howard University and further cemented the relationship between Azikiwe and Padmore. Lloyd attended Howard University, too, and he studied at the City College of New York. Lloyd, like Ollivierre, had an accomplished medical career, but Lloyd is best known for his political career. In 1942, he was one of the People's National Party's first elected officials for the legislative council. Letter from George Padmore to Cyril C. Ollivierre, 5 July 1932, George Padmore Letters, SCRC; Hooker, *Black Revolutionary*, 6–7; Colin A. Palmer, *Freedom's Children: The 1938 Labor Rebellion and the Birth of Modern Jamaica* (Chapel Hill: University of North Carolina Press, 2014), 337–38, 349; Howard Campbell, "Icon: Ivan Lloyd South East St Ann's Champ", *Jamaican Gleaner*, 26 June 2007.

36.   James, "Notes on George Padmore", 9–10.

37.   Letter from George Padmore to Alain Locke, 31 December 1942, 22 Cranleigh House, Cranleigh St., London N.W.1, ALP, 164/76 Folder 16.

38.   Robert A. Hill, "In England, 1932–1938", *Urgent Tasks* 12, Special Issue on C.L.R. James: His Life and Work (Summer 1981): 26; Marc Matera, "Black Internationalism and African and Caribbean Intellectuals in London, 1919–1950" (PhD diss., Rutgers University, 2008), 152–53; Robert L. Tignor, *W. Arthur Lewis and the Birth of Development Economics* (Princeton, NJ: Princeton University Press, 2005), 33, 231n43; "Eric Williams", Arthur Lewis Papers, Princeton University Library, Department of Rare Books and Special Collections, Seeley G. Mudd Manuscript Library, Princeton, NJ, Box 13.

39.   In 1936, Padmore occupied two rooms in the basement of a building inhabited by the African Church Stories Limited, an organization that acted as a cooperative selling agent for native wares from the Gold Coast. He shared the rooms with Kenyatta and Griffiths. Jomo Kenyatta from J.L. Stone, Sergeant, 27 April 1936, KV2/1797.

40.   *Special Branch Report*, 8 June 1938, KV 2/1824.

41.   Ryan, *Eric Williams*, 24.

42.   I want to thank Patricia Mohammed, University of the West Indies, Trinidad

and Tobago, for her suggestion at the "New Perspectives on the Life and Work of Eric Williams" conference at St Catherine's College, Oxford University, 25 September 2011, that I view Eric Williams's association with various leftist groups from an outsider-insider perspective.

43. Letter from Eric Williams to Ralph Bunche, 27 May 1937; Letter from Eric Williams to Alain Locke, 2 July 1936, ALP, Box 164–93, Folder 2; James, "Notes on George Padmore", 46. The typist Padmore recommended was Dorothy Pizer. She became Padmore's partner, and, in the 1950s, she went with Padmore to Ghana, where he was adviser to Nkrumah (a role Dorothy assumed after his death in 1959).

44. Williams, *Negro in the Caribbean*, 95.

45. Letter from George Padmore to W.E.B. Du Bois, 12 April 1945, WEBD, Reel 57, 1035.

46. Letter from George Padmore to W.E.B. Du Bois, 9 August 1946, Paris, WEBD, Reel 59, 370.

47. Letter from George Padmore to W.E.B. Du Bois, 12 April 1945, WEBD, Reel 57, 1035.

48. "League of Coloured People Formed in UK", *Daily Gleaner*, 16 March 1931, 16; "Dr Moody Elected Head of League of Coloured People", *Daily Gleaner*, 8 June 1931, 4; "Abolish Colour Bar Barrier Plea of Jamaican in the UK", *Daily Gleaner*, 8 June 1931, 32; "League of Coloured People in England", *Daily Gleaner*, 30 March 1932, 31; Harold A. Moody, "Communications", *Journal of Negro History* 18 (January 1933): 92–101.

49. Hooker, *Black Revolutionary*, 44, 132; Stephen Howe, *Anticolonialism in British Politics: The Left End of Empire, 1918–1964* (New York: Oxford University Press, 1993), 84–89.

50. Editorial, *Keys* 1 (July 1933): 1–2.

51. "*The Keys* Disclose –", *Keys* 1 (October 1933): 32; Carter J. Woodson, "Review of *Capitalism and Slavery*", *Journal of Negro History* 30 (1945): 93–95.

52. See Eric Williams, "The Abolition of the Slave System in Britain", *Keys* 7 (July–September 1939): 11. This issue of the *Keys* also included Williams's review of the anthology *Gems of Modern Poetry*. Here Williams engaged in literary criticism of the book, which contained works by poets who were not known in either Britain or the West Indies. He thought that the work was uneven, ranging from rather immature expressions of thought to a splendid, sweeping imagining of Toussaint. *Keys* 7 (July–September 1939): 11.

53. E.W., "That Emancipation Complex", *Keys* 6 (October–December 1938): 11. The sentiments in the articles so closely mirror Williams's dissertation that it must be his work. At the point when the first article went to press, he probably had

not completed the defence of his dissertation, which would explain why he might not have wanted to be explicit about his authorship. Williams submitted his doctoral dissertation to the Faculty of Modern History of Oxford University in 1938, and his degree was conferred in December 1938. Williams, *Capitalism and Slavery*, 264; Williams, *Inward Hunger*, 51.

54.   Woodson, "Review of *Capitalism and Slavery*", 93–95.

55.   Palmer, *Eric Williams*, 30–31.

56.   Claudia Jones (1915–64) was a communist, journalist, Marxist social critic, theoretician, anti-colonialist, feminist and activist. She arrived in England in December 1955 after being deported from the United States because of her affiliation with the Communist Party of the United States of America. She advanced liberation paradigms that linked the questions of race, class, gender, anti-colonialism, anti-imperialism and anti-fascistm into one struggle for humankind. In the United States, through the 1930s and early 1950s, Claudia Jones edited the *Weekly Review* and *Spotlight* magazine, wrote a column for the *Worker*, was the editor for the Negro Department for the *Daily Worker* and wrote major discussion articles for the CPUSA journal, *Political Affairs*. In 1945, she became a member of the CPUSA leadership as secretary of the National Women's Commission. When she was deported, she was the highest-ranking black woman in the CPUSA. The depth of her relationship with Williams is blurred, but Buzz Johnson, Jones's biographer, said that Williams and Jones met, and there are letters to Williams concerning her passport. Buzz Johnson also has some of Claudia Jones's papers in his possession in London. I have spoken with him briefly about these materials, but I have not yet reviewed these sources. Letter from Claudia Jones to Eric Williams, 23 July 1957, 25 March 1958, Claudia Jones Memorial Collection, Schomburg Center for Research in Black Culture, Manuscripts, Archives and Rare Books Division, New York Public Library, New York, Box 1 Folder 9.

57.   Claudia Jones, "Books: *Capitalism and Slavery*: What Determined Abolition of Slavery by Eric Williams", *West Indian Gazette*, November 1964, n.p.

58.   Jones, "Books: *Capitalism and Slavery*".

59.   Ibid.

60.   *Nation*, 7 Aug 1959, n.p.; Ryan, *Eric Williams*, 44–45.

61.   Brent Hayes Edwards, *The Practice of Diaspora: Literature, Translation, and the Rise of Black International* (Cambridge, MA: Harvard University Press, 2003), 276, 377n99; Boodhoo, *Elusive Eric Williams*, 158–60.

62.   C.L.R. James, "George Padmore: Marxist Revolutionary", in *At the Rendezvous of Victory* (London: Allison and Busby, 1984), 256, 260. In addition to James's *The Black Jacobins* and *History of Negro Revolt*, he published Padmore's *How Britain Rules Africa* and *Africa and World Peace*. He also published a pamphlet

titled *The Native Problem in South Africa* along with Jomo Kenyatta's study of the Kikuyu tribe, *Facing Mount Kenya*. Makonnen, *Pan-Africanism from Within*, 119, 128, 145; Hakim Adi and Markia Sherwood, *Pan-African History: Political Figures from Africa and the Diaspora since 1787* (London: Routledge, 2003), 119.

63.   Palmer, *Eric Williams*, 19–20.

64.   Williams, *Negro in the Caribbean*, 93–94, 103–9.

65.   Williams, *Inward Hunger*, 84, 86–87.

66.   Before *IAO*, there were two other publications by the IASB: *African Sentinel* and *Africa and the World*. Between the fall of 1937 and the spring of 1938, there were about four or five bimonthly issues of *African Sentinel*, while *Africa and the World* was a monthly newssheet that was published in 1937. The first issue of the *IAO* appeared in July 1938. It functioned as the monthly organ of the IASB. The first issue's editorial stated that the *IAO* was "the mouthpiece of black workers and peasants, and those intellectuals who see the necessity of making the cause of the masses their own". The *IAO* was not a "literary journal" or a "giver of advice from the mountain tops". It was to be "a journal of action". It was to be "a living weapon in the struggle, a reflection of every day demands of the masses as they fight their way to the larger goal". The original intent was to have the new publication appear in May 1938. In June, MI5 reported that efforts were being made to raise the sum of £16 in order to start a periodical which would be called the *IAO*. The Colonial Office believed that there "were special clandestine arrangements for smuggling the journal into the Colonies". Letter from E.B. Boyd to Sir Thomas Southorn, Sir Arnold Hodseon and eleven others, Downing Street, 19 April 1938, CO 232/1601/2; International African Service Bureau, 9 June 1938, MEPO 38/91; *Report Wallace-Johnson and the IASB*, 27 January 1938, CO 232/1601/2; editorial, *IAO* 1 (July 1938): 2; *Report on Investigating*, CO 295/606/4.

67.   Despite his ill health, James found the time to give talks to various groups. At all of his meetings, he directed the attention of his listeners to the existence of the IASB as an organization of Africans and peoples of African descent in London. Letter to Sir Thomas Southorn, Sir Arnold Hodseon and eleven others, CO 232/1601/2; C.L.R. James Cross-Reference, 8 June 1938, KV 2/1824; "Expulsion Notice", *IAO* 1 (Feb–March 1939): 9; *Communism and the West Indian Labour Disturbances*, 1938, CO 295/606/4; "Good Will Ambassador in America", *IAO* 1 (Feb–March 1939): 16.

68.   Kenyatta, IASB, 27 Feb 1939, KV 2/1797.

69.   Letter from George Padmore to Alain Locke, 3 October 1938; Letter from Eric Williams to Alain Locke, 1 January 1939, ALP, Box 164–76 Folder 16.

70.   Letter from George Padmore to Alain Locke, 3 October 1938, ALP.

71. Letter from Alain Locke to Malcolm [Nurse alias George Padmore], 11 October 1938, ALP, Box 164–76 Folder 16.
72. Letter from Eric Williams to Alain Locke, 1 January 1939.
73. Letter from Eric Williams to Alain Locke, 30 March 1939, 32 St Catherine's, Oxford, ALP, Box 164–93 Folder 23.
74. Kenyatta, IASB, 27 Feb 1939, KV 2/1797; Extract relating to C.L.R. James and West Indies, 25 May 1939, KV 2/1824.
75. E.E. [Williams], "Editorial: An Open Letter to West Indian Intellectuals", *IAO* 1 (May–June 1939): 1–2.
76. Letter from Eric Williams to Alain Locke, 30 March 1939.
77. E.E. [Williams], "The Trinidad Scene", *IAO* 1 (May–June 1939): 11–12.
78. Ibid.
79. Ibid.
80. E.E. [Williams], "Child Labour in the British West Indies", *IAO* 1 (May–June 1939): 8–9. Historian Charles H. Wesley shared an interest with Williams in black education in the British Empire. He published two articles on the subject. See Charles H. Wesley, "The Rise of Negro Education in the British Empire – I", *Journal of Negro Education* 1 (October 1932): 354–66; Charles H. Wesley, "The Rise of Negro Education in the British Empire – II", *Journal of Negro Education* 2 (January 1933): 68–82.
81. There appear to have been several editions of *The West Indies To-day*. In 1937, Arthur Lewis wrote a pamphlet in conjunction with Padmore, also titled *The West Indies To-day*. In a letter to Hooker in 1965, Lewis did not recall Padmore having any hand in writing the pamphlet. Lewis remembered writing it, and the IASB published it. He said that the pamphlet was not written in Padmore's style. But Lewis admitted that it had happened thirty years earlier and he could not be sure. Parts of Williams's 1939 pamphlet also seem to have had some connection with the Bronze Booklet Series for the Associates in Negro Folk Education, of which Locke was the editor. Eric Williams, *The West Indies To-day* (London: IASB, 1939); Letter from Arthur Lewis to Hooker, 19 Aug 1965, in Hooker, *Black Revolutionary*, 48.
82. Eric Williams, *Capitalism and Slavery* (1944; reprint, Chapel Hill: University of North Carolina Press, 1994), 7–29; Williams, *West Indies To-day*, 9, 42.
83. Williams, *West Indies To-day*, 14.
84. In 1964, the *West Indian Gazette* printed that the mere contemplation of a state visit from Ethiopian Emperor Haile Selassie to Trinidad in January 1965 had raised much interest. The *Gazette* also reported that, according to the *Trinidad Guardian*, the anticipated visit of the Ethiopian emperor had provoked "more interest throughout the West Indies than the visit of any other African personage

bar Ghana's Dr Nkrumah". "Haile Selassie Visit", *West Indian Gazette*, November 1964, n.p.

85.   Eric Williams Memorial Collection, folio 1914, 4, in Ryan, *Eric Williams*, 26–25. The opening of Aggrey House became a focal point for rising anti-colonial sentiments. A main purpose of WASU was to open a hostel for students in search of accommodations. In seeming support of this aim, the Colonial Office opened Aggrey House in 1933. In the meantime, WASU opened its own hostel, partly with contributions from West Africa secured by Solanke. After Aggrey House's opening, the Colonial Office was accused of providing a hostel not out of compassion but out of a desire to control the colonial students. Colonial Office reports show that WASU's fight against Aggrey House was extremely effective and that officials were not sure how to handle it. Despite its government sponsorship, the Aggrey House became a popular meeting place. Adi, *West Africans in Britain*, 57–65.

86.   Ralph Bunche's diary, March 1937, in Brian Urquhart, *Ralph Bunche: An American Odyssey* (New York: W.W. Norton, 1993), 69; Charles P. Henry, *Ralph Bunche: Model Negro or American Other?* (New York: New York University Press, 1999), 80; Colonial Office Comments, June 1937, CO 323/1517/2; "Italian Anti-Fascists Denounce Massacre in Addis", *Crusader News Service*, 15 March 1937, n.p.; Eric Williams Memorial Collection, folio 1914, 4, in Ryan, *Eric Williams*, 26–25.

87.   E.E. [Williams], "Trinidad Scene", n.p.

88.   Sam Bornstein and Al Richardson, *Against the Stream: A History of the Trotskyist Movement in Britain, 1924–38* (London: Socialist Platform, 1986), 183.

89.   Williams, *Inward Hunger*, 50; Langely, *Pan-Africanism and Nationalism*, 325–31.

90.   The British public assumed that the League of Nations would assert its authority and would apply sanctions against Italy; Prime Minister Stanley Baldwin's policy was to stay out of the Italian-Ethiopian crisis. In December 1935, the Hoare-Laval Pact was made with the French, by which Mussolini would be allowed to seize about half of Ethiopia. In this instance, British statesmen were softer than was the British public. The plan was leaked to the press, and there was a storm of protest over the action of the government. Baldwin thereupon dropped his foreign secretary, Sir Samuel Hoare, and annulled the agreement, but, in the meantime, Mussolini had completed his conquest. Makonnen, *Pan-Africanism from Within*, 113; Ralph Bunche's diary, May 1937, in Urquhart, *Ralph Bunche*, 64–65; Asante, "The Italo-Ethiopian Conflict", 294.

91.   Williams, *Inward Hunger*, 50.

92.   Tignor, *W. Arthur Lewis*, 34. The original name was International African Friends of Abyssinia, and this is how it appears in the Secret Service files, the *Manchester Guardian*, *Negro Worker* and the *Daily Gleaner* in June, August, September and

October 1935. In August and September, the name appears as the International African Friends of Ethiopia in Secret Service files and in the *Chicago Defender*. The reason for the name change is not clear. This paper will use the International African Friends of Ethiopia. See Johnston Kenyatta, Cross-Reference, 28 June 1935, KV 2/1797; Johnston Kenyatta, Cross-Reference, 26 August 1935, KV 2/1797; Johnston Kenyatta, Cross-Reference, 16 September 1935, KV 2/1797; Johnston Kenyatta, Cross-Reference, 12 October 1935, KV 2/1797; "Friends of Abyssinia", *Manchester Guardian*, 30 August 1935, n.p.; "International Actions in Support of Abyssinia", *Negro Worker* 5 (September 1935): 12–13; "London Protests Against Arms Embargo", *Daily Gleaner*, September 1935, n.p.; "Londoners Demonstrate in Favor of Ethiopia", *Chicago Defender*, 7 August 1935, n.p.

93.   It seems that the IAFE was established in the summer of 1935. The Communist Party papers include a letter written by Arnold Ward, in which he speaks about the activism of the IAFE in June. The two Kenyatta sources give two different months. The Kenyatta's Secret Service file said that he spoke at a meeting of the IAFE on 28 June 1935 at Memorial Hall, Farrington. But in a letter dated 14 August 1935 to Sylvia Pankhurst, Kenyatta said that the group had just formed, though it had been publicly active since July. It is possible that the 28 June date could have been a typographical error. There are other accounts that the IAFE held a meeting on 28 July at Memorial Hall. *The West Indian* reported that the first mass meeting of the Association was held on 22 July at the Aggery House, and the second on 28 July at Memorial Hall. What can be agreed on is the sequence of events – that is, the IAFE began in the summer of 1935 after Padmore's article was published in the *Crisis*. Letter from W. [Arnold Ward], 26 June 1935, RGASPI 495/155/102; Johnston Kenyatta, Cross-Reference, 28 June 1935, KV 2/1797; "International Actions in Support of Abyssinia", *Negro Worker* 5 (Sep 1935): 12–13; George Padmore, "Ethiopia and World Politics", *Crisis* 42 (May 1935): 138–39, 156–57; Samuel Rohdie, "The Gold Coast Aborigines Abroad", *Journal of African History* 6 (1965): 391; "Letter To Sylvia Pankhurst from Jomo Kenyatta", *New Times and Ethiopian News*, 30 January 1954, 3, in P. Olisanwuche Esedebe, *Pan-Africanism: The Idea and Movement, 1776–1991*, 2nd ed. (Washington, DC: Howard University Press, 1994), 98.

94.   Letter from W. [Arnold Ward], 26 June 1935, RGASPI 495/155/102.

95.   George Padmore, "Ethiopia and World Politics", *Crisis* 42 (May 1935): 138–39, 156–57; Tony Martin, *Amy Ashwood Garvey: Pan-Africanist, Feminist and Mrs Marcus Garvey No. 1 or, A Tale of Two Amies* (Dover, MA: Majority Press, 2007), 142; Letter from Colonel Sir Venom Kell to General Mac Brien, London, 12 December 1936, KV 2/1824.

96.   Tony Martin, *Amy Ashwood Garvey*, 142; *Communism and the West Indian Labour*

Disturbances, 1938, CO 295/606/4; Letter from Colonel Sir Venom Kell to General
Mac Brien, KV 2/1824.

97. T.A. Marryshow, "London Notes", *West Indian,* 19 June 1935, 4; "Mr. Marcus
Garvey Campaigns for British Parliament Seat: Receives Support of London
Colonials", *West Indian,* 12 July 1935, 4; "Mr. Marcus Garvey's Campaign for Seat
in Br. Parliament", *Daily Gleaner,* 20 June 1935, 8; Rudolph Dunbar, "Things
Theatrical Mills Club Opens in London", *Plaindealer* (Kansas City), 24 July 1936,
n.p.; "Rudolph Dunbar and Sam Manning Launch New London Night Spot",
West Indian, 8 September 1936, n.p.

98. Lionel M. Yard, *Biography of Amy Ashwood Garvey, Co-founder of the Universal
Negro Improvement Association* (Washington, DC: Associated, 1990), 109–10.

99. Padmore remembered the IAFE growing out of the ad hoc committee that he
formed in 1934 to help the Gold Coast delegation in London in the midst of
a conference on "Negro in the World Today". The lapse of time between the
convening of the 1934 ad hoc committee and the emergence of the IAFE in the
summer of 1935 suggests that there were two ad hoc meetings – one in 1934 and
another in 1935 – or that the 1934 ad hoc committee was revived as the IAFE.
Historian Immanuel Geiss suggests that there were two distinct ad hoc commit-
tees. George Padmore, *Pan Africanism: The Coming Struggle for Africa* (London:
Denis Dobson, and Accra: Guinea Press, 1956), 144; Esedebe, *Pan-Africanism,*
98; Immanuel Geiss, *The Pan-African Movement: A History of Pan-Africanism
in America, Europe, and Africa* (New York: African Publishing, 1968), 35; editorial, *Keys* 2 (July–September 1934): 1; Peter Fryer, *Staying Power: The History of
Black People in Britain* (London: Pluto, 1987), 344; "African Friends Abyssinia in
London", *Daily Gleaner,* 10 September 1935, 7; Makonnen, *Pan-Africanism from
Within,* 130; Tony Martin, "Amy Ashwood Garvey Wife No. 1", *Jamaica Journal*
20 (August–October 1987): 34, 35; "Mrs Amy Garvey", *Daily Gleaner,* 26 October
1935, 2.

100. Our London Correspondent, "How London's Harlem Heard Joe Louis's Victory",
People, 2 October 1937; Leslie Elaine James, "'What We Put in Black and White':
George Padmore and the Practice of Anti-imperial Politic" (PhD diss., London
School of Economics, 2012), 12, accessed 8 January 2013, http://etheses.lse
.ac.uk/399/1/James_What%20we%20put%20in%20black%20and%20white.pdf.

101. Makonnen, *Pan-Africanism from Within,* 130; Martin, "Amy Ashwood Garvey
Wife No. 1", 34. According to James, Amy Garvey's West End restaurant was
the only place in town where good food was served. It specialized in Caribbean
cuisine and music. So, if you wanted to tap your feet to "the 78s of Trinidadian
calypsonian Sam Manning, Garvey's partner, [would] spin late into the night".
Makonnen recalled going there after two or three hours at Hyde Park or some

other meeting and getting a lovely meal, dancing and just enjoying himself. London, the heart of the Mother Country, was the "junction box", where Africans and West Indians in 1930s and 1940s forged anti-colonialism – the "junction box" is a concept borrowed from historian Stephen Howe. Delia Jarrett-Macauley, *The Life of Una Marson, 1905–1965* (Manchester: Manchester University Press, 1998), 84; Martin, "Amy Ashwood Garvey Wife No. 1", 34; Makonnen, *Pan-Africanism from Within*, 130; Howe, *Anticolonialism in British Politics*, 85, 191.

102. Williams, *Negro in the Caribbean*, 92.

103. Sam Manning was a successful actor, singer, comedian and recording artist. He was an expert on West Indian music and had become politically active in black politics through his relationship with Amy Ashwood. They were business partners between 1926 and 1936, and verbal accounts suggest a more intimate relationship. Richard L. Osborne of the West Indies National Council (based in New York) and Amy Ashwood Garvey carried on voluminous correspondence. In 1958, Osborne passed on a "confidential story" obtained by Sam Manning "which, if true would turn a lot of heads in the West Indies gray were they to see what I saw and hear from his lips". Osborne wrote, "The story involves no less a person than Dr Eric Williams . . . what grounds for speculation! I am hoping that Sam does not talk in his sleep." Osborne left Amy hanging, however; he did not unearth the shattering information. After showing him a "rather chummy" letter from the vice-president of the Alcoa Steamship Company, Osborne said that Manning had passed the story on to him. See Letter from Herman Osborne to Amy, 28 March 1958, in Martin, *Amy Ashwood Garvey*, 264. Rudolph Dunbar was well known within British music quarters. He was a Guyanese clarinetist and a foreign correspondent for the Associated Negro Press. The Colonial Office was suspicious of Dunbar; J.L. Keith wrote that they should be careful in their dealings with him. They thought that Dunbar may be responsible for the anti-British propaganda which was being shared among blacks in the United States. Although Dunbar purported to embrace British sentiments, they wanted to make sure that he was not misleading them into believing that he was 100 per cent loyal. John Cowley, "Cultural 'Fusion': Aspects of British West Indian Music in the USA and Britain 1918–51", *Popular Music* 5 (1985): 83; Letter from George Padmore to Alain Locke, 28 February 1944, Press Room, Ministry of Information, London, W.C.1, ALP, Box 164–76 Folder 16; Note from J.L. Keith, 16 May, CO 875/11/14.

104. "Urges Wrecking of Ethiopia, Than Bow to Italy", *Daily Gleaner*, 30 July 1935, 1.

105. "What Africa Was and May Be Again", *Daily Gleaner*, 14 August 1935, n.p.; T.A. Marryshow, "Meeting of the International African Friends of Ethiopia;

At Memorial Hall, Farringdon Street, Sunday July 28th 1935", *West Indian*, 28 August 1935, 5.

106. Minkah Makalani, *In the Cause of Freedom: Black Radical Internationalism from Harlem to London, 1917–1939* (Chapel Hill: University of North Carolina Press, 2011), 211.

107. "Friends of Abyssinia", n.p.

108. "Africans and Abyssinia: Meeting of London Sympathisers", *West Africa*, 3 August 1935, 872–73.

109. Wood and Moore were one of two deputations from the Gold Coast. One mission represented the traditional rulers and unofficial members of the legislative council that was led by Nana Sir Ofori Atta with J.B. Danquah as secretary. The other mission, which included Wood and Moore, was made up of officials of the Gold Coast Aborigines' Rights Protection Society. Padmore convened an ad hoc committee to help the delegation in London. "Africans and Abyssinia", 878; "Hon. A.T. Marryshow on His Return Home", *Daily Gleaner*, 8 October 1935, n.p.; "Friends of Abyssinia", n.p.; Rohdie, "The Gold Coast Aborigines Abroad", 391; Kenyatta, Cross-Reference, 28 July 1935, KV 2/1797; Padmore, *Pan Africanism: The Coming Struggle*, 144; Esedebe, *Pan-Africanism*, 98.

110. "Africans and Abyssinia", n.p.

111. "Friends of Abyssinia", n.p.; "International Action in Support for Abyssinia", *Negro Worker* 5, no. 9 (July–August 1935): 12–14.

112. "Londoners Demonstrate in Favor of Ethiopia", *Chicago Defender*, 7 August 1935, n.p.

113. "Friends of Abyssinia", n.p.

114. Yard, *Biography of Amy Ashwood Garvey*, 109–10.

115. The crowd at Trafalgar Square started with about two hundred people, and, after an hour, the number had grown to nearly five hundred people. The *Manchester Guardian* was critical of the black turnout. The paper noted that there were about "two to three thousand negroes in London", but there were few blacks present "to support the first mass demonstration of their race". The *Negro Worker* reported that there were many "Negro actors and musicians". There were a number of resolutions passed by ships' crews and delegations from Cardiff to protest Mussolini's action. "Africans and Abyssinia", 878; "Hon. A.T. Marryshow on His Return Home", 2; "Friends of Abyssinia", n.p.; "International Action in Support for Abyssinia", 1; Eric Williams Memorial Collection, folio 1914, 4, in Ryan, *Eric Williams: The Myth and the Man*, 26–25. Other speeches delivered by members of the IASB were from Johnstone Kenyatta of Kenya, Arnold Ward of Barbados, Sam Manning, I.T.A. Wallace-Johnson and Mohammed Said of Somaliland. James, "George Padmore: Marxist Revolutionary", 256, 260.

116. Yard, *Biography of Amy Ashwood Garvey*, 113.

117. "Friends of Abyssinia", n.p.

118. Under Williams, Woodford Square became a seat of learning. Karl Douglas, "Historic Woodford Square", *Trinidad Guardian*, 29 July 1962, n.p.; "Substitute Political Thinking for Personalities – Pro. Gordon Lewis", *West Indian Gazette*, September 1960, n.p.; Gordon Lewis, *The Growth of the Modern West Indies* (New York: Monthly Review Press, 1968), 213; Claudia Jones, "Profile: Dr Eric Williams", *West Indian Gazette*, December 1960, n.p.

119. After Padmore left the Communist Party, he charged that the ITUCNW had been liquidated by the RILU and the Comintern without consulting the secretary or staff. Padmore claimed this was the result of a Comintern decision to placate the British government, which had strongly protested the ITUCNW's agitation among English colonies in Africa and the West Indies. In a letter to his friend Cyril C. Ollivierre, Padmore confided that since "last August [1933] the Communist International wanted us to close down our activities in order to appease the British Foreign Office: which was raising hell because the Blacks in Africa were beginning to wake up". Padmore maintained that the interests of blacks in the colonial areas had been sacrificed by the Politburo, which was attempting to come to terms with the imperialist states in launching its united front programme following Hitler's rise to power. Padmore charged that the Soviet Union would have been quite willing to sacrifice Ethiopia to Mussolini in the interests of the socialist fatherland. The continued publication of the *Negro Worker* for several years contradicts Padmore's assertion that the ITUCNW was liquidated, but Padmore is correct in insisting that its strategy and tactics changed. James recalled Padmore remembering that, in 1935, after foreign secretary "Anthony Eden visited Moscow to discuss a rapprochement between Great Britain and Russia", he was informed that one of the conditions that was "laid down was the cessation of anti-imperialist propaganda in Africa". Letter from George Padmore to Cyril C. Ollivierre, 28 July 1934, George Padmore Letters, SCRC; "George Padmore Dies in London", *Pittsburgh Courier*, 3 October 1959, "Matche's Diary", *West Africa*, 3 October 1959, 799; "George Padmore Cremated", *West Africa*, 3 October 1959, 81; "Expulsion of George Padmore from the Revolutionary Movement", *Negro Worker* 4 (June 1934): 2, 14–15; James, "Notes on George Padmore", 11–12, 17–19.

120. Earl Browder, the Communist Party secretary in the United States, asserted that George Padmore had been dismissed from the ITUCNW for arguing that the emperor of Japan was the legitimate protector of the world's darker people. Furthermore, Browder contended that Padmore was not removed by the Comintern but by his black associates in the ITUCNW, whom Padmore had

ignored and attacked. Browder denied that the ITUCNW had been abolished, pointing out that Otto Huiswoud had succeeded Padmore as executive secretary and editor of the official organ. As usual, the truth was somewhere in between Browder's and Padmore's contentions. On one hand, Browder was correct in saying that the ITUCNW was not disbanded at the time Padmore had claimed. Otto Huiswoud did function for a while as executive secretary, and Padmore was expelled from the Comintern as a petty bourgeois nationalist. On the other hand, Padmore's underlying charges were not baseless. Huiswoud, a prominent member of the Communist Party of the United States, with the help of his wife Hermina, tried to re-establish the ITUCNW. Huiswoud advocated "class before race", but, at the same time, he fervently attacked the virulent racism both inside and outside communist organizations. In 1935, the Seventh World Congress of the Comintern delivered the final blow to the RILU and, subsequently, the ITUCNW, by embracing the Popular Front doctrine. A few years later, the *Negro Worker*, together with the ITUCNW, was erased from the scene. Wilson Record, *The Negro and the Communist Party* (Chapel Hill: University of North Carolina Press, 1951), 84–85, 138; George Padmore, "Ethiopia and World Politics", *Crisis* 42 (May 1935): 138; George Padmore, "An Open Letter to Earl Browder", *Crisis* 42 (October 1935): 320, 315; Mark Naison, *Communists in Harlem during the Depression* (Urbana: University of Illinois Press, 1983), 131, 156; Fryer, *Staying Power*, 334–35; Hooker, *Black Revolutionary*; Richard Hart, "Oral Interviews about Claudia Jones", ICS, Tape Three, 9; *Negro Worker* 2 (January–February 1932): inside cover page; "Policy of Negro Champion", 7 September 1928, RGASPI/1/104/1366; "Minutes from the First Meeting to Re-organize the Negro Committee", 14 August 1928, RGASPI/ 515/1/ 104/1566; "National Sub-committee of the CEC on Negro Work", 17 August 1938, RGASPI/515/l/104/1366; National Negro Committee Meeting, 26 October 1928, RGASPI /515/1/ 104/1366. The Colonial Office reported that Padmore quarrelled with the Political Bureau of the French Communist Party and was expelled from the Communist Party by the International Control Commission on a charge of "deviation". *Communism and the West Indian Labour Disturbances*, 1938, CO 295/606/4.

121. Makonnen, *Pan-Africanism from Within*, 120.
122. CO 295/606/4, Letter from H[enry] Moore to R. Beaumont, 17 June 1938; Letter from D.G. White to F.J. Howard, London, 26 May 1938, CO 295/606/4.
123. RA 495/64/132/13, in Joyce Moore Turner, *Caribbean Crusaders and the Harlem Renaissance* (Urbana: University of Illinois Press, 2005), 213. The controversy over why Padmore left the Comintern continues. Both Hakim Adi's and Holger Weiss's recent, massive studies address this controversy and offer new details about the circumstances in which Padmore famously broke from the Comintern

around 1933–34. Hakim Adi's *Pan-Africanism and Communism* argues that there should be greater challenges to Padmore's assertion on why he left the party. Adi maintains that the monolithic understanding put forth by Padmore has become the general consensus accepted by historians and that it is inaccurate. He argues that this historical inaccuracy prevents any real understanding of the aims, complexities and significance of the Comintern and of the ITUCNW. Hakim Adi, *Pan-Africanism and Communism: The Communist International, Africa and the Diaspora, 1919–39* (Trenton, NJ: African World Press, 2013), xiii–xvii. Holger Weiss's *Framing a Radical African Atlantic* is more magnanimous in its assessment of Padmore's separation from the party. He suggests that Padmore's "fierce criticism of the lax attitude" of the party was, perhaps, because he was not "fully aware of the aversion and disinterests to Negro work in certain circles in metropolitan parties and labor unions". Weiss tells the story from Moscow's viewpoint and concludes that Padmore's expulsion was due to his alleged failure in leading the Hamburg secretariat of the ITUCNW and to the fact that the African students he had been sending to Moscow lacked the necessary screening. Furthermore, Padmore was undermining the directives of the Comintern as he became more and more engaged in pan-African activities and as he became more and more disillusioned by the directives from Moscow and the practices of metropolitan communist parties. Moscow pulled the strings. As Weiss put it, Padmore had "to choose sides – race or class first?" Holger Weiss, *Framing a Radical African Atlantic: African American Intellectuals and the International Trade Union Committee of Negro Workers* (Leiden, the Netherlands: Brill, 2014), 452–56, 608. Both studies offer powerful first-hand testimony regarding the betrayals and crimes of the Stalinist bureaucracy with respect to the struggle for black and colonial liberation and are critical reading for historians seeking to understand the experience of "black Bolshevism" in its full richness and complexity – but I am sure that neither study will be the last word on this subject.

124. "Africans Will Help Padmore: Black Students Refuse to Condemn Leader on 'Sellout' Charges", *New York Amsterdam News*, 4 August 1934, n.p.; James, "Notes on George Padmore", 25.

125. Eric Williams, "Trinidad and Tobago: International Perspectives", *Freedomways* 4 (Summer 1964): 335.

126. Williams, *Negro in the Caribbean*, 105; Jones, "Profile: Dr Eric Williams"; E.E. [Williams], "Trinidad Scene".

127. William Patterson, "George Padmore: The Theoretician of Pan-Africanism", William Patterson Papers, MSRC, Box 8, Folder 79; "More Super-Profits from Us", *West Indian Gazette*, February 1963, n.p.

128. "IASB", 4, MEPO 38/91; Ras Makonnen, *Pan-Africanism from Within*, 117–19, 120.

129. Williams, *Inward Hunger*, 85.

130. George Padmore, *Pan-Africanism or Communism* (New York: Doubleday, 1972), 159.

131. Abrahams, *Black Experience in the 20th Century*, 36; editorial, *IAO* 1 (July 1938): 2.

132. In the first issue of the *African Sentinel* the general secretary explained the aims and objects of the IASB. The organization represented "progressive and enlightened public opinion among Africans and Peoples of African descent". The *IAO* explained that the IASB's position in London made it more immediately familiar with "the problems of Negroes in the British Colonies", yet its appeal was "for collaboration with Negroes" wherever they were, "in French and Belgian colonies, in the United States and in South America. Problems differ from country to country, but there is a common bond of oppression, and as the Ethiopian struggle has shown, all Negroes everywhere . . . [have] the necessity for international organization and unification of their scattered efforts." "International African Service Bureau", 4, MEPO 38/91; Makonnen, *Pan-Africanism from Within*, 117–19, 120.

133. Padmore, *Pan-Africanism or Communism*, 159.

134. Williams, *Inward Hunger*, 85–87.

135. Williams, *West Indies To-day*; Letter from Eric Williams to Alain Locke, 11 December 1938, St Catherine's Oxford, ALP, MSRC, 164/93 Folder 23; Boodhoo, *Elusive Eric Williams*, 70; Letter from Alain Locke to Malcolm [Nurse alias George Padmore], 11 October 1938, ALP, Box 167/96 Folder 27.

136. Letter from Eric Williams to Alain Locke, 1 January 1939, St Catherine's Oxford, ALP, Box 164/93 Folder 23; Letter from Eric Williams to Alain Locke, 30 March 1939, St Catherine's Oxford, ALP, Box 164/93 Folder 23.

137. In letters between Padmore and Williams, the tone does not suggest that Williams was being begged by the IASB to publish *The Negro in the Caribbean*. Padmore wrote to Williams explaining how he had explored the possibility of getting the book published in England, but, because of the wartime paper shortage, publishers in England were giving priority to their regular authors. As an alternative, Padmore suggested that the IASB would publish the book using money donated by Makonnen. Williams accepted the terms Padmore offered with a 10 per cent royalty, and publication proceeded. Williams reminded Padmore to advertise the book in the West Indies, because "they were anxious to get it". Letter from George Padmore to Alain Locke, 31 December 1942; Letter from George Padmore to Eric Williams, 29 April 1944; Letter from Eric Williams to George Padmore,

May 1944, Eric Williams Memorial Collection, University of the West Indies, St Augustine, Trinidad, Folder 96, in Polsgrove, *Ending British Rule In Africa*, 166; Williams, *Inward Hunger*, 85–87.

138. Adi and Sherwood, *Pan-African History*, 186; Worcester, *C.L.R. James*, 254n19, n20; Williams, *Inward Hunger*, 85–87; Polsgrove, *Ending British Rule in Africa*, 68; Ralph Bunche's diary, March 1937, in Urquhart, *Ralph Bunche*, 69; Henry, *Ralph Bunche*, 80; Colonial Office Comments, June 1937, CO 323/1517/2.

139. Williams, *Inward Hunger*, 85–87.

140. Eric Williams, "My Relations with the Caribbean Commission, 1943–1955", in Selwyn R. Cudjoe, ed., *Eric E. Williams Speaks: Essays on Colonialism and Independence* (Wellesley, MA: Calaloux Publications, 1993), 145–46.

141. *Nation*, 7 August 1959, n.p.

142. Communism and the West Indian Labour Disturbances, 1938, CO 295/606/4.

143. The IASB was spawned by IAFE and Pan-African Brotherhood, also known as the Pan-African Federation, Pan-Afro Federation, Pan-Afro League and the Pan-Afro Group. "Appeal to Readers", *IAO* 1 (Feb–March 1939): 3; *Wallace-Johnson Report*, 5 July 1937, MEPO 38/91; *Report Wallace-Johnson and the International African Service Bureau*, 27 January 1938, CO 232/1601/2; Derrick, *Africa's "Agitators"*, 388.

144. Langely, *Pan-Africanism and Nationalism*, 325–31; Fenner Brockway, *The Colonial Revolution* (New York: St Martin's, 1973), 35–36.

145. Williams, *West Indies To-day*, 41–42.

146. Langely, *Pan-Africanism and Nationalism*, 35–36.

147. *Report on Investigating*, CO 295/606/4.

148. Williams, *West Indies To-day*, 41–42.

149. "Editorial: An Open Letter to West Indian Intellectuals", *IAO* 1 (May–June 1939): 1–2.

150. *Report on Investigating*, CO 295/606/4.

151. *Africa and the World* 1 (1 September 1937): 1–3, CO 847/11/16.

152. Letter from M. Kirkwood to Marquis of Dufferin and Ava, the West Indies Co., 17 May 1938, CO 295/606/4; Letter from D.G. Whit to F.J. Howard, CO 295/606/4; *Report on Investigating*, CO 295/606/4.

153. *Communism and the West Indian Labour Disturbances*, 1938, CO 295/606/4. On 13 November 1937, it was reported to the Colonial Office that a barrister from Barbados named Adams, who recently had been in Britain to see the secretary of state about the situation in the colony, had been in close touch with Padmore and others in the IASB. Adams visited "Padmore's flat and gave him a detailed account of the events leading up to the recent difficulties in the West Indies". The Colonial Office was not able "to identify Mr. Adams", but it is reasonable

to assume this was Grantley Adams. At the time, Padmore was in correspondence with Adrian Cola Rienzi, secretary of a militant native group in Trinidad, through the medium of a woman. Adams also revealed that Uriah Butler, an ex-serviceman and labour leader, was working behind the scenes in Trinidad on behalf of Rienzi. Letter to F.J. Howard, Colonial Office, from MI5, 30 November 1937, CO 323/1517/2; *Report West African Matters*, 17 August 1937, MEPO 38/91.

154. Williams, *Negro in the Caribbean*, 95–96.

155. "Self-Determination for West-Indies", *Negro Worker* 2 (April 1932): 4.

156. Letter to Henry Moore from Selwyn Grier, 12 April 1938, CO 295/606/4.

157. Williams, *Negro in the Caribbean*, 95–96.

158. Ibid.

159. E.E. [Williams], "Trinidad Scene".

160. The Colonial Office believed that the NWA had been absorbed by the IASB and Ward was still on tap for his services. *Report on Investigating*, CO 295/606/4; Communism and the West Indian, CO 295/606/4; C.L.R. James Cross-Reference, 8 August 1937, KV 2/1824; Trafalgar Square IASB Meetings, 26 June 1938, MEPO 38/91.

161. Trafalgar Square IASB Meetings, MEPO 38/91.

162. "Activities of the Bureau", *IAO* 1 (August 1938): 16. After the demise of the League against Imperialism, historian Stephen Howe suggests there was no lobby that specifically dealt with a whole range of Caribbean colonial problems. The IASB, though most of its members were West Indians, devoted the lion's share of its attention to African colonies, and especially Ethiopia. There is much in Howe's contentions, but, in the early period of the IASB, it does not appear that it paid Caribbean affairs any less attention than African conditions. Howe, *Anticolonialism in British Politics*, 100–3.

163. Letter from Ben Bradley to Richard Hart Jamaica, London, *Colonial Information Bulletin*, 17 April 1939, KV2/1824.

164. Letter from Ben Bradley to Richard Hart Jamaica, KV2/1824. In May 1939, a British government official described C.L.R. James as "a rat". He was viewed with some apprehension by the communists, as he was a Trotskyist who could develop a following among West Indian workers. There was some concern that he might split the groups and destroy some of the framework of the movement. It was suggested that, if James were to appear on the scene in the West Indies, it was not recommended that any attempt be made to use him. He was regarded as being too "fanatically disposed" and his approach to agitation work as too divisive. See Extract relating to C.L.R. James and West Indies, 25 May 1939, KV 2/1824.

165. Williams, *West Indies To-day*, 41.

166. On 29 September, some of the black West Indians who gave evidence in support of the memorandum included T.R. Makonnen of the IASB, who prepared the supplement on agriculture; Dr Harold Moody of Jamaica, president of the LCP; and Rev. Peter Blackman, a former missionary who was then associated with the NWA. "Lord Olivier and the West Indies" and "Summary of the Memorandum", *IAO* 1 (October 1938): 7.

167. The first signature on the memorandum was George Padmore as chairman of the IASB. Other signatories were T.R. Makonnen, secretary, IASB; Harold Moody, chairman, and Clement Phillips, secretary, LCP; Peter Blackman, president, and Rowland Sawyer, secretary, NWA. "Memorandum on Economic, Political and Social Conditions in the West Indies and British Guiana Presented by the International African Service Bureau, the League of Coloured Peoples and the Negro Welfare Association", 9 September 1938, CO 950/30.

168. Other white members of the commission were Sir Reginald Stubbs, who was the vice-chairman; Sir Walter Citrine; Ralph Assheton, MP; Dame Rachel Crowdy; Morgan Jones, MP; Hubert Douglas Henderson of All Souls College, Oxford; Sir Percy Graham Mackinnon; and Dr Mary Blacklock. "Lord Olivier and the West Indies" and "Summary of the Memorandum", *IAO* 1 (October 1938): 7.

169. "Stop the Press" and "The West Indian Commission", *IAO* 1 (August 1938): 1–2.

170. Williams, "My Relations with the Caribbean Commission", 163.

171. Williams, *Inward Hunger*, 85; Williams, *Negro in the Caribbean*, 38–39, 67, 96, 104; Claudia Jones, "British Citizen Second Class", *West Indian Gazette*, December 1961, n.p.

172. Eric Williams, *From Columbus to Castro: The History of the Caribbean* (New York: Vintage, 1970), 476. In 1931, Cecil Rawle was elected chairman of the Dominica Conference. The purpose of the meeting was to discuss political and socio-economic possibilities of the future. The conference, which became known as The West Indies Conference, helped to pave the way for the West Indies Federation.

173. Ryan, *Eric Williams*, 24.

174. Woodson, "Review of *Capitalism and Slavery*", 93–95.

175. Ryan, *Eric Williams*, 24–27, 55; James, *Convention Appraisal*, 4–5, 7. On 24 January 1956, a new political party, the People's National Movement, was founded; it was a black-dominated party. The aims of the PNM included self-government, a reorganization of the economy to make the fullest use of the resources of the island, and dominion status for the West Indies Federation within five years. In 1956, Williams took the first draft of the People's Charter, the founding document of the PNM, to London, where he discussed it with C.L.R. James, George Padmore and William Arthur Lewis. The Charter stated that it was for "a comprehensive and social security programme for the general welfare of all

the people of Trinidad and Tobago". Padmore's and James's theoretical finger-prints were all over the document. Selwyn R. Cudjoe, "Eric E. Williams and the Politics of Language", *Callaloo* 20 (Autumn 1997): 51–65; Adi and Sherwood, *Pan-African History*, 187. For James's discussion on his Trinidad years from 1958 to 1960, see his *Party Politics in the West Indies*.

176. James, *Convention Appraisal*, 6–7.

Chapter 3

Eric Williams as a Man of Culture

SELWYN R. CUDJOE

> If I turn into earth, water, grass,
> Flower or fruit – if it comes to pass
> I return to Earth in the animal class,
> Why in the world should I care?
> In the limitless bond wherever I pass,
> A kinship is ever there.
>
> – Rabindranath Tagore, *Of Myself*

There is a paradox. Many people in Trinidad and Tobago are wont to say that Dr Eric Williams was a racist and that he despised people of Indian descent. Such a categorization was given greater validity when, after the 1958 federal elections, Williams claimed that the PNM was defeated because of a recalcitrant minority within the Democratic Labour Party. An interpretation was extended to suggest that Williams had characterized the entire Indian population as a recalcitrant minority, a statement that Kamla Persad-Bissessar repeated after she was elected the first woman prime minister of Trinidad and Tobago.[1] Yet, when we turn to examine the major religious and philosophical influences on Williams's life, we ought to look no further than his exposition on the works of Rabindranath Tagore, the great Bengali poet and author, whose philosophical and religious thinking are mirrored in Williams's writings and in his life.[2] This fact is lost on those who see only the outer dimension of the man rather than his resilience, his beliefs and his understanding of the world. We can use Tagore's observation on religion as a starting point to get a glimpse into Williams's inner thoughts and deeply held beliefs.

Everyone has something special called "my religion". But he has no clear knowledge of it. He knows "I am a Christian, I am a Muslim, a Vaishnavite, a Shakta", and so on. But even if he is certain from birth till death that he belongs to an established religion, he may be mistaken. The very assumption of a name erects such a screen that the inner religion itself escapes his notice.

Which is his religion? The one that lies hidden in his heart and keeps on creating him. An inherent religion and instinct of life builds up all that is animal and living. The animal need not have any sense of religion. Man has another being, greater than his physical being – his humanity. The creativity that is inside this being is his religion. For this reason, *dharma* (religion) is a very significant word in our language. The wateriness of water is the religion of water, the fieriness of fire the religion of fire. Similarly, man's religion is his innermost truth.[3]

Williams's admiration of Tagore came from his deep appreciation of literature and art "as sources for the understanding and appraisal of historical development".[4] He used literature and art as means of organizing and expressing his truths. He subscribed fully to Tagore's conviction: "In a literary work the author's purer being reveals itself unconsciously; the work thereby is a purer thing. That is why I go to poetry and drama for evidence."[5] And so Williams titled his autobiography *Inward Hunger,* from three lines of the verse in Dante's *Inferno* where Ulysses says: "[I] could conquer the inward hunger that I had / To master earth's experience, and to attain/ Knowledge of man's mind, both good and bad."[6]

Thirty years after Williams's death, it is propitious to look at his record in the area of culture (especially in his appreciation of poetry) to get a feel for the man who governed Trinidad and Tobago for twenty-five of the sixty-nine years that he lived. Such an examination also seems appropriate on the centenary of Williams's birth and the one hundred and fiftieth anniversary of the birth of Rabindranath Tagore, who, I argue, had such a profound impact on Williams's philosophical and religious life. Although we know of Williams's influence on our political life, we have not paid sufficient attention to his importance in shaping our cultural history or race relations. An examination of his writings in this area (particularly his three essays on Mahatma Gandhi,

Jawaharlal Nehru and Rabindranath Tagore) and his thoughts on culture give us a deeper insight into the man and his way of thinking.

Eric Williams was a private man. Nowhere else, to the best of our knowledge, does he spell out his religious beliefs, open himself up to public scrutiny or even try to come to grips with his nationalist position (both as political leader and historian) as he does in these three essays. His public discourses drew on verses and aphorisms from the Bible and local sayings to elaborate his meanings, to offer succinct summations of his themes and to serve as points of inspiration to his listeners. He loved Tagore, primarily a poet,[7] who on his seventieth birthday could say of his vocation: "Now I have followed this long orbit of life I can take a look at the circle in its entirety at the hour of farewell, and I understand that I have only one identity, and it is this: I am simply a poet."[8] When Williams delivered his lecture on Tagore at Queen's Hall, Port of Spain, Trinidad, on 6 May 1961, at the invitation of India's high commissioner, he came closest to disclosing his religious views. In this context, we should thank the Central Bank of Trinidad and Tobago and Ewart Williams for republishing the three speeches that Williams delivered on the "great Trinity of India's Nationalist figures": Mahatma Gandhi (1959), Rabindranath Tagore (1961) and Jawaharlal Nehru (1964).[9]

Williams's Relationship to Poetry

Williams was familiar with the major poets of the Western and Eastern world and read their work widely. Although we tend to see him primarily as a historian and a politician, his ruminations on poetic luminaries reveal much about his philosophical thinking. It is, I believe, the tendency of poetry to go "from Nature towards the domain of man", as Tagore notes, that allows Williams to express many of his deeply felt sentiments through it. Tagore captures this in the following observation:

> Who is it forever playing
> in the heart's deep plot
> rich tunes on Time's instrument? –
> some hear them, some do not.
> To their meaning I am blind –

sages seek it, do not find.
The tides of the great human mind
are as the songs allot.[10]

Probably because he was the prime minister of the country (primarily a political position), Williams sought to listen to the "rich tunes on Time's instrument". He was determined to demonstrate that "the sentient and discerning being" had an obligation to drive "the history of universal man through every obstacle and impediment on a path of perilous ups and downs".[11] Discouraged by what he characterized as a tendency towards "anti-intellectualism" in West Indian life, Williams emphasized the role that culture plays in the life of a nation and the obligation of the political leader to be in tune with the currents of his or her time. Williams's promotion of the steel-band movement, the delight he took in listening to calypsonians and his inauguration of the Best Village Competition once he became prime minister demonstrated his awareness of the vital source of his people's feelings.[12]

Williams's embrace of popular or people's culture (although he paid more attention to African-based rather than Indian-based culture) demonstrated the sensitivity of a man who understood the importance of culture in national development. With the same enthusiasm that displayed in embracing the people's culture, he could show disdain for what Naipaul called the philistine nature of the intellectual life of society. As he noted in his autobiography, "A Head of Government cannot be limited to such narrow and materialistic considerations [that is, the banal of everyday life in the Caribbean]. So I read deliberately, in silent protest against the bastardization of so-called West Indian intellectualism."[13]

Four Poets of the Greater Antilles

In spite of his historical and political pursuits, Eric Williams always possessed an eye for the enduring truths that poetical wisdom (or culture, broadly speaking) revealed. Between 1938, when he received his doctorate from Oxford, and 1944, when he completed *Capitalism and Slavery*, Williams had a chance to discover the Caribbean as he transformed his doctoral thesis into a finished book manuscript. In 1952, at a public lecture sponsored by the Trinidad and Tobago Literary League of Cultural and Debating Clubs, he offered his analysis of four outstanding non-British Caribbean poets: Nicolás Guillén of Cuba; Jacques Roumain and Jean-Fernand Brierre of Haiti; and Luis Palés Matos of Puerto Rico, whom he discovered during the time he was doing research in those islands.[14] At this early stage, Williams saw literature as one of the activities that could fill the cultural gap that existed in the larger geographical area and as a means through which to express his thoughts on certain political tendencies. He noted: "In my opinion, the development and organization of this common body of knowledge of the Caribbean, based on the deliberate cultivation of the multi-lingual facility, is the great political desideratum and intellectual truth of the age and the area."[15]

Williams believed the two major influences on these Caribbean writers were elements of African culture (Africanisms) and the economic impact (perhaps interference) of the United States in the Caribbean. Palés Matos's poetry, he argues, "is full of sonorous Africanisms".[16] Then he asks of Palés Matos, "But what else is Africa to the Caribbean?" to which Palés Matos answers, "It is an amalgam of dance, drums, voodoo and sex."[17] Guillén had a different take that was fundamentally economic. Williams notes that, while Guillén also "has his Africanisms and emphasizes the African origin, his Negro is a poor worker, working in the sun whilst the Arabs sell their wares and the Frenchmen take a stroll or a rest".[18] Roumain and Brierre are more international. They are concerned about "the Negro in the world as a whole and place their emphasis on racial discrimination", which leads Roumain to affirm nostalgically: "I have kept your memory, Africa. You are in me."[19] Brierre, on the other hand, "is bitter at the thought that the broom, the tool, the elevator and the kitchen are the Negro's share, and reminds us that behind the music, the love and the dance there are concealed dope and loneliness".[20] He also celebrates the contribution Haiti made towards "breaking the bars of slavery", thereby inaugurating "The birth of liberty / For all Latin America".[21]

Williams then directs his readers' eyes to the resentment that the poets feel at the exploitative tendencies of the United States. Palés Matos sees the Puerto Rican solution as emanating out of what he calls "cultural" or "linguistic nationalism", whereas Guillén's solution was a united front of blacks and whites against capitalist exploitation. Like Palés Matos, Roumain urged the adoption of the communist ideology and international solidarity as solutions to the problem of the working people in the Caribbean. From the foregoing, Williams concludes on a harsh note:

> This, then, is the choice we are offered by these four poets: to sing the International with Guillén and Roumain, or bleat like a stewed goat with Palés Matos; to die under the Red Flag with Guillén and Roumain or stagnate and die from nothing with Palés Matos. Guillén and Roumain call on Stalin; Palés Matos harks back to Tchekov and betrays a weariness and sadness reminiscent of the *mal de siècle* of the French Romantic movement in the nineteenth century. As opposed to the insistent propaganda of Guillén and Roumain regarding the racial equality of world Stalinism, Palés Matos offers us his sonorous Africanisms. It would be a tragedy for the Caribbean if these were the only alternatives. Fortunately they are not.[22]

What, then, are the alternatives that Williams presents? He cites the nationalism of Munoz Marin and the poetry of Walt Whitman, the poet of democracy. He does not see communism as an answer to our problems and argues that

> it is wholly false to think that communist ideology has a monopoly of the theory of racial equality. Nearly a hundred years ago, seven years after the *Communist Manifesto*, to be precise, the doctrine of racial equality was stated by one of the brightest stars in the nineteenth century democratic constellation – the United States poet, Walt Whitman . . . with this little known manifesto of fraternity, entitled *Salut au Monde*.[23]

From his entry into national politics, Williams was committed to a nationalist rather than an internationalist solution to Caribbean problems, although he understood that international currents affected his nation. Communism may have had its attractions, but it did not possess a monopoly on political wisdom. It took the poetic voice of Whitman, an American, to express Williams's deeply held political position: a form of Caribbean nationalism to solve Caribbean problems. Inherent in this approach was a commitment to a religion of man (rather than an abstract philosophy) that was grounded in humanitarian values. In Whitman's words, it was a world in which

> Each of us inevitable,
> Each of us limitless – each of us with his or her right upon the earth,

Each of us allow'd the eternal purports of the earth,

Each of us here as divinely as any is here . . .

My spirit has pass'd in compassion and determination around the
whole earth,

I have look'd for equals and lovers and found them ready for me in
all lands,

I think some divine rapport has equalized me with them.

You vapours, I think I have risen with you, moved away to distant
continents, and fallen down there, for reasons,

I think I have blown with you, you winds;

You waters I have finger'd every shore with you,

I have run through what any river or strait of the globe has run through,

I have taken my stand on the bases of peninsulas and on the high embedded
rocks, to cry thence:

Salut au monde![24]

The Political Leader as a Man of Culture

In April 1959, Williams used an international forum to expand upon his
views about the role of culture in the liberation process. Once more, he
emphasized the importance of literature in articulating the nascent consciousness of Caribbean peoples. This opportunity was provided when
Alioune Diop, the editor of *Présence Africaine*, invited him to write a paper
for the Second Congress of Negro Writers and Artists that was held in Rome
from 26 March to 1 April, 1959. In "The Political Leader Considered as a Man
of Culture", Williams elaborated upon an observation that Diop had made at
the First International Congress of Negro Writers and Artists, held in Paris
in 1956: "There is no people without culture. But we often lose sight of the
natural bond . . . between politics and culture. It is the State that guarantees
a culture, the memory of its traditions, and a sense of its personality. A community deprived of political liberty has great difficulty in creating the image
of its past."[25] Although Williams drew upon the Ancient Greeks to set up his
argument, he was convinced that Diop was only "seeking to translate to the
African struggle what has already been established on the Indian field of

battle. For it is modern India which most clearly demonstrates the natural tie between politics and culture as symbolized by Gandhi and Nehru."[26] He noted that Gandhi, in his struggle to free India from colonial rule, emphasized the importance of a national culture by saying, "I must cling to my mother-tongue as to my mother's breast, in spite of its shortcomings. It alone can give me the life-giving milk. I love the English tongue in its own place, but I am its inveterate opponent, if it usurps a place which does not belong to it."[27] This does not mean that the movement towards the adoption of a national culture was made any easier by the several languages that were spoken in India. It only means that one could not cultivate a national culture if one did not give precedence to the language of one's people.[28]

If European colonization implied a displacement of local languages and cultures, independence demanded its reversal: that is, an emphasis on local languages and culture. In this context, Williams quoted Kwame Nkrumah, prime minister of Ghana, who observed:

> We must work a greater glory and majesty, greater than the civilization of our grandfathers, the civilization of Ghana, the civilization of the Mali Empire and the civilization of the Songhay Empire. Long before the slave trade, long before imperialistic rivalries in Africa began, civilizations of the Ghana Empire were in existence. And here, you even discover that at one time, at the great University of Timbuctoo, Africans versed in the science of art and learning were studying their works translated [from Latin] in Greek and Hebrew, and at the same time exchanging professors with the University of Cordoba in Spain. These were the brains, and today they come and tell you that we cannot do it.[29]

Culture, as Williams observed and the congress emphasized, was not an embellishment. It was a way of thinking about one's society and an integral part of the nationalist struggle for independence.

In contrasting India and Africa with the Caribbean, Williams pointed out the absence of local languages among Caribbean people. For the most part, they used the languages of the societies from which they had come. Such an absence created difficulties in offering a rallying point for the nationalist movement and prevented greater collaboration among the people of the islands, a condition made worse by the absence of a regional university to hold the society together. The failure of the West Indian federation in which

Williams and other leaders had held such high hopes only aggravated the situation. However, it was our West Indian literature that offered the promise of bridging the territorial divide and a forum for regional cooperation. In this regard, he may have been echoing the sentiments of Tagore, who argued: "In the treasure-house of art and literature the gems of a people's aesthetic enjoyment are created and accumulated in every age and clime. In this wide world we can tell from literature alone to whom or to what the people of a country have given their love and admiration. Indeed, it is by their love that we should judge people."[30]

Williams believed that the leader, as a man of culture, had an important role to play in welding the society together. This could not be achieved if the people's culture was not at the vanguard of the nationalist movement and the educational system was not rooted in the national culture. This is why he affirmed that "the struggle for the national culture today is not only a part of the struggle for political independence but also the struggle for building a new social order as well".[31] Therefore, when the people of Trinidad and Tobago started their quest for national independence, Williams saw culture or the practice of culture as integral to the construction of the new society. He did not start with the premise that we needed to adopt a multicultural policy because a segment of the community felt alienated.[32] He offered his analysis against a backdrop of the colonizing powers' tendency to privilege their culture and languages over local languages and culture, which led leaders of newly independent states, both in India and Africa, to insist on the revitalization of their indigenous cultures and languages as central ingredients in the construction of these new states. This still remains the challenge of postcolonial nationhood.

Gandhi and Nehru

A lecture on Gandhi in October 1959 allowed Williams another opportunity to elaborate on the role that culture plays in developing societies and to continue the discussion he began in *Présence Africaine*. Even before Williams's conference paper, Gandhi was venerated by the people of Trinidad and Tobago. Both C.L.R. James and Beatrice Greg, an Englishwoman living in Trinidad, had alerted the public to Gandhi's accomplishments in the

Beacon in 1931 and 1932.[33] Williams reminded his listeners that Gandhi, "one of the most gifted human beings who has ever lived", centred his work around the Indian peasant "by whose progress and emancipation from misery and poverty the standard of Indian civilization was to be judged". Gandhi believed that "the process of education must centre around some form of manual and productive work in the shape of a craft. The craft chosen should not be any craft, but a basic craft around which the different subjects of the curriculum can be grouped and a craft intimately bound up with the life of the children". He also emphasized the teaching of social sciences, which he saw as "an indispensable prerequisite of good citizenship", a lesson that should interest many educators in Trinidad and Tobago today. Gandhi put it this way: "The history of Indian national awakening combined with a living appreciation of India's struggle for social, political and economic freedom should prepare the pupils to bear their share of the burden joyfully and to stand the strain and stress of the period of transition."

In his lecture, Williams pointed out the lessons that Gandhi's life had for the citizens of Trinidad and Tobago. He noted: "The traditions against which he fought in South Africa and developed his capacities were in some respects very similar to those which existed in the Trinidad of the time. Gandhi's relations with the Indians and the Africans in South Africa should form a chapter of his history which should not only be of interest but of profit to all of us at this particular time." He ended his lecture by highlighting Gandhi's method of passive resistance and "the highly spiritual quality of his personal life. . . . To acquaint ourselves with it [his life], to whatever degree, can only lead to the enrichment of our own."[34]

Williams felt closer to Nehru politically than he did to Gandhi, in spite of Gandhi's spiritual qualities and the tremendous contribution he made to revolutionary theory and practice in the twentieth century. While Gandhi played down the importance of academic learning and attempted to spiritualize poverty, Nehru was more politically inclined and was determined to reduce poverty through scientific methods.[35] This was also true of Tagore, who "thought little of Gandhi's alternative economics, and found reason to celebrate, with a few qualifications, the liberating role of modern technology in reducing human drudgery as well as poverty".[36] It helped that Nehru, an amateur historian,[37] was the leader of a nationalist movement, who had a close attachment to his people. Like Williams, he became "alive before a large audience; his speeches, whether in Hindi or English, were always clear, direct, easily understood if somewhat lecturing (the communists' nickname for him was 'the Professor')".[38] Trinbagonians fondly called Williams "the doc". Although he compared Gandhi's accomplishments with those of Marx and others "in the sense that he discovered and invented a new method of political struggle, carried it through successfully over a vast area of human activities and has left it as a heritage which has been studied and followed in areas as far apart as Ghana and Montgomery, Alabama",[39] Williams's ideas and ideals of national independence were closer to those of Nehru than they were to those of Gandhi.

Williams acknowledged his spiritual kinship to Nehru, "an Anglicized product of Harrow and Cambridge who spent over ten years in British jails; an agnostic radical who became an unlikely protégé of the saintly Mahatma Gandhi", and who carried the fight for independence against the British. Like Williams, Nehru was "the glamorous face of Indian nationalism just as Gandhi was its other-worldly deity".[40] Even Tagore hailed Nehru "as the embodiment of spring itself, 'representing the season of youth and triumphant joy' ",[41] although he "rebelled against the strongly nationalist form that the independence movement often took, and this made him refrain from taking a particularly active part in contemporary politics".[42]

As a historian, Williams appreciated Nehru's "analysis on Britain's imperialism in India".[43] One may remember that Williams did a similar thing for British capitalism in the Caribbean. He also restated Nehru's contention that British imperialism led to "the total destruction of Indian community life and community values", which subsequently led to the pauperism of Indian peasants that sent millions of them to Burma, Malaya, Sri Lanka, Kenya, South Africa, Guyana, and Trinidad and Tobago.[44] This exploitation led to the "demoralization and sapping of the spirit of the people"; hence the goal of the independence movement was to restore that dignity to the Indian people.[45]

Although Nehru was a trained lawyer – a profession he entered to please his father, who was also a lawyer and prominent figure in the Indian independence movement – Williams appreciated Nehru's masterful writing of history. *Glimpses of World History*, written while Nehru was in prison, revealed

Nehru's "vision of human progress, advancing through periods of inhuman-
ity and suffering but teleologically moving onward towards better lives for
the world's ordinary people. . . . There is great praise for the Indian epics, the
Ramayana and the *Mahabharata* (in particular the *Bhagavad Gita*), but as
works of literature rather than as sacred texts."[46] Williams calls *Glimpses of
World History* "a classic in the literature of intellectual decolonization" that
places "the history of India in true perspective", and he singles out Nehru's
description of the Dravidian civilization as one of the finest chapters of his
work. India's cultural unity comes in for special praise even as its caste system, "the enemy of every kind of progress",[47] is condemned. No progressive
leader – Tagore, Gandhi or Nehru – could be silent about its debilitating effect
on the progress of India.

In his analyses, Williams was concerned about the role of the historian
in the nationalist project, both as a leader and as an interested participant.
He argued that "Nehru was not only a nationalist historian analyzing the
colonialism from which his country had suffered. He was much, much, more
than this. He was the historian of the colonial peoples, protesting against the
glitter of Europe, and claiming a place in the sun of civilization for all the
subject peoples. He was the colonial historian against the arrogant assumption that civilization is the monopoly of Western Europe."[48] This conclusion
echoes the theme of the Second Congress of Negro Writers and Artists.

Williams was inspired by Nehru's internationalist perspective. Speaking of the new creative spirit that was being reborn in India, Williams says
of Nehru: "[He was] internationalist because he was nationalist, just as he
was the champion of all colonial peoples because he was an Indian colonial,
Nehru, with the universal vision of a Walt Whitman or a Victor Hugo."[49] In
1932, as Nehru compared India's struggle for freedom with Europe's dominance and authoritarianism, he could declare in confidence: "So while we
struggle for the freedom of India, we must remember that the great aim is
human freedom, which includes the freedom of our people as well as other
peoples."[50] Williams could invoke Whitman to demonstrate how these literary
personalities assisted in the construction of his vision.

From these essays, one gets the impression that Williams felt a certain
anxiety[51] about his role as historian and nationalist leader, trying as he did to
locate himself and his activities within the decolonizing process and seek-

ing to understand his place as a colonial intellectual and historian within the larger international process. In Nehru, Williams saw "a man who was at one and the same time a national symbol, a philosopher of anti-colonialism and a student of world history",[52] whose task it was to build up "that inner strength of the people that we were after, knowing that the rest would inevitably follow. We had to wipe out some generations of shameful subservience and timid submission to an arrogant alien authority."[53] Williams might have uttered these words. He said as much when he declared: "Massa Day Done".[54] Each man believed that greatness was thrust upon him.[55]

Williams identified with Nehru's legacy in a meaningful way. He concluded his lecture in the following manner: "India today would not be what it is if India had not achieved independence and if Nehru had not been there for forty years to learn and to teach, to guide and be guided, to inspire and be inspired, to aspire and to achieve. He stands out as one of the greatest champions of freedom for all times."[56] Interestingly enough, the national motto, "Together we aspire; together we achieve", is inscribed on the coat of arms of Trinidad and Tobago. It is tempting to think that Nehru's influence might have been essential in the coining of the national motto of Trinidad and Tobago.

Rabindranath Tagore

Williams admired Gandhi and was inspired by Nehru's political achievements, but it was Tagore in whom Williams found a measure of spiritual guidance and a canvas upon which to reflect upon his humanity. Unlike Gandhi and Nehru, Tagore was still in vogue during Williams's adolescent years, having been awarded the Nobel Prize in literature in 1913 and being a towering international figure during the first twenty-five years of the twentieth century. It helped also that Tagore's "outlook was persistently nonsectarian, and his writings – some two hundred books – show the influence of different parts of the Indian cultural background as well as that of the rest of the world".[57] He was committed also to the humanitarian ideal. "As early as 1908, he put his position succinctly in a letter replying to the criticism of Abala Bose, the wife of a great Indian scientist, Jagadish Chandra Bose: 'Patriotism cannot be our final spiritual shelter; my refuge is humanity. I will not buy glass for the price of diamonds, and I will never allow patriotism to triumph over humanity as long as I live.'"[58]

Although Tagore, Gandhi and Nehru knew each other, worked together and were committed to India's independence, the Amritsar Massacre of 1919 brought them together in a common cause and "made Indians out of millions of people who had not thought consciously of their political identity before that grim Sunday. It turned loyalists into nationalists and constitutionalists into agitators [and] led the Nobel Prize–winning poet Rabindranath Tagore to return his knighthood to the king and a host of Indian appointees to British offices to turn in their commissions."[59] The Trinidad awakening and the Bandung conference had a similar impact upon Williams. Caught up in the intensity of a rising nationalist movement in Trinidad and Tobago, and anxious about his role as a historian/intellectual in the movement, Williams regarded the philosophical reflections of Tagore as guides to his behaviour. He admired Tagore's aesthetic sensibilities, his participation in India's nationalist movement, the breadth of his internationalist concerns and what Amartya Sen called his "reasoned understanding of the world around us . . . his wholehearted support for scientific education . . . [and] his cultural evaluations".[60]

Tagore's epistemic approach to his work and his concern for the common people appealed to Williams, who must have been impressed by Tagore's belief in the "freedom of mind", the expansion of education as "central to social progress", the importance of science in understanding the world and the use of modern technology to develop India.[61] Amartya Sen put it this way: "The poet who was famous in the West only as a romantic and a spiritualist was in fact persistently guided in his writings by the necessity of critical reasoning and the importance of human freedom."[62] Most of all, Tagore believed that "truth is realized through men".[63] Like Tagore, Williams believed that if you gave people the information (in Williams's case, historical and political information) they required, they would be able to make intelligent choices about where they wanted to go as a people. His association with C.L.R. James during the early phases of the nationalist movement tended to reinforce this position.

Tagore, like Williams, "hated foreign rule but believed that as a sick body easily falls prey to outside infection, so a society where the individual had lost all initiative and backbone must invite foreign exploitation. . . . He was therefore more concerned with rousing in his people a sense of their own dignity than with finding fault with the foreigner."[64] Both Tagore and Williams believed in the capacity of art and literature to lift a society and be a means of getting at what people were thinking during a particular period. Given the opportunity, Williams used his lecture "to penetrate, for the benefit of our own people, the political significance of Tagore's poetry, dramas and novels in order to draw lessons for our society in the West Indies. Few have written as powerfully as he did of the role of personality in human affairs, and of the superiority in this respect of art over science."[65] He understood only too well that "no history of any epoch of human civilization, least of all our own, can exclude a chapter on art and society. This evening, therefore, I shall consider not so much the art and personality of Tagore, the poet, as the importance of Tagore's art for our West Indian society."[66]

In his autobiography, Williams noted that literature allowed him to see that "history was not a record of battles and politicians, dates and events, or even of the follies and foibles of mankind, but rather a record of the development of humanity, of life and of society, in all their various manifestations".[67] He observed:

> The themes of [Tagore's] poetry, his dramas, his songs are the people of India, the beauty of India, the life of India. He had a special tenderness, as he himself confessed for the peasants of India, those "big, helpless, infantile children of Providence", as he called them. The subject matter of his poetry is the girl tending a buffalo, the worker returning from work, the emaciated beggar, the death of a little boy, the unwanted daughter; in general what Tagore called the poorest and lowliest and lost.[68]

According to Williams, Tagore represented "one of the best examples that we can ever hope to find of the role of the intellectual in the Nationalist Movement in colonial countries".[69] It may have helped if Williams had emphasized that, although Tagore fought for the independence of India, he "was critical of the display of excessive nationalism in India, despite his persistent criticism of British imperialism. And notwithstanding his great admiration for Japanese culture and history, he would chastise Japan late in his life for its extreme nationalism and its mistreatment of China and east and southeast

Asia."[70] Yet it remains true that this was a role that Williams tried to emulate as he gave himself more and more to his nationalist movement.[71]

As an intellectual at the head of a nationalist movement, Williams drew on Tagore's inspiration to assist him in understanding the demands of our nationalist movement and his own humanity. Although he never articulated his religious beliefs, his conception of the Godhead was close to that of Tagore, who prayed that "he may never lose the bliss of the touch of the One in the play of the many".[72] In his final tribute to the oneness of the world, Tagore declared: "I have come to the brink of eternity from which nothing can vanish – no hope, no happiness, no vision of a face seen through tears. Oh dip my emptied life into the ocean, plunge it into the deepest fullness. Let me for once feel that lost sweet touch in the allness of the universe."[73] It was this magnanimous, all-embracing spirit that Whitman, whom Tagore also admired, tried to capture in his poetical rendering of the world. It was a vision of the world that Williams also shared.

Williams never wanted any monuments built to commemorate his achievements or to perpetuate his glory or his memory. He wanted to be cremated and have his ashes thrown into the Gulf of Paria to merge once more with the great confluence of nature out of which he had come. Eternity rather than the passing moments of time mattered to him. This is why he quoted Tagore so approvingly when he said, "There, where spreads the infinite sky for the soul to take her flight in, reigns the stainless white radiance. There is no day nor night, nor form nor color and never a word."[74]

Tagore was also fascinated by the play between life and death. Williams writes, "His principal concern was death."[75] In *Phalguni*, a celebration of spring, Tagore captured this *pas de deux* between life and death when he observed, "those who fear death do not know life; they embrace decay and exist in a living death, cut off from the life-rich universe".[76] Men and women, as Tagore said, yearned to experience life in a fuller and truer way, leading him to believe that "the life that is continually in blossom in the journey of human civilization, is so by continually conquering death".[77] It is in this conflict between "death and life, might and love, self-interest and welfare, this struggle of opposites to which only man's religious instinct can glimpse a true solution – a solution that is supreme peace, supreme good and supreme unity".[78]

This was Williams's yin and yang – the dialectic that undergirded his life. He believed that we could not understand ourselves if we did not understand what those in the Eastern world were saying about existence. Aware of the importance of Tagore's work and the rich insights of Eastern philosophy, Williams bemoaned that little of this rich thought can be found in Western universities. Relating this richness to Trinidad and Tobago, a nation that was on the verge of independence, Williams acknowledged that "the polyglot descendants of these castaways of Asia and Africa, uprooted and detribalized by European slave traders, we, as we move on to independence have an enormous reservoir at our disposal in the presence, in our midst of these ancient cultures of India, Africa, China and Syria".[79]

There are those who insist that Williams was a racist who had no time or interest for Trinbagonians of East Indian descent. The record, for those who choose to peruse it, tells a different story. Now that the People's Partnership is in power, they will have to revise their interpretation of our mutual past if they hope to create a united society. They will also have to accept the enormous reservoir of intelligence, philosophical wisdom and religious strength that was contained in the person of Williams, all that he tried to give to us and the enormous legacy that he has left us. Like Williams, they will have to join in the struggle to immunize themselves from the poison of racial hatred and, like Tagore, exclaim:

> Again and again to death succumb,
> In order death to overcome.
> Only later life will come,
> Itself to take the throne.[80]

In their introduction to Tagore's autobiographical essays, Devadatta Joardar and Joe Winter say of Tagore: "If literature was a focus for his inner energies the village of Santiniketan was where Tagore's practical life sought an ideal. In the deepest of ways he lived for his people. From 1901, when he started his school there, to his death, he worked continuously to let the creative currents of the society find their freedom."[81] From the moment he entered politics in 1956 until his death in 1981, Williams strove continuously to let the creative currents of our people find their freedom in an understanding of their sensuous activities. In committing his life to *re-searching* and serving his people, he was aware, as Thucydides wrote, that the essence of historical inquiry was "to correct and eliminate legends, false beliefs, [and] mistakes",[82] without which a people could not understand themselves. That is what Williams sought to do throughout his life.

Tagore's life and contribution to India's society are similar to those of Williams. In his biography on Tagore, Kripalani observed that

> Tagore's main significance lies in the impulse and direction he gave to the course of India's cultural and intellectual development, and in the example he presented of a genius passionately devoted to his art and no less passionately dedicated to the service of his people and of humanity in general. He gave them faith in their own language and in their cultural and moral heritage. The contemporary renaissance in Indian languages is due largely to his inspiration and example.[83]

This is a point I made about Williams's contribution to Trinidad and Tobago in my essay "Eric E. Williams and the Politics of Language".[84]

Williams believed in the growth and freedom of the human personality in spite of all the dross and inanities of racial chauvinism, blind egotism and an inordinate love of self. This is a message that he learned from Tagore, Gandhi and Nehru. Tagore, he said, "was an intellectual nationalist, not a nationalist politician. . . . Magnificent individualist, [he] blandly went his way, refusing to subordinate his poetry to their politics, glorifying Ancient India's 'Message of the Forest', exalting the individual personality three centuries before him as Shakespeare had done in *Hamlet*, Montaigne in his *Essays* and Pascalin in his *Pensées*."[85] It was a description that he could have applied to himself.

In *The Future of History*, John Lukacs has argued that "the purpose of history is understanding even more than accuracy (though not without a credible respect for the latter)".[86] He cites this as a major reason why historians ought to read literature, even more than statistics, "to truly widen and deepen their acquaintance with their chosen subject, but also to recognize that their main task is a kind of literature, rather than a kind of science".[87] Like the novelist, the historian must weigh each word. In the essay "History", Thomas Macaulay observed that it "could be laid down as a general rule, though subject to considerable qualifications and exceptions, that history begins in novel and ends in essay".[88] As a historian turned politician, Williams had to be even more careful in his choice of words and how he told his stories. He understood, as T.S. Eliot did, only too well that "the motive to write is the desire to vanquish a mental preoccupation by expressing it consciously and clearly".[89] I suspect that this is one reason why Williams used the insights of literature so closely to express his meanings.

After fifty years of independence, we ought to rededicate ourselves to the dreams and aspirations of the father of our nation. Eric Williams read widely and drew his inspiration from the best that was said and thought in the world, a concession he might have made to Matthew Arnold, who would have understood him perfectly. He was committed to "freedom of mind", freedom of the press and an open democracy. His sympathies knew no racial barriers as he embraced us all. He understood fully that "to be ignorant of what happened before you were born is to remain a child forever",[90] which is why he believed that the study of history and literature holds the keys to understanding the peoples of Trinidad and Tobago. He would have been sympathetic to the imperative that they ought not to be trapped by their past. The least they can do is come to terms with his teachings and the interracial message that he left, seeking to find kinship everywhere they pass and, perhaps, proclaiming as Tagore did in *Gitanjali*:

> Where the mind is without fear and the head is held high;
> Where knowledge is free;
> Where the world has not been broken into fragments by narrow domestic walls
> . . .
> Where the clear stream of reason has not lost its way into the dreary desert sand of dead habit . . .
> Into that heaven of freedom, my Father, let my country awake.[91]

NOTES

1.   See my discussion of this matter in *Indian Time Ah Come* (Wellesley, MA: Calaloux, 2010).

2.   Bengali, the language of West Bengal and Bangladesh, is one of the major languages spoken in India.

3. Rabindranath Tagore, *Of Myself: Atmaparichay*, trans. Devadattta Joardar and Joe Winter (London: Anvil, 2007), 45.
4. Eric Williams, *Inward Hunger* (Chicago: University of Chicago Press, 1971), 42.
5. Tagore, *Of Myself*, 67.
6. Williams, *Inward Hunger*, 343.
7. Krishna Kripalani points out that Tagore "was poet in the traditional Indian sense of the word, *kavi*, a seer, an intermediary between the human and the divine. His genius enriched whatever it touched. Like the sun after which he was named (*Rabi* in Bengali, derived from Sanskrit *ravi*, means the sun), he shed light and warmth on his age, vitalized the mental and moral soil of his land, revealed unknown horizons of thought and spanned the arc that divides the East from the West." Krishna Kripalani, *Rabindranath Tagore: A Biography* (New Delhi: UBSPD, 2008), xi. In African thought, one would call Williams a seer man, given his capacity to "see" things and act with a certain perspicacity. It is noteworthy that the Spiritual Baptists were his staunchest supporters.
8. Tagore, *Of Myself*, 75. Tagore loved poetry immensely, although he captured the lives of his Indian compatriots most intensely in his short stories. In a letter to a friend in May 1892, he rhapsodizes: "The joy of writing one poem . . . far exceeds that of writing sheaves and sheaves of prose. . . . If I could only write one poem a day." Quoted in Kripalani, *Rabindranath Tagore*, 176.
9. See *Commemorating the Centenary of the Birth of Dr Eric Eustace Williams, 1911–2011* (San Fernando: Viren Annamunthodo, 2011); hereafter cited in the text as *Birth of Dr Williams*. This essay was written initially for a book entitled *Mother Trinidad and Tobago* (forthcoming).
10. Tagore, *Of Myself*, 52.
11. Ibid.
12. Culture in this sense does not simply mean music, plays, literature and so on. It is also "taken to indicate patterns of thought and understanding, modes of language, rituals of life, and ways of thinking. Cultural historians have taken Marx's idea, that economic circumstances affect the way people think and behave, and have changed its emphasis: arguing that the ways in which people think affect their relationship to society and economics. Getting at the ways in which people think can involve studying the art and literature of a certain period." John H. Arnold, *History: A Very Short Introduction* (Oxford: Oxford University Press, 2000), 87.
13. Williams, *Inward Hunger*, 327.
14. Between 1900 and 1950, the literary and debating societies in Trinidad and Tobago made heroic attempts to cultivate the literary culture of the islands.

15.   Eric Williams, "Four Poets of the Greater Antilles", *Caribbean Quarterly* 2, no. 4 (1951–52): 8.
16.   Ibid., 9.
17.   Ibid.
18.   Ibid., 10.
19.   Ibid.
20.   Ibid.
21.   Ibid., 11.
22.   Ibid., 13.
23.   Ibid., 14.
24.   Quoted ibid., 15.
25.   Quoted in Eric Williams, "The Political Leader Considered as a Man of Culture", *Présence Africaine* 24–25 (February–May 1959), 98. It was reproduced in the *Nation* (29 November 1959). All quotations are taken from the *Présence Africaine* translation, although I have made slight changes. Adrian Bodlain also assisted with this translation.
26.   Williams, "Political Leader", 103.
27.   Quoted ibid., 104–5.
28.   Margery Sabin, my colleague at Wellesley College, observed: "Although Gandhi was an outspoken critic to the effect of English on Indian culture, his native language was Gujarati, and he openly acknowledged that he was not good at learning languages. He championed the idea of Hindi as a national language, but was not fluent in it. All his writing was in Gujarati which was then translated into English and other languages. Gandhi managed to develop non-linguistic ways of affirming a nation through his long marches, the use of the spinning wheel, etc." Correspondence with author, 13 September 2011.
29.   Quoted in Williams, "Political Leader", 105–6.
30.   Tagore, *Of Myself*, 91–92.
31.   Williams, "Political Leader", 110–11.
32.   See Selwyn R. Cudjoe, "Multiculturalism and Its Challenges in Trinidad and Tobago", *Society* 48, no. 4 (July/August 2011): 330–41, for a discussion on this point.
33.   See C.L.R. James's review of C.F. Andrew's "Mahatma Gandhi: His Own Story", *Beacon* 1, no. 2 (August 1931); and Beatrice Greig, "Mahatma Gandhi", *Beacon* 2, No. 4 (August 1932).
34.   The preceding quotations are taken from *Birth of Dr Williams*, 46, 48, 51–53.
35.   I am indebted to Margery Sabin for this insight into the differences between these two men.
36.   Amartya Sen, "Poetry and Reason", *New Republic*, 30 June 2011, 26.

37. John Lukacs differentiates between professional historians (men and women with PhD degrees in history) and amateur historians (those without a PhD in history). Lukacs comments that "it is more than possible that in the twenty-first century the best, the greatest writers of history may not be certified professionals but erudite and imaginative 'amateurs'". To his credit, Williams saw the realization of this possibility in the historical writings of Nehru. See John Lukacs, *The Future of History* (New Haven, CT: Yale University Press, 2011). The quotation is from page 22.

38. Shashi Tharoor, *Nehru: The Invention of India* (New Delhi: Penguin, 2003), 99.

39. *Birth of Dr Williams*, 52.

40. Ibid., 99.

41. Ibid., 99–100.

42. Amartya Sen, *The Argumentative Indian* (New York: Farrar, Straus and Giroux, 2005), 107.

43. *Birth of Dr Williams*, 13.

44. Ibid.

45. Ibid., 18–19.

46. Ibid., 89–90.

47. *Birth of Dr Williams*, 20–24.

48. Ibid., 20.

49. Ibid., 27.

50. See Victor Hugo's connection to Trinidad and Tobago in Selwyn R. Cudjoe, *Beyond Boundaries* (Wellesley, MA: Calaloux, 2003), 312–13.

51. I use the term "anxiety" in the psychoanalytical sense to capture the state of apprehension in which Williams found himself: he had to balance the demands of being an intellectual and man of culture (that is, to be reasonable, dispassionate, controlled) with those of being a nationalist leader who was expected to be a firebrand, contentious and passionate in his demands for independence. Frantz Fanon speaks about the danger in which the native intellectual finds himself: "The interest of this period is that the oppressed comes to be no longer satisfied with the objective non-existence of the dominated nation and culture. Every effort is made to induce the colonized to confess the inferiority of his culture, transformed into instinctive behavior, the unreality of his Nation, and in the extreme case, the unorganic and incomplete character of his own biological structure. In the face of this situation the reaction of the colonized is not unequivocal. While the masses preserve intact those traditions which are most heterogeneous in the light of colonial conditions, while the style of craftsmanship becomes solidified in an increasing stereotyped formalism, the Intellectual hurls himself frantically into the frenzied acquisition of the Culture of the Occupant, taking great pains

to disparage his national culture, or immures himself in the circumstantial, methodological, passionate and rapidly sterile enumeration of his culture." See Frantz Fanon, "The Reciprocal Basis of National Cultures and the Struggle for Liberation", *Présence Africaine* 24–25 (February–May 1959): 89–90. Richard Wright, a famous African American author, dedicated his book of essays, *White Man Listen* (New York: Harper Perennial, 1957) to Williams and "the Westernized and tragic elite of Asia, Africa, and the West Indies", describing them as "the lonely outsiders who exist precariously on the clifflike margins of many cultures – men who are distrusted, misunderstood, maligned by Left and Right, Christian and pagan – men who carry on their frail but indefatigable shoulders the best of two worlds – and who, amidst the confusion and stagnation, seek desperately for a home for their hearts: a home which, if found, could be a home for the hearts of all men". In his autobiography, Williams refers to Wright as an "old friend". *Inward Hunger*, 142.

52. *Birth of Dr Williams*, 42.

53. Ibid., 28.

54. See Eric Williams, "Massa Day Done", in Selwyn R. Cudjoe, *Eric E. Williams Speaks* (Amherst: University of Massachusetts Press, 2006), 237–64.

55. In 1920, in a letter to his father, Nehru wrote: "Greatness is being thrust upon me" (Tharoor, *Nehru*, 30). In *Inward Hunger*, Williams observes: "Some are born great, some achieve greatness, some have greatness thrust upon them. Greatness, Trinidad style, was thrust upon me from the cradle" (Williams, *Inward Hunger*, 30). Nehru may well have been Dr Williams's inspiration with regard to his being singled out to be great.

56. *Birth of Dr Williams*, 43.

57. Sen, *Argumentative Indian*, 90.

58. Ibid., 108.

59. Tharoor, *Nehru*, 33.

60. Amartya Sen, foreword, in Rabindranath Tagore, *Boyhood Days* (London: Hesperus Worldwide, 2007), xi.

61. Sen, *Argumentative Indian*, 113–14. Sen writes, "Tagore was concerned not only that there be wider opportunities for education across the country (especially in rural areas where schools were few), but also that the schools themselves be more lively and enjoyable. He himself had dropped out of school early, largely out of boredom, and had never bothered to earn a diploma. He wrote extensively on how schools should be made more attractive to boys and girls and thus more productive. His own co-educational school at Santiniketan had many progressive features. The emphasis here was on self-motivation rather than on discipline, and on fostering intellectual curiosity rather than competitive excellence." Sen,

a big supporter of Tagore and his educational method, attended Tagore's school, Santiniketan, as his mother did before him. Former Indian prime minister Indira Gandhi was also a student at Santiniketan.

62.   Sen, "Poetry and Reason", 26.

63.   Ibid., 104.

64.   Kripalani, *Rabindranath Tagore*, 173.

65.   *Birth of Dr Williams*, 57.

66.   Ibid.

67.   Williams, *Inward Hunger*, 42.

68.   *Birth of Dr Williams*, 60–61.

69.   Ibid., 57.

70.   Sen, "Poetry and Reason", 27.

71.   There is some evidence that Williams believed that he was not as successful in his endeavours (as a nationalist and as a leader) as he wished. A few weeks before his death, as he saw the public protest of the civil servants marching around the Red House, he is reputed to have exclaimed, "Lord! What have I wrought?"

72.   *Birth of Dr Williams*, 68.

73.   Ibid., 68–69.

74.   Ibid., 68.

75.   Ibid.

76.   Tagore, *Of Myself*, 68.

77.   Ibid., 69.

78.   Ibid., 66–67.

79.   Ibid., 80.

80.   Ibid., 69.

81.   Tagore, *Of Myself*, 12.

82.   Lukacs, *Future of History*, 57.

83.   Kripalani, *Rabindranath Tagore*, xii.

84.   See Selwyn R. Cudjoe, "Eric E. Williams and the Politics of Language", in *Eric E. Williams Speaks*, 35–110.

85.   *Birth of Dr Williams*, 68, 85.

86.   Lukacs, *Future of History*, 89.

87.   Ibid., 89.

88.   Thomas Macaulay, *The Miscellaneous Writings and Speeches of Lord Macaulay* (London: Longmans, Green, 1889), 133.

89.   Lukacs, *Future of History*, 96.

90.   Quoted ibid., 78.

91.   Quoted in Sen, *Argumentative Indian*, 98.

Chapter 4

Eric Williams and the Challenges of Caribbean Integration

COLIN A. PALMER

Meeting in 2011, the leaders of the Caribbean governments placed "on pause" their plans to strengthen the Caribbean Economic Community. This decision to postpone the making of difficult decisions reflected the triumph of petty nationalism over far-sighted and progressive thinking about the future of these mostly small and impoverished political units. This was hardly the first time that Anglo-Caribbean leaders had failed to act expeditiously and courageously to address their common problems. Attempts to promote some kind of collective behaviour by the anglophone units can be traced to the late seventeenth century, but the challenges have remained essentially unmet over time.

Eric Eustace Williams was the most aggressive and persistent proponent of the concept of an integrated Caribbean in the twentieth century. There were others, to be sure, such as T. Albert Marryshow, Grantley Adams, Norman Manley and Forbes Burnham, but none addressed it with the passion and intellectual vigour that Williams invested in the cause. Williams brought an unparalleled understanding of the Caribbean and its political, social and economic realities to his advocacy, supplemented by his considerable analytical prowess and acerbic tongue. His research for his books *Capitalism and Slavery* and *The Negro in the Caribbean* broadened his knowledge of the Caribbean and its peoples and added power, authenticity and urgency to his arguments.

Williams began his advocacy of the economic and political integration of the Caribbean in the 1940s. His views were shaped, in part, by the domination of the region's economies by sugar and the dependence on foreign capital. In the early 1940s, for example, sugar cane cultivation accounted for four-fifths of the arable land in Antigua, three-fifths in Cuba and two-fifths in Puerto Rico. Sugar constituted nine-tenths of Barbados's exports, four-fifths of Cuba's exports and two-thirds of the exports from the Dominican Republic and Puerto Rico. The cultivation of sugar cane engaged 50 per cent of the population of Puerto Rico and 33.3 per cent of that of Cuba and Antigua.

Although Williams questioned the economic viability of sugar cane's domination in these economies, he saw it "as neither accidental nor arbitrary". He believed that the islands "are too small and their arable land too inadequate to permit of any extensive diversification". The islands tried a number of alternative crops over the years, Williams said, "but they have all succumbed to world competition". The list included cotton, cocoa, arrow root and lime. It was only in sugar cane, Williams stressed, that "the islands had been able to hold their own in the world market".[1]

The concentration on sugar cane and other export crops led to a dependence on imported foodstuffs. Jamaica, for example, was importing one-quarter of its food, Trinidad one-fifth and Grenada one-third. Williams did not believe, however, that any of the islands could become self-sufficient in food production, given the limited amount of land available for agriculture, as well as population pressures. But he held the view that the encouragement of sugar refining and the development of secondary industries would relieve "the pressure of population on the land".

Williams observed that "inter-insular relations were virtually non-existent". This led him to conclude that "the Caribbean, in fact, is a geographical expression". It was "a collection of isolated units, each functioning independently of the others". Williams emphasized that if change were to occur in the region, "it must be carefully planned and must involve a closer union of the now separated Caribbean units". Elaborating, he said: "No worthwhile industries could be developed in Barbados for 190,000 people; or in Jamaica for one and a quarter million; or in Cuba for four million. But combine the different units, you get a total population of some fourteen or fifteen million people. Then on the basis of these pooled resources, you can work out industrialization plans, and talk of the greater self-sufficiency or a planned economy."[2]

In order to strengthen his argument, Williams approvingly quoted Colonel Stanley, the secretary of state for the colonies. Stanley maintained that the future of the British West Indies resided in the creation of "some organization which will bring together the West Indies and the rest of the Caribbean area which will enable them to find some solution of [to?] problems which are as common in Puerto Rico or indeed to Cuba and Haiti as to Jamaica". He thought that if the Caribbean were to survive and prosper, it "must be fitted into the world as a whole".[3]

Williams shared this assessment, adding: "Trinidad by itself, Puerto Rico by itself, Cuba by itself, can only continue at the economic mercy of the more advanced and more powerful countries of the world. Federation will make possible an economic development now impossible, and give the Caribbean area a bargaining power in the world which its isolated units do not have now."[4]

Paraphrasing President Roosevelt, who had recently visited Mexico, Williams said that "the peoples of the Caribbean have for some years increasingly recognized the principle of independence; it is time now for them to recognize the privilege of interdependence".[5]

Williams saw no merit in these units remaining separate. These "tiny isolated communities" constituted "eighteenth century fossils in a twentieth century world", he asserted. He noticed signs, however, of a developing "unity". It was "fostered by the increase of inter-island travel, the improvement of communications, the unifying effects of the aeroplane, and by the contact made by students and tourists in England, America, Canada and the various universities of those countries". There were other enabling factors as well. These included the location of the colonies "in the same climatic zone, endowed with a similar economic structure, burdened by the same difficulties and problems, peopled by the same race". Williams declared that "nothing less than a Caribbean Federation made sense". He saw no justification "for the expensive duplication of necessary administrative and social services in islands whose budgets and revenues are exceeded by the wealth of many private individuals in larger countries".[6]

Williams was sensitive to the obstacles in the path of the economic and political integration of the territories in the region. He recognized "difficulties of distance – as between Trinidad to the South and Jamaica to the East –, difficulties of uneven economic development – as between Trinidad with its oil and Barbados with nothing but sugar". But he did not believe that "these difficulties are of the magnitude that is often contended", predicting that the federation would not be "built in one day".[7] Still, Williams emphasized that "some form of a federation is demanded at least by common sense".[8]

Eric Williams endorsed the Anglo-American Caribbean Commission when it was founded in March 1942. Its purpose was to promote and strengthen a more extensive social and economic cooperation among the British and American territories in the Caribbean. This enhanced cooperation, it was hoped, would provide the foundation for the political and economic integration that some were proposing for the region. Williams accepted an appointment with the commission in 1944, ultimately becoming the deputy chairman of its Caribbean Research Council. His responsibilities included research and the organization of conferences. During his tenure at the commission, Williams was unable to comment publicly on proposals for federation advanced by Caribbean governments, because they "were associated with the work of the Commission".[9]

The potential creation of a West Indies federation received a strong endorsement from the commission's report. Appointed in 1938 in the aftermath of the labour rebellions, the commission was mandated to explore the social and economic conditions that precipitated them and to recommend appropriate reforms. Led by Lord Moyne, the commission concluded that the future of the West Indies resided in the creation of a political federation. The first tentative step towards the formation of the union occurred in Montego Bay, Jamaica, in 1947. Invited by the secretary of state for the colonies, all of the British West Indian governments met to lay the foundation for the creation of the federal unit. The attendees at the conference agreed to create the Standing Closer Association Committee to draft a federal constitution.

Eric Williams did not participate in the conference at Montego Bay since he was not an official of a Caribbean government. He was not hesitant, however, to voice his ideas about the federal union in succeeding years. Williams reiterated his support for the political and economic integration of the territories but insisted that the union be accorded dominion status. He welcomed "an autonomous British Caribbean community equal in status to the other members of the British Commonwealth, in no way subordinate to any of the others in any aspect of its domestic or external affairs".[10] Williams also advocated for substantial economic support from the imperial government for the federation. The author of *Capitalism and Slavery* stressed that the colonies had a special claim on the British treasury. As he expressed it:

> The British Caribbean Federation has a claim on the United Kingdom's government which no other part of the Empire has. That is that the very presence of the two largest racial stocks, the African and the Indian, is the result of deliberate British policies designed to produce sugar and other products in the West Indies to meet British needs. We can get grants from Britain for past services which need not be regarded as charity or need not afford a basis for continued political control.[11]

Williams's tenure at the Caribbean Commission had allowed him to develop a very sophisticated understanding of the economy of the various islands and British Guiana. More than any other West Indian leader of the time, Eric Williams could speak authoritatively about the weaknesses and strengths of these economies, both individually and as a region. It was this understanding that made him advocate a massive infusion of capital as a necessity if the region were to experience substantial and sustained economic growth and development.

Not until 1957 did Williams become actively involved in planning for the federation. He had assumed the office of chief minister of Trinidad and Tobago the previous year. The selection of Trinidad as the federal capital in 1957 gave him an important role in shaping the union. When Chaguaramas was chosen as the actual site of the capital, Williams initiated a long and acrimonious dispute with the Americans to vacate the naval base they had built there. Williams did not stand for election to the federal parliament in 1958, but he became a strong and persistent critic of the federation's constitutional structure and its impoverished condition.

Williams denounced the "anaemic" West Indies Federation, describing its constitution as "colonial" and declaring that Trinidad wanted "nothing else than a consolidated Nation, free and independent, a strong federal Government, and economic development on a national scale".[12] Williams explained:

> We were not raising the question of independence and a strong Federal Government for abstract reasons either of pride in the first place. . . . For us

it was the very life of the federation which was at stake. Independence meant turning of the minds and ideas of the West Indies from London and the Colonial Office, which had hitherto been our centre, to the Federal Capital, where the politics and economics of the West Indies would be decided. It was through such a political medium also that we of the West Indies would be able to unite ourselves.[13]

Williams strongly believed that the federation needed a strong centre if it were to succeed. He supported tightly knit federation, "adequately empowered at the Centre, to shape and direct the future of the Nation . . . the centre should have a far wider range of powers than it at present possesses".[14] The Jamaican leaders, Norman Manley and Alexander Bustamante, feared that a federation that was constructed along these lines posed a threat to their island's autonomy, preferring a union with much weaker powers. The smaller islands endorsed Williams's position, effectively isolating Jamaica.

When the leaders of the federating units held an intergovernmental conference in 1959, they failed to resolve their principal differences. These included the structure of the federal government, the formula for the allocation of seats in the federal parliament, the creation of a customs union and the pace at which freedom of movement among the units should be introduced. Eric Williams was the dominant personage at the conference, according to reports in the *Daily Gleaner*. "The Conference went wherever Dr Williams went", observed the newspaper's political reporter.[15]

Williams knew, however, that Trinidad and Tobago and Jamaica had to establish a modus vivendi to ensure a positive future for the union. The first step in this process occurred in August 1960 when Manley and Williams met in Antigua to discuss and resolve their political differences. Eric Williams made significant concessions, including granting Jamaica a virtual veto power over some decisions of the federal parliament and retreating somewhat from his advocacy of a strong federal centre.[16] Williams was genuinely trying to save the federation from an early demise. As he explained:

> We could see no other way of saving the Federation, because we were convinced that to insist on our conception would break up the Federation. We disagreed with Jamaica's thinking. . . . We believe Jamaica's fears exaggerated. But if to save the Federation it was necessary to respect these fears, to respect apprehensions which would, at worst, drive Jamaica out of the Federation, or might,

at best, jeopardize Jamaica's stability and thus endanger Jamaica's capacity to
contribute jointly with Trinidad and Tobago, over 80% of the Federal resources
. . . then we of Trinidad and Tobago decided that Jamaica was not to be pushed
to the wall; Jamaica was to be saved for the Federation and the growth of Federal
power would be more gradual than in our hearts we had originally anticipated.[17]

This extraordinary agreement had little practical effect. Manley's colleagues were delighted by Williams's concessions. Williams, however, was
unable to get the endorsement of his senior colleagues. He retreated from
some of the concessions he had made, even denying that he had agreed that
Jamaica could exercise a veto power over some of the decisions made by the
federal parliament. "We don't propose", Williams said, "to agree to any condition which provides any single unit with a power of veto. We have never been
committed to such a suggestion." The minutes of the meeting with Manley
contradict this assertion.[18]

In the end, the two men were unable to save the federation. Led by Alexander Bustamante, the anti-federation movement in Jamaica became more
virulent. There was no strong support for the union in Jamaica anyway, and
the continuing squabbles among the leaders of the territories exacerbated the
situation. Seeking to resolve the question of Jamaica's political future, Manley called a referendum in September 1961 to determine whether the island
would remain in the union. The voters supported secession, and the West
Indies Federation ended. "One from ten leaves nought", was Eric Williams's
comment. He flirted, however, with the idea of creating a smaller Eastern
Caribbean federation under Trinidad's leadership, but this was stillborn. He
eventually led his country to independence in August of 1962. Williams also
tried to absorb Grenada into a union with Trinidad and Tobago, but these
efforts were unsuccessful.[19]

Despite the failure of the West Indies Federation, Williams never abandoned his faith in the efficacy of the political and economic integration of
the Caribbean. He realized that it was politically injudicious to revisit the
question of a political federation too soon after the demise of the first experi-
ment. Under the circumstances, Williams began to emphasize the question
of economic integration. Shortly after he decided to opt for the independence
of Trinidad and Tobago, Williams told a meeting of the British Caribbean
Association in London that he planned to promote "the undertaking of some

form of Caribbean Economic Community, with powers within the economic sphere which might ultimately extend to political spheres".[20] Given the political climate in the region, this made practical sense. But Williams's principal objective remained the founding of a political union. "I don't see any future for the West Indian area that excludes planning in that direction", he told an interviewer from the British Broadcasting Corporation in August 1962. "In so far as we in Trinidad and Tobago, with independence and a large population majority can influence things, we have been moving in that direction, not limiting ourselves to our former colleagues in the Federation, we have begun discussions with Guiana, that are going on now."[21]

Continuing to believe that the region as a whole benefited from a common approach to similar problems, Williams proposed regular meetings of the heads of the governments of the independent and self-governing states. Patterned after the Organization of African Unity, these gatherings would include representatives of all such countries in the region with the exception of Cuba, Haiti and the Dominican Republic. Williams viewed the dictatorial regimes in these islands with disfavour, hence his desire to exclude them. He would later change his position.

Although Jamaica's withdrawal from the West Indies Federation had precipitated its demise, Prime Minister Alexander Bustamante was receptive to Williams's proposal, provided that the meetings were confined to Anglo-Caribbean governments. The first meeting, including Jamaica, Trinidad and Tobago, and British Guiana (later Guyana), occurred in Port of Spain in 1963. Additional meetings were convened in 1964 and 1965, and in subsequent years. The leaders addressed issues relating to regional cooperation, but they did not agree on much of major significance.

Still fiercely committed to the realization of the political and economic integration of the Caribbean writ large, Williams held discussions with the secretary of state for the colonies in mid-1964 as well as with the leaders of the governments of Puerto Rico and the Netherlands Antilles. In his meeting with Nigel Fisher, the secretary of state, Williams proposed the creation of a new union, including Trinidad and Tobago, Puerto Rico, Suriname, Jamaica, Haiti, the Netherlands Antilles, the French Islands, British Guiana and the Dominican Republic. He pointedly excluded Cuba because of the Marxist nature of its regime. Williams was not proposing a political union, but what appears to be an embryonic confederation. Initially, the association would consist of a customs union, a shipping service and a regional airline.[22]

The time was hardly propitious for such meaningful collective action. Lacking in vision and blinded by their insularity, the other Caribbean leaders were not likely to greet such proposals with enthusiasm. Eric Williams also had the capacity to sabotage his own initiatives. Arrogant and abrasive, Williams was frequently at odds with his Caribbean peers. The chronic disharmony exacerbated the difficulty of obtaining support for his proposals, no matter how meritorious they seemed. Three years after the demise of the West Indies Federation, the governments of Antigua, British Guiana and Barbados agreed to establish a free trade area, removing barriers on trade between them. The agreement that established the Caribbean Free Trade Association was signed at Dickenson Bay, Antigua, in December 1965. Eric Williams was not a party to the agreement, and he responded to the creation of the association with a feigned and lofty disinterest.

The agreement at Dickenson Bay was not enforced, because of other developments. Its signing, however, became a catalyst for discussions on the creation of a larger Caribbean free trade area. The region's leaders were concerned that, if the United Kingdom joined the European Economic Community, this would have a deleterious impact on Caribbean exports. Consequently, they became increasingly more receptive to the notion of Caribbean integration and to reducing their dependence on foreign markets. The fledgling movement towards Caribbean integration received a significant boost when two University of the West Indies economists presented a report on the subject in April 1967. Havelock Brewster and C.Y. Thomas, the two economists, advocated an integrated production of goods by the territories in the region. They proposed a sectoral approach to the problem, beginning with "the basic resource inputs of the particular sector to the disposition and scale of final output yielded by the sector". This would require a high degree of central planning and coordination, both of which were alien to the traditions of the territories.

The Caribbean Free Trade Agreement took effect in May of 1968. It provided for the establishment of a common external tariff, the development of regional industries requiring the entire market of the signatory territories, the implementation of a common regional policy regarding fiscal incentives for the introduction of new industries, and so on. The CARIFTA reflected the ideas and influence of Eric Williams, but it had other parents as well. It did not, however, include the sectoral integration that the two University of the West Indies economists had recommended.

Four territories signed the CARIFTA agreement on 1 May 1968. They included Trinidad and Tobago, Barbados, Antigua, and Guyana. Dominica, Grenada, St Kitts–Nevis–Anguilla, St Lucia and St Vincent joined on 1 July, and Jamaica and Montserrat joined a month later. The signatories had a combined population of about 4.5 million, with Jamaica constituting almost 50 per cent of the potential market. Within eighteen months of the implementation of the agreement, Jamaica, Barbados, Guyana, and Trinidad and Tobago had increased their domestic exports by 60 per cent. Trinidad and Tobago outdistanced the others, boasting an increase of 70 per cent in its interregional exports. Jamaica and Barbados saw 50 per cent increases and Guyana saw 25 per cent.[23]

Statistics such as these must have delighted Williams. But he continued to display a deep and strong affection for a political union. This could be an exercise in delusion, as Williams demonstrated in 1972. Sir Peter Tennant, an official of the London-based West India Committee, was invited to lunch with Williams when he visited Port of Spain in December 1972. Williams asked him to convey a secret message to Edward Heath, the British prime minister. Williams, according to Tennant, was asking Heath to "never mention the matter publicly nor allow any of your colleagues to leak". Williams, Tennant informed Heath, said that he left the last CARIFTA conference that was in Trinidad "with the firm conviction that a Caribbean political federation, at first without Jamaica is round the corner". Tennant said he asked Williams for his reasons, but "he said the matter was too delicate, and I must believe him and let you know". Tennant was hoping, however, that Williams "is right as nothing on the face of it looks less likely from what I have seen, at least in the near future which is what he means" – but Williams was indulging in a fantasy, an unusual behaviour for him.[24]

Despite this misreading of the prospects for a new political union, Williams was still trying to foster closer relations among the territories of the region for much of the 1970s. On 18 June 1971, for example, his government announced that it was creating a nine-member National Task Force to examine closer relations between Trinidad and Tobago and the rest of the Caribbean. It was empowered "to assess the various initiatives towards closer association in the Caribbean which have been developed in the past ten years". Specifically, Williams wanted the task force to examine "the disbandment of the West Indies Federation", the heads of government conferences, CARIFTA, the harmonization of fiscal incentives in the region, the rationalization of agriculture and so on. It was also asked "to make recommendations for the future . . . on integration of the Caribbean territories, not excluding political association, and taking into account the possibility of closer collaboration with non-commonwealth countries".

The task force received an ambitious and wide-ranging charge. Its terms of reference reflected the vision of the Caribbean that Williams wanted to call into being, a region integrated both politically and economically. Given the enormity of the challenges it confronted, it is not surprising that the task force took three years to present its report.[25]

The creation of the task force was greeted with some criticism. Some critics argued that the task force should have included representatives from the other Caribbean territories. Others questioned Williams's motives for establishing it. The task force, however, was intended to gather and evaluate information upon which the government of Trinidad and Tobago could formulate an effective and informed Caribbean policy. This kind of study was unprecedented in the region and could be beneficial to all of its constituent territories. The task force's four-hundred-page report contained no surprises in its recommendations, but it underscored the necessity to foster a higher degree of regional integration and cooperation. It merely added teeth to Williams's well-known views on those matters.[26]

Although the task force's report may have helped to shape Trinidad and Tobago's policy towards the region as a whole, Eric Williams could not wave a magic wand to achieve the integration it recommended. This required collective action inspired by far-sighted leadership. CARIFTA had constituted a necessary first step in that direction. It was replaced by the CARICOM, a larger unit with more extensive powers.

CARICOM officially came into existence in 1973. Its principal provisions included the creation of an integrated regional market, the adoption of a common external tariff and the implementation of a common protective policy. The fifteen signatories to the Treaty of Chaguaramas that created CARICOM pledged themselves to adopt and promote joint policies and actions to enhance regional economic development. They agreed to jointly negotiate external trade agreements and to create a Caribbean Investment Corporation. These principal objectives would be enlarged and clarified over time.

Eric Williams would have liked a regional economic organization empowered to engage in central planning for the region. He also wanted closer cooperation among its members to counter the increasing influence of Venezuela and Cuba in the region. Frustrated by his inability to achieve these objectives, Williams became increasingly critical of CARICOM and the behaviour of some of its member states. When Jamaica and Guyana curtailed imports from Trinidad and Tobago in 1977 to protect endangered industries, an angry Williams announced that he intended to impose a "system of selected control of imports into Trinidad and Tobago. It is tit for tat."[27] This was an unworthy response from the principal architect of Caribbean integration in the twentieth century. In fact, Williams devoted less of his energy to the cause of integration in the Caribbean after 1977, allowing some critics to accuse him of practising Trinidadian isolationism.

Three decades after the passing of Eric Williams, his vision for the economic and political integration of the Caribbean remains largely unfulfilled. Few contemporary academics and even fewer politicians provide intellectual leadership on the promise and challenge of a political union. CARICOM still exists, hobbling along on crutches. There are other examples of regional cooperation, most notably the University of the West Indies. But there is a paucity of bold and far-sighted leadership in a region increasingly characterized by the mediocrity of its elected officials. Eric Williams imagined a Caribbean with a common future, not the debilitating parochialism and insularity that bedevil the region.

NOTES

1. This and the following quotations came from Eric Williams, "An Analysis of the Economic Development of the Caribbean" (typescript, Eric Williams Memorial Collection). A slightly revised version of the paper was published in E. Franklin Frazier and Eric Williams, eds., *The Economic Future of The Caribbean* (Washington, DC: Howard University Press, 1944), 19–24. This book was reprinted by the Majority Press, Dover, MA, in 2004, with a new introduction by Tony Martin.

2. Williams, "Analysis of the Economic Development", n.p.

3. Quoted ibid., n.p.

4. Ibid.

5. Ibid.

6. See Eric Williams, "The Anglo-American Caribbean Commission: Its Problems and Prospects" (typescript, Eric Williams Memorial Collection, 14 March 1943), n.p.

7. Ibid.

8. See Eric Williams, "My Federation Record" (typescript, Eric Williams Memorial Collection, n.d.), n.p.

9. Ibid.

10. Eric Williams, "Federation in the World Today" (Eric Williams Memorial Collection, 25 February 1955), n.p.; Eric Williams, "The Proposed Federal Constitution for the British Caribbean" (Eric Williams Memorial Collection).

11. Williams, "Federation in the World Today", n.p.

12. Eric Williams, *Inward Hunger: The Education of a Prime Minister* (Princeton, NJ: Markus Wiener, 2006), 17.

13. Ibid., 185.

14. John Mordecai, *The West Indies: The Federal Negotiations* (Evanston, IL: Northwestern University Press, 1968), 161.

15. "A Failure and a Success?" *Daily Gleaner*, 11 October 1959, 6.

16. *Report on Meeting between the Premiers of Jamaica and Trinidad at the Anchorage, Antigua on the 7th and 8th August 1960*, Norman Manley Papers, Jamaica Archives, Spanish Town.

17. Quoted in Mordecai, *West Indies*, 250.

18. Ibid., 279.

19. See Colin Palmer, *Eric Williams and the Making of the Modern Caribbean* (Chapel Hill: University of North Carolina Press, 2006), 70–75, 179–97.

20. R.B. Manderson-Jones, *Jamaican Foreign Policy in the Caribbean, 1962–1988* (Kingston: CARICOM Publishers, 1990), n.p.; Palmer, *Eric Williams*, 70.

21.   "Eric Williams BBC Interview", 9 August 1962, Records of the Dominions Office and of the Commonwealth Relations and Foreign Offices, Public Record Office, London 200/95.

22.   Palmer, *Eric Williams*, 71.

23.   For a discussion of the formation of CARIFTA, see Joseph A. Tyndall, "The Development of the Caribbean Free Trade Area", Records of the Foreign and Commonwealth Office and Predecessors, Public Record Office, FCO63/635.

24.   Letter from Peter Tennant to Edward Heath, 2 December 1972, Records of the Prime Minister's Office, Public Record Office, PREM15/1255.

25.   Letter from David Burnikell to F.D. Milne, esq., 6 August, 1971, FCO63/864.

26.   "Report of The Caribbean Task Force", 21 June 1974, FCO63/1264.

27.   Letter from J.R. Patterson to R.W. Newsam, esq., 27 October 1977, FCO44/1410.

Chapter 5

Eric Williams and the Construction of a Caribbean History

FRANKLIN W. KNIGHT

The Caribbean has always had a history, and historians have been trying to capture that history ever since Christopher Columbus wrote his famous journal of his first voyage in 1492 and, two years later, commissioned Father Ramón Pané to write an account of the early inhabitants that he found living on the island of Hispaniola. Columbus wrote, as did every early explorer, to describe his experiences and authenticate his achievements in the manner of his idol, Marco Polo.[1] Pané's short treatise is considered to be "the first book written on American soil in a European language".[2] Neither Columbus's journal nor Pané's report constitutes a proper history, but they do represent important sources for the then-emerging historiography of the Caribbean. As a new site for the expansion of European social and political forms as well as a new arena for religious proselytization during the sixteenth century, the Caribbean became the locus for an impressive historiography, as illustrated by the significant historiographical studies of Elsa Goveia, Gordon Lewis, Barry Higman and Nigel Bolland.[3] Much of this rich historiographical tradition emanated from the quests of empire and the subsequent rivalries produced in the Caribbean by the successive, and often conflicting, aims of imperialists, settlers and sojourners.[4] Different audiences required different types of "histories", and so, throughout time, histories of the Caribbean have reflected the changing perspectives by their authors. Not surprisingly, the majority of these early authors were from Europe, and their attempts to portray the region of the Caribbean responded to a strong desire to establish hegemony, support

European expansion and attain private and collective wealth. Any attempt to assess the role of Eric Williams in the writing of Caribbean history and the expansion of Caribbean historiography must begin with the recognition that behind every history is a rich contextual bonding of ideas and culture.

Unlike the large, complex, sophisticated mainland empires, the indigenous Taino people of the Caribbean were relatively recent arrivals from disparate mainland locations, beginning around the seventh century of the modern era. They did not have an easily recoverable or self-evident history. Their precipitate disappearance inhibited the sort of contact information that was available for Mexico or Peru.[5] The Taino of the Caribbean left no written records, no pictographs of how they viewed their island world and no specific notion of how they related to other known or unknown peoples. This led the English historian John Parry and his Jamaican colleague Philip Sherlock to write, in the original version of their well-known history of the British Antilles, that "the recorded history of the West Indies does not grow gradually, as most Old World histories grow, out of a more remote mythological past. It begins abruptly with a definite event: the arrival of the European discoverers in Columbus's fleet in 1492. The present aspect of the islands has been shaped largely by events which took place after that date."[6]

The falsity of the statement is self-evident, but it does highlight the considerable extent to which early Caribbean historiography became distorted by writers who failed to adjust their parochial and myopic lenses. The Tainos might not have had a written history, but they did have a history that can be recovered, although not from conventionally written sources or oral accounts.[7] To a certain extent, the distorted vision reflected by Parry and Sherlock is common in almost all the historiography of the Caribbean before Eric Williams's seminal work, *Capitalism and Slavery*.[8] Williams became the first to fundamentally change the observation point of Caribbean history and to bring an entirely different set of cultural values to bear on his work. Indeed, his national *History of the People of Trinidad and Tobago* begins with a chapter on "Our American Ancestor".[9] By so doing Williams correctly stretched the Caribbean antiquity to include the pre-Hispanic inhabitants, whose culture and DNA would indelibly influence the original European attempts to transform the Caribbean world.

The long tradition of Europeans placing the Caribbean marginally to the mainstream of European interests should not be surprising. The earliest Spanish historians and chroniclers of the Caribbean sought to justify the Iberian presence in their newly encountered sphere, although their reasons varied. Columbus and Pané were genuinely intellectually curious, but they also needed hard evidence to support claims of a Castilian possession, which was the only way Columbus could earn his reward. He was desperate to justify his error in not arriving in China and accessing its immense riches for his Castilian benefactors. Gonzalo Fernández de Oviedo y Valdés (1478–1557), Peter Martyr d'Anghiera (1457–1526) and Antonio de Herrera y Tordesillas (1549–1626) were official court historians, of whom only Oviedo had any first-hand experience of the Americas. Oviedo served as a gold assessor in Hispaniola between 1514 and 1523 and made about five subsequent visits to the New World. Herrera, although he never went to the Indies, was court historian for Philip II with access to important people and valuable, imperially generated official documents. A prolific and experienced writer, Oviedo's four-volume *Historia general de los hechos de los Castellanos en las islas y tierra firme del Mar Oceano*[10] presents a detailed narrative of the first century of Spanish activities in the Americas. The basic intention of the author, however, is to give the monarch a detailed inventory of his newly acquired royal estates. The Italian, Peter Martyr, never visited the Americas but, like Herrera, who came later, was very important at court. As chaplain to Ferdinand and Isabella, Peter Martyr also had access to official records as well as individuals who had travelled to the New World.[11] In 1524, Martyr was appointed the absentee abbot of Jamaica, but, although he authorized the construction of the first church to be built with stone material, he never visited the island before his death in 1526. Martyr's writings were descriptions of the overseas royal realm with marginal concern for the autonomous legitimacy of the inhabitants.

Two early historians whose work influenced almost all other the early historians, official as well as unofficial, were Bartolomé de las Casas (1484–1566), the Dominican priest who made a personal fortune in Hispaniola and Cuba between 1502 and 1514, and Bernal Díaz del Castillo (1492–1585), the poignantly articulate captain in the expedition of Hernán Cortés to Mexico in 1519.

Las Casas, the itinerant priest, designated defender of the indigenous population and an indefatigable polemicist, wrote several accounts of the Spanish in the Americas.[12] Las Casas reflected the dominant mode of intellectual thought of his age. He was neither a pacifist nor an anti-imperialist nor a genuine anti-slavery advocate. He believed in wars, provided they were just wars. He believed in slavery, provided the slaves were legally acquired and treated well. Like other Europeans, Las Casas tended to homogenize the indigenous population and to treat them as one large, intellectually and technologically inferior community.[13]

Díaz del Castillo wrote his history while he was living in Guatemala, largely to refute the notion that only important people such as the eminent conquistador Hernán Cortés (1485–1547) achieved the incredible conquest of the Americas in the early decades of the sixteenth century.[14] In his introduction, Díaz del Castillo wrote:

> My relation will give to historians sufficient whereby to celebrate our general [Hernán] Cortés, and the brave conquerors by whose hands this holy and great undertaking succeeded; for this is no history of distant nations, nor vain reveries; I relate that of which I was an eyewitness, and not idle reports and hearsay: for truth is sacred. [Francisco López de] Gomara received and wrote such accounts as were intended to enhance the fame and merit of Cortés; no mention being made by him of our valiant captains and soldiers; and the whole tenor of the work shows how much he was influenced by his attachment to the family by whom he and his were patronized.[15]

Díaz del Castillo has little positive to say about the past or the reality of the indigenous Indians, although he provides a poignant and precise description of the reality of conquest and a good reason for the Spanish intrusion in the New World:

> of the five hundred and fifty soldiers who left the island of Cuba with Cortés, at the moment that I am writing this history in the year one thousand five hundred and sixty eight no more than five are living, the rest having been killed in wars, sacrificed to idols, or died naturally. In answer to your question concerning their tombs and monuments, I tell you that their tombs are the maws of cannibal Indians, who devoured their limbs, and of tigers, serpents, and birds of prey, which feasted on their mangled bodies. Such were their sepulchers, and such their monuments! But to me it appears that the names of those ought to be written in letters of gold, who died so cruel a death, for the service of God and his Majesty, to give light to those who were in darkness, and to procure wealth which all men desire.[16]

By the seventeenth century, the Spanish and Portuguese monopoly of the Americas had been effectively shattered as, beginning in the late 1620s, English, French and Dutch settlements were established on the eastern Caribbean periphery of the Spanish-American settlements. Accounts of the new developments in the Caribbean began to proliferate, most of them informative and promotional about specific locations. Sometimes the accounts were regional, covering the entire Caribbean, such as the religious travel-writer Samuel Purchas's politically motivated *Purchas his Pilgrimage, or Relations of the World and the Religions Observed in all Ages and Places Discovered from the Creation unto this Present* that appeared around 1613. In a similar vein, the remarkable seventeenth-century ex-Dominican friar Thomas Gage issued his *English American his Travails by Sea and Land* in 1648, a work that partly inspired Thomas Cromwell's military expedition to Jamaica in 1655.[17] More general in scope were the remarkable histories of Jean-Baptiste Du Tertre (1610–87), who served as a missionary to the French Antilles between 1640 and 1658. Du Tertre was the author of a *Histoire générale des îles Saint-Christophe, de la Guadeloupe, de la Martinique et autres de l'Amérique*; the *Histoire naturelle et morale des îles Antilles de l'Amérique avec un vocabulaire caraïbe*; *La Vie de Sainte Austrebert*; and the four-volume *l'Histoire générale des Antilles habitées par les Français*, all appearing in Paris between 1654 and 1671. Increasingly, these histories were territory-specific, such as Diego de Torres Vargas's *Descripción de la Isla y Ciudad de Puerto Rico* of 1647 or Richard Ligon's *History of Barbados* that appeared in 1659. The Caribbean was a changing place, and that was reflected in the historical literature.

By the eighteenth century, a new Caribbean had appeared. The initial attempts to reproduce microcosms of European settler society in the Caribbean, as described by Diego de Torres Vargas (1592–1649) for Puerto Rico or Richard Ligon (c. 1585–1662) in Barbados in the middle of the seventeenth century, had been rapidly replaced by a new product generated by the Caribbean sugar revolutions that arrived in the region from Brazil around 1647. This new product was the artificially constructed exploitation society of European planters and merchants, with veritable armies of coerced and exploited enslaved Africans producing plantation-based export commodities such as sugar, cotton, indigo and coffee for an overseas European market.[18]

Two historians who captured these panoramic changing times in the

Caribbean are Père Jean-Baptiste Labat (1663–1738) and Edward Long (1734–1813). Their writings are bookends for the transformative eighteenth century.

The peripatetic and exceptionally able French Dominican Père Labat sojourned as a clergyman and innovative sugar planter in the Caribbean between 1694 and 1714. His multitalented experience on many islands lent authority to his writings, especially his six-volume *Nouveau voyage aux îles de l'Amerique* that appeared in Paris in 1722. Labat, besides being a clergyman and sugar-making landowner, was also a botanist, writer, explorer, ethnographer, soldier and engineer. Labat's charming, nostalgic descriptions of the Caribbean barely disguise the hard-nosed business acumen of a slave-exploiting Caribbean sugar producer.

Edward Long was born in Cornwall, England, but his family had extensive interests in Jamaica from its capture in 1655, and Long spent twelve years on the island as a well-connected and successful planter as well as prominent member of the island legislature. His encyclopaedic three-volume history published in 1774 reveals in its title the ambitiously comprehensive nature of the work: *The History of Jamaica: Reflections on Its Situation, Settlements, Inhabitants, Climate, Products, Commerce, Laws, and Government*.[19] In her insightful study of Caribbean historiography, the distinguished historian Elsa Goveia wrote of Long:

> Although he was not born in Jamaica, Edward Long . . . was nevertheless completely Creole in his sympathies. . . . Unlike some of the true Jamaican Creoles of his time, he was not an untraveled man: he had experience in a larger world than that of the island. For this reason he shows a marked tendency to consider himself superior in outlook and general culture to many of his fellow-whites in the island. He often criticized the manners of the Creoles, and especially of their womenfolk, who appeared to him a little uncouth, for the taste of any gentleman. He had little sympathy for what he considered to be the follies of their way of life. He spoke with sarcasm of their extravagance, with disapproval of their wasteful agricultural management, with impatience of the abuses tolerated in their government. . . . The object of his work was to make Jamaica better understood, not more despised, or as he himself expressed it, to "obviate slanders and explode those prejudices which malice or error have generated".[20]

Long wrote under the strong influence of the Enlightenment – a time when a new style of broadly based analytical history, relying on multiple sources, was being introduced to a new, international market of sophisticated, intellectually curious readers and shrewd businessmen.[21] In an opinion that is uncontestable, Goveia calls Long's work "one of the truly great achievements in the writing of West Indian history".[22] Despite its Enlightenment influence, or maybe because of it, Long's monumental study is unapologetically racist and Eurocentric. And indeed those qualities would become, with few exceptions, the normal pattern in imperial histories of the Caribbean during the nineteenth century and well into the early twentieth century.[23]

The important observation is that the long historiographical trajectory that Eric Williams railed against in his *British Historians and the West Indies*, published in 1964, is a complicated trajectory, although with one common characteristic. Most histories accepted the marginal and subordinate position of the Caribbean as normal in the universal scheme of things and tended to patronize, denigrate or neglect the achievements of Caribbean peoples.

In some respects, the historical treatment was understandably the result of ignorance rather than malice. The Caribbean territories were, after all, an entirely new location, outside the scope of the writings of the ancients like the Roman historian Livy (59 BC–17 AD), with completely new peoples in an environment entirely unfamiliar for all the arriving immigrant populations. Caribbean communities were the quintessentially Creolized societies, a unique amalgam of peoples and cultures from around the globe.[24] The ignorance was compounded by the ethnocentricity and racism created by the ruthless subordination, enslavement and exploitation of Africans over centuries to produce the wealth which Europeans, by the nineteenth century, had quickly come to take for granted – and which reinforced a sort of self-confidence that drove modern imperialism around the world.[25]

Other chapters of this work are devoted to a detailed examination of the biography, temper, temperament and literary works of Eric Williams. Here I will restrict myself to a general examination of the role of Eric Williams in the development of the modern Caribbean historiography. In many ways, Eric Williams was a typical product of his times – times that produced several distinguished individuals from many fields in the Caribbean – although, as an individual, he was more competent and certainly more successful than most. In this regard, Eric Williams may be compared to Christopher Columbus, who brought the Americas into the intellectual and political consciousness of Europe. Columbus brought no unique skills to navigation, and, had he not "discovered" the Caribbean in 1492, it is quite possible that some other explorer of the time would have done so within a few years. But Columbus certainly catalysed exploration in the way that Williams catalysed Caribbean historical scholarship. Williams was not afraid to challenge the powerful historical tradition that the abolition of the transatlantic slave trade and British imperial slavery resulted primarily from an irresistible wave of British religious humanitarianism at the end of the eighteenth century and the beginning of the nineteenth century. But Eric Williams also had a more ambitious agenda than merely challenging the principal thrust of one aspect of the larger historiography. He wanted to develop a new Caribbean school of history that demolished the imperial perspectives on the Caribbean and integrated the individual island histories within the framework of a wider regional approach.

This chapter examines the major historical publications of Eric Williams. In chronological order of publication, they are: *Capitalism and Slavery* (1944); *History of the People of Trinidad and Tobago* (1962); *British Historians and the West Indies* (1964); *Inward Hunger: The Education of a Prime Minister* (1969); and *From Columbus to Castro: The History of the Caribbean, 1492–1969* (1970). While these titles certainly do not exhaust the publications of the author, they do cover the spectrum of his historical work.[26]

In the thesis of his major work, *Capitalism and Slavery*, Williams connected, in a more direct and sophisticated way than had previously been done, the relationship between imperialism, slavery and the rise of industrial capitalism.[27] It focused on the British Atlantic slave trade, slave production in the British West Indies and the growth of capitalism in Europe during the nineteenth century. As the author explained in the preface of the original first edition, his study was "an attempt to place in historical perspective the relationship between early capitalism as exemplified by Great Britain, and the Negro slave trade, Negro slavery and the general colonial trade of the seventeenth and eighteenth centuries".[28] Some analysts have noted that *Capitalism and Slavery* reflects the incipient Marxism of its author and even has overtones of C.L.R. James's *The Black Jacobins*.[29] Yet the novelty and enduring appeal of the work lies less in its ideology than in its contagious originality. Despite the extensive controversy surrounding the thesis, no historian has been able to demolish the basic argument set forth by Williams in 1944.[30] This publication remains a major milestone in the writing of Caribbean history. While I am confident that much more light will be offered on the essential argument relating slavery to the rise of British (and wider European and North American) capitalism, it is important to make two initial observations.

The first is that Williams did not couch his language narrowly in simple profit accrual and reinvestment but rather in a complex, catalytically inducing process in which the employment of slaves represented market capital with the additional capacity to produce capital. Slaves were a marketable commodity that also directly produced other marketable commodities in a system that stimulated forward and backward economic linkages. The sugar business, after all, ranks among the earliest forms of factory production in the modern age. Moreover, the Caribbean sugar colonies were some of the highest-yielding commercial enterprises that exported commodities as well as considerable capital to Europe and North America.[31]

The second observation is that, in the absence of a reliable international banking system, the operation of international transatlantic slave complexes facilitated the transition from bullionism – or the use of bullion to estimate national and individual wealth – to mercantilism, the attempt to restrict imperial trade to national carriers within imperial borders – and eventually to free trade capitalism, where participants need not be connected at all except by capital involvement. The development of capitalism opened the marketplace to associated private participants, allowing them to operate with a minimum of governmental controls and government regulations, as exemplified by the English East India Company.[32]

Williams saw the imperial activities of Europeans as driven by the urge to promote capitalism via non-restricting, market-driven mechanisms – an idea that goes back to the eighteenth century and to the Scottish philosopher Adam Smith (1713–90) as well as the French philosopher Guillaume-Thomas François Raynal, better known as the Abbé Raynal. Williams's *Capitalism and Slavery* touched a metaphorical nerve because it countered the conventional British conviction that a religiously based humanitarianism was at the forefront of British slave abolition, both of the trade and later of the system of slavery.

Yet the economic perspective should not be considered the focus of

Williams's thinking, because it was not. Instead, his focus was the reorientation of European historical thought relating to the Caribbean. As Higman has pointed out, "Williams . . . set out to unsettle and destroy the pillars of the old colonial order, not the least of all in its intellectual aspect. . . . For him history was a battleground on which imperialist politics struggles against nationalist politics."[33] The historical works of Eric Williams are permeated with a potent mix of Caribbean nationalism and anti-colonialism, served up in an unabashedly confrontational style.

History of the People of Trinidad and Tobago was written in about one month, while the author was serving as chief minister of his country and preparing himself to accept the role as first prime minister of an independent state. It is a straightforward, chronological narrative, with long extracts from public documents and little analysis. But it was consciously designed to set a model for popular Caribbean national histories, which were noticeably lacking at a time when the British West Indian territories were negotiating their political independence. Williams was unapologetic about its challenging tone. "No apology", he wrote in his preface, "is made either for its form, or its content, or its timing . . . it is the manifesto of a subjugated people".[34] Although he promised to publish similar popular histories for "British Guiana, Jamaica, Cuba, Barbados and either Martinique or Guadeloupe . . . in the next few months", he failed to do so.[35] In any case, the *History of the People of Trinidad and Tobago* has been superseded by a number of excellent publications that comprehensively cover the themes addressed in that preliminary effort.

Although it was in gestation for a very long time, Williams admits that *British Historians and the West Indies* was, like his previous effort, hastily written. Nevertheless, it demonstrates impressive erudition, despite the narrowness of its historical selection and the linearity of the narrative. Beginning with colonial trade around the middle of the eighteenth century, Williams shows that British historians reflected the arrogance of imperial power afforded by the relative superiority of Great Britain in international commercial competition and that, in general, their attitude towards the Caribbean sugar colonies and their inhabitants was conditioned by their relationship to the main engines of the imperial economy. He does not equally condemn all his historical writers, however, and not all are from Britain. He is contemptuous of the histories of Edward Long and Bryan Edwards and more sympathetic to Adam Smith than was probably warranted. He has a very long discussion on two North American writers – the journalist William Sewell, who visited the Caribbean in 1859 and of whom Williams wrote admiringly, and Frank Tannenbaum, whose book *Slave and Citizen* Williams found to be full of shortcomings and errors.[36] While interesting, *British Historians* cannot be considered a major contribution to Caribbean historiography.

Inward Hunger is a quite remarkable autobiography. With its informed insights, incredible wisdom and poignant passion, it may be compared to Simon Bolivar's famous letter from Jamaica in 1815 (which lacks the autobiographical details) and C.L.R. James's *Black Jacobins* (which lacks the political perspectives). Like in his other publications, Williams does not provide footnotes for his numerous quotations, but he does provide good bibliographies and commendable indexes for all his works. *Inward Hunger* is a sober and sobering reflection on Caribbean realities in the 1960s, with some manifest exasperation at local social mores and marked impatience at the pace of general political change. Williams is also disappointed in the way that major powers treat minor states like the new states of the Caribbean. Although Williams still had many productive years ahead of him, there is within this book the inward disquiet and apprehension of a "lion in winter", and an acknowledged resignation that many local Caribbean political and economic problems appeared to be insoluble.

The political incentive for the writing of *From Columbus to Castro: The History of the Caribbean, 1492–1969* was admitted by the author in his brief introduction. He felt there was no general history of the entire region, and he wanted to fill the gap: "But in intellectual, as well as in political matters the Caribbean is a geographical expression. There is no history of the Caribbean area as a whole. Indeed, histories worthy of the name exist for only a few of the Caribbean territories. . . . The present work is designed to fill this gap and to correct this deficiency."[37]

Sometimes it seems that great minds do think alike: in the very year that Williams published his work, the outstanding intellectual from the Dominican Republic, Juan Bosch, also published an equally long book with a similar title in Spanish.[38] The books complement each other. Although Williams's work is strongly slanted towards the British Caribbean while Bosch orients his to the Hispanic Caribbean, both authors attempt to provide a regional approach to their narratives of Caribbean events, with Williams emphasizing the seminal importance of sugar and slavery and Bosch emphasizing that of competing imperial designs in the Caribbean.

Eric Williams had a deep conviction shared by many others of his generation that Caribbean peoples had a history no less worthy than that of peoples from other parts of the globe, especially from Europe. His writings gave dynamic agency to the people of the Caribbean in the same way that C.L.R. James's *Black Jacobins: Toussaint L'Ouverture and the San Domingo Revolution* gave agency to the rebellious slaves in that exploited French colony at the end of the eighteenth century.[39] This agency is also found in most modern histories of the Caribbean beginning with Elsa Goveia's *Slave Society in the British Leeward Islands*.[40]

Another aspect found in Williams's works, as indicated before, is a conscious attempt to look at the Caribbean regionally rather than as peripheral subdivisions of European activities and empires. This is especially evident in *From Columbus to Castro*. But Williams had already presented this regional conception in his short study *The Negro in the Caribbean*, published in 1945.[41] The attempt to view the region as an integrated whole remains a rare concept even today – but far less uncommon than a few decades ago.

Finally, in his writings and his speeches, Williams conveyed a strong conviction, one more commonly found among Caribbean artists and writers, that the people of the region needed to understand their history better – and that only by understanding that history better could they control their affairs more efficaciously in the modern world.[42] That conviction remains more hope than reality. But, gradually, the professional historians of the Caribbean are beginning to constitute a significant mass that give increasing weight to the avant-garde ideas that Williams promulgated during his professional lifetime. The writings of Eric Williams provided a solid foundation on which rich Caribbean historiography was constructed after World War II. He was not alone – but his role was extraordinarily important.

NOTES

1. David Henige, *In Search of Columbus: The Sources for the First Voyage* (Tucson: University of Arizona Press, 1991), 232; Gianni Granzotto, *Christopher Columbus: The Dream and the Obsession – A Biography,* trans. Stephen Sartarelli (New York: Doubleday, 1985), 38–39.

2. Fray Ramón Pané, *An Account of the Antiquities of the Indians,* rev. ed. with an introductory study, notes, and appendixes by José Juan Arrom, trans. Susan C. Griswold (Durham, NC: Duke University Press, 1999), xi. Many editions and translations of the Columbus journals exist. Two excellent examples are *The Four Voyages of Christopher Columbus,* trans. J.M. Cohen (London: Penguin, 1969); and John Fuson, *The Log of Christopher Columbus,* trans. Robert H. Fuson (Camden, ME: International Maritime Publishing, 1987).

3. Elsa Goveia, *A Study on the Historiography of the British West Indies to the End of the Eighteenth Century* (Mexico City: Instituto Panamericano de Geografía e Historia, 1956); Gordon K. Lewis, *Main Currents in Caribbean Thought: The Historical Evolution of Caribbean Society in Its Ideological Aspects, 1492–1900* (Baltimore: Johns Hopkins University Press, 1983); B.W. Higman, ed., *General History of the Caribbean,* vol. 4: *Methodology and Historiography of the Caribbean* (London: UNESCO/Macmillan Education, 1999); O. Nigel Bolland, ed., *The Birth of Caribbean Civilization: A Century of Ideas about Culture and Identity, Nation and Society* (Kingston: Ian Randle, 2004).

4. See, for example, Stanley J. Stein and Barbara H. Stein, *Silver, Trade, and War: Spain in the Making of Early Modern Europe* (Baltimore: Johns Hopkins University Press, 2000); J.H. Elliott, *Empires of the Atlantic World: Britain and Spain in America, 1492–1830* (New Haven, CT: Yale University Press, 2006); Franklin W. Knight and Peggy K. Liss, eds., *Atlantic Port Cities: Economy, Culture, and Society in the Atlantic World, 1650–1850* (Knoxville: University of Tennessee Press, 1991).

5. Bernardo de Sahagun, *Florentine Codex: General History of the Things of New Spain,* trans. Arthur J.O. Anderson and Charles E. Dibble, 13 vols (Salt Lake City: University of Utah Press and School of American Research, 1950–1982); Frances Berdan and Patricia Anawalt, eds., *The Codex Mendoza,* 4 vols (Berkeley: University of California Press, 1992); Miguel Leon-Portilla, ed., *The Broken Spears: The Aztec Account of the Conquest of Mexico* (Boston: Beacon, 1972); Gary Urton, *Signs of the Inka Kipu: Binary Coding in the Andean Knotted-String Records* (Austin: University of Texas Press, 2003).

6. J.H. Parry and P.M. Sherlock, *A Short History of the West Indies,* 3rd ed. (New York: St Martin's, 1971), v.

7. The best example of this pre-Hispanic Caribbean reconstruction may be found in Jalil Sued-Badillo, ed., *General History of the Caribbean*, vol. 1: *Autochthonous Societies* (London: UNESCO/Macmillan, 2003).

8. Eric Williams, *Capitalism and Slavery* (Chapel Hill: University of North Carolina Press, 1944).

9. Eric Williams, *History of the People of Trinidad and Tobago* (Port of Spain: PNM Publishing, 1962).

10. Published in Madrid between 1601 and 1614.

11. Goveia, *Study on the Historiography*, 12.

12. The Lascasian bibliography is immense. See Bartolomé de las Casas, *An Account, Much Abbreviated, of the Destruction of the Indies*, ed. Franklin W. Knight, trans. Andrew Hurley (Indianapolis: Hackett Publishing, 2003).

13. Daniel Castro, *Another Face of Empire: Bartolomé de las Casas, Indigenous Rights, and Ecclesiastical Imperialism* (Durham, NC: Duke University Press, 2007).

14. Bernal Díaz del Castillo's work was written mainly in response to the history of Cortés's chaplain, Francisco López de Gomara, published in 1552. Gomara had never travelled to the New World.

15. Bernal Díaz del Castillo, *The True History of the Conquest of Mexico*, trans. Maurice Keatinge, Esq. (1568; reprint, London: J. Wright, 1800), iv–v.

16. Díaz del Castillo, *True History*, 502.

17. Lewis, *Main Currents in Caribbean Thought*, 90–91.

18. Elsa V. Goveia, *Slave Society in the British Leeward Islands at the End of the Eighteenth Century* (New Haven, CT: Yale University Press, 1965); Franklin W. Knight, *The Caribbean: Genesis of a Fragmented Nationalism*, 3rd ed. (New York: Oxford University Press, 2012), 62–112; B.W. Higman, "The Sugar Revolution", in *The Economic History Review* 53, no. 2 (May 2000): 213–36.

19. Ian Randle Publishers brought out a lovely facsimile edition of Long's three-volume history in 2002 with an excellent introduction by Howard Johnson.

20. Goveia, *Study on the Historiography*, 53–54.

21. See, for example, Guillaume-Thomas François Raynal, *L'Histoire philosophique et politique des éstablissements et du commerce des Européenes dans les deux Indies*, 4 vols. (Amsterdam: n.p., 1770). Several editions of this highly influential work appeared across Europe, with a six-volume English translation appearing in 1796.

22. Goveia, *Study on the Historography*, 55.

23. Among the exceptions noted by Lewis, *Main Currents of Caribbean Thought*, 36, are "Raffles in Singapore, Lawrence in Arabia, Olivier in Jamaica, and Wingate in Palestine . . . regarded by London as eccentrics, unreliable types, odd men out".

24. Anthony Pagden, "The Challenge of the New", in *The Oxford Handbook of the Atlantic World, 1450–1850*, ed. Nicholas Canny and Philip Morgan (Oxford: Oxford University Press, 2011); Alfred Crosby, *The Columbian Exchange: Biological and Cultural Consequences of 1492* (Westport, CT: Greenwood Publishing, 1972); Stuart Schwartz, ed., *Tropical Baylons: Sugar and the Making of the Atlantic World, 1450–1680* (Chapel Hill: University of North Carolina Press, 2004); Peter Emmer and German Carrera Damas, eds., *General History of the Caribbean*, vol. 2: *New Societies: The Caribbean in the Long Sixteenth Century* (Paris: UNESCO/Macmillan, 1999); John Elliott, *Empires of the Atlantic World: Britain and Spain in America, 1492–1830* (New Haven, CT: Yale University Press, 2006).

25. See, for example, Barbara L. Solow, ed., *Slavery and the Rise of the Atlantic System* (New York: Cambridge University Press, 1991); Alfred W. McCoy and Francisco Scarano, eds., *Colonial Crucible: Empire in the Making of the Modern American State* (Madison: University of Wisconsin Press, 2009).

26. A list of the major publications of Eric Williams may be found in Colin A Palmer, *Eric Williams and the Making of the Modern Caribbean* (Chapel Hill, NC: University of North Carolina Press, 2006), 336. For *Capitalism and Slavery*, I have used the 1961 Russell and Russell edition as well as the reissued 1994 Chapel Hill edition with its excellent new introduction by Colin A. Palmer. For *History of the People of Trinidad and Tobago*, I consulted the original 1962 paperback edition. I consulted the Scribner's 1966 edition of *British Historians and the West Indies*. The edition of *Inward Hunger* I used was from University of Chicago Press, 1969. And the edition of *From Columbus to Castro* was from Harper and Row Publishers, 1970.

27. The bibliography on this subject is extensive. See B.W. Higman, *Writing West Indian Histories* (London: Macmillan Education, 1999), 90–97.

28. Eric Williams, *Capitalism and Slavery* (Chapel Hill: University of North Carolina Press, 1944), vii.

29. Francisco Scarano, "Slavery and Emancipation in Caribbean History", in B.W. Higman, ed., *General History of the Caribbean*, vol. 6: *Methodology and Historiography of the Caribbean* (London: UNESCO/Macmillan, 1999), 249–50.

30. Roger Anstey, *Atlantic Slave Trade and British Abolition, 1760–1810* (London: Macmillan, 1975); Seymour Drescher, *Econocide: British Slavery in the Era of Abolition* (Pittsburgh: University of Pittsburgh Press, 1977; reprint, Chapel Hill: University of North Carolina Press, 2010); Barbara L. Solow and Stanley Engerman, eds., *British Capitalism and Caribbean Slavery: The Legacy of Eric Williams* (New York: Cambridge University Press, 1987); Selwyn H.H. Carrington, *The British West Indies during the American Revolution* (Dordrecht, Holland: Foris Publications, 1988); Heather Cateau and Selwyn H.H. Carrington, eds., *Capitalism and Slavery Fifty Years Later: Eric Eustace Williams – A Reassessment of the Man*

and His Work (New York: Peter Lang, 2000); Selwyn H.H. Carrington, *The Sugar Industry and the Abolition of the Slave Trade, 1775–1810* (Gainesville: University of Florida Press, 2002). The principal positions of the debate may be followed in B.W. Higman, ed., *General History of the Caribbean*, vol. 6: *Methodology and Historiography of the Caribbean* (London: UNESCO/Macmillan, 1999), 81–94.

31. Victor Bulmer-Thomas, *The Economic History of the Caribbean since the Napoleonic Wars* (Cambridge: Cambridge University Press, 2012), 10–11.

32. See John Keay, *The Honourable Company: A History of the English East India Company* (London: Harper Collins, 2010).

33. B.W. Higman, ed., *General History of the Caribbean*, vol. 6: *Methodology and Historiography of the Caribbean* (London: UNESCO/Macmillan, 1999), 196.

34. Williams, *History of the People of Trinidad and Tobago*, viii.

35. Ibid., viii.

36. Williams, *British Historians*, 96–102, 225–32.

37. Williams, *From Columbus to Castro*, 11–12.

38. Juan Bosch, *De Cristóbal Colón a Fidel Castro: El Caribe, frontera imperial* (Madrid: Alfaguara, 1970). A new edition has recently appeared: Juan Bosch, *De Cristóbal Colón a Fidel Castro: El Caribe frontera imperial* (Mexico: Porrua, 2009). According to Pablo Maríñez in his introduction to this 2009 edition, Bosch's title was created by his Spanish publishers in 1970.

39. C.L.R. James, *The Black Jacobins: Toussaint L'Ouverture and the San Domingo Revolution*, 2nd ed. (New York: Vintage Books, 1963).

40. Goveia, *Slave Society*.

41. Eric E. Williams, *The Negro in the Caribbean* (Manchester: Panaf Services, 1945).

42. Selwyn R. Cudjoe, *Eric Williams Speaks: Essays on Colonialism and Independence* (Wellesley, MA: Calaloux, 1993).

Chapter 6

Capitalism and Slavery Revisited

The "Williams Thesis" in Atlantic Perspective

DALE TOMICH

Capitalism and Slavery *and the "Williams Debate"*: *Conceptual* *Frameworks*

Since its publication in 1944, Eric Williams's classic *Capitalism and Slavery* has remained an essential source for the study of Atlantic slavery and a focus of scholarly controversy. A work of engaged scholarship, *Capitalism and Slavery* directly challenged the prevailing historiographical canon at the time of its publication. In seeking to systematically disclose the economic processes and interests that shaped the course of slavery and abolition in the British West Indies, Williams sharply contrasted economic factors to moral and political ones, in his account of the abolition of slavery. The book's enduring interest lies in Williams's comprehensive, systematic and forceful effort to interpret capitalism, colonialism and slavery within a unified historical framework. *Capitalism and Slavery* has exercised a powerful influence not only on scholars of the Caribbean and Africa but also on historians of Britain, the Industrial Revolution, colonialism and empire. In addition, it has remained a fundamental reference for social scientists interested in questions of development, dependency and world-economy.

Especially since the 1960s, *Capitalism and Slavery* has been subject to intense scrutiny and criticism, particularly from economic historians. The

"Williams thesis" and slavery have provided fertile ground for the New Economic History, a highly quantitative approach that combines neoclassical economic theory and computer technology. Scholars employing these techniques have turned to previously unused sources and systematically analysed great quantities of data in ways that otherwise would not have been possible. From this perspective, they have engaged in a broad examination of the economy of slavery and the slave trade and have interrogated the "Williams thesis". They have produced impressive results. Over the course of the past fifty years, their work has reshaped the study of slavery and economic history more generally.

The debate has been conducted in such a way as to attempt to prove or disprove Williams's propositions on empirical grounds. While the debate over Williams's work has focused on questions of empirical proof, the historical framework in which he posed the problem has been generally accepted. Although many continue to support Williams's arguments, the majority of economic historians feel that their research has resolved the issues raised by Williams. In their view, there is not an economic cause for the abolition of slavery and the slave trade. Instead, they propose that scholars should turn their attention to political, social and ideological explanations. (However, I do not believe that it would be unfair to suggest that the economic historians have been more effective in disqualifying Williams's arguments than in providing an alternative interpretation.) This chapter addresses the conceptual frameworks deployed in the debate. My purpose is, on the one hand, to examine methodological problems entailed both in the conceptual structure of Williams's argument and in the application of economic theory to historical analysis; and, on the other hand, to propose a reinterpretation of the arguments of *Capitalism and Slavery* from the perspective of Atlantic history.

Eric Williams

Eric Williams's overriding concern was to understand the historical relation of capitalism and slavery. His innovation and the source of his radical critique is his integration of colonial slavery, industrial capitalism and abolitionism in a single account. In it, he seeks to explain the West Indian contribution to British development and the sources of what a later generation of scholars would characterize as colonial underdevelopment. Williams's interpretation is anchored in a conception of capitalism as a *national* phenomenon. He identifies the origin of modern capitalism with the Industrial Revolution. While, in his view, the slave trade and slavery in the West Indian sugar colonies provided the capital that financed the Industrial Revolution, the Industrial Revolution itself was a British phenomenon. He regards Britain as the site of industrialization, proletarianization, the rise of an industrial middle class and the emergence of liberal ideologies. Conversely, Williams construes slavery as a non-capitalist phenomenon and treats it as a property of the Caribbean.

In his interpretation, British industrial capitalism appears as the dynamic source of change acting on the increasingly backward, static and archaic West Indian colonies. For Williams, industrial capitalism requires free trade. Indeed, he regards free trade as the natural and necessary outcome of industrialization. Hence, the Industrial Revolution in Britain is the sole source of Britain's free trade policy. In contrast, the "law of slave production" – soil exhaustion and the need for more slaves and livestock to secure the same level of production – retarded the expansion of production in the British slave colonies.[1] Slavery was inextricably linked to the colonial system and mercantilist monopoly. Taken together, they represented an obstacle to expanding industrial capitalism in Britain, and the new industrial interests progressively removed them in favour of free trade.

> The attack on the West Indians was more than an attack on slavery. It was an attack on monopoly. Their opponents were not only the humanitarians but the capitalists. . . . The attack falls into three phases: the attack on the slave trade, the attack on slavery, the attack on the preferential sugar duties. The slave trade was abolished in 1807, slavery in 1833, and the sugar preference in 1846. The three events are inseparable.[2]

Williams thus inscribes the political events resulting in the abolition of the slave trade and slave emancipation in the movement leading from the Industrial Revolution to the establishment of free trade. A unilinear process of industrialization and free trade *in Britain* produces a similarly unilinear sequence from abolition to emancipation *in the West Indies*.

Williams's conception of capitalism and industrialization as British national phenomena provides the foundation around which he constructs the spatial and temporal framework of his analysis. In his formulation, capitalism and slavery are not regarded as constitutive of one another. Rather, Williams takes British capitalism and West Indian slavery as conceptually discrete and separate terms, each with its own characteristics. In this dualistic construction, these conceptually independent entities are conjoined with one another through their interaction. Consequently, the integral relations between metropolis and colonies that produce the links between the two terms, and therefore the relational character of the categories themselves, disappear from view. Instead, the terms are brought into relation with one another through complex linkages of colonial domination, mercantilist economic policy, trade, forced and unforced migration, ideology and social movements. These links are treated as if they form the relation. As a result, the categories of capitalism and slavery, or metropolis and colony, are transformed into classificatory terms without analytical value.[3]

The British Empire provides the organizing structure within which these integrating processes occur. Williams's conception of the empire in its relation to the more comprehensive Atlantic or world-economy exhibits the same dualistic structure. The empire forms a closed and internally integrated unit that conceptually and substantively bounds Williams's analysis. Relations outside this sphere – including with the French and Spanish empires, Brazil, and the United States – are treated as external to the fundamental relation between Britain and its colonies. They enter into his account only insofar as they influence British industrialization, West Indian slavery or imperial policy, but they are not themselves accounted for in his explanatory framework. Thus, even as Williams proposes a broadly comprehensive *historical* interpretation, the world he describes extends beyond the limits of his explanatory framework. His focus on the British Empire continuously excludes the full range of causally significant relations and processes.

The New Economic History

Since the 1960s, the "Williams thesis" has become fertile ground for criticism by scholars of the New Economic History. Their challenge has in large measure set the parameters of the "Williams Debate". The new economic historians have generally accepted Williams's analytical framework, but they have submitted his claims to quantitative scrutiny based on neoclassical economic theory. With few exceptions,[4] they feel that they have disproved his claims on empirical grounds. Most prominently, Seymour Drescher contends that the British West Indies were not in decline at the time of the abolition of the slave trade in 1807 and that abolition was the cause of the economic crisis, not the other way around. Others concur and find no other impediment to what they view as the prospect for continued West Indian prosperity.[5]

The innovation of the New Economic History has been the application of sophisticated econometric models and statistical methods to the study of historical problems. Such quantitative methods combined with computer technology have allowed scholars to treat large quantities of data in ways that were not previously possible. However, this approach has been more oriented towards economic theory than towards historical analysis. The quantitative economic historians have generally operated within the conceptual framework of Britain and its colonies posited by Williams. But they have subtly shifted the analytical terms of the debate from Williams's concern with capitalism to a focus on an abstract and universal concept of "economy". They may have valid reasons for doing so, but we would do well to recognize that the two concepts are not the same.

The economic theory upon which the New Economic History is based is regarded as a purely technical instrument for determining the optimal allocation of scarce resources independently of particular social or historical contexts. Its fundamental theoretical categories are treated as technically determined universals. Taking price formation as its central object and point of departure, this approach is concerned only with the technical determination of the proportions in which factors of production are employed in order to produce goods. Production is treated from a purely technical point of view. Land, labour and technology are abstracted from the historical relations and conditions through which they are employed, and they are treated as conceptually independent production functions – that is, as quantifiable inputs that affect the allocation of resources.

In this model, the analysis and interpretation of slavery focuses on the evaluation of the "profitability" and "efficiency" of the slave "economy". It is presumed that continued profitability and efficiency are sufficient to maintain the viability of slavery as an economic institution. Profitability and efficiency are also understood as technical terms. The calculation of profitability is based upon the comparison of the price of factor inputs to the price of output. It depends upon market prices and the capacity of the rational entrepreneur to efficiently allocate production factors. On the other hand, efficiency is measured by either output per worker (labour productivity) or by output per average unit of all inputs – here, land, labour and capital (total factor productivity). Thus, these two categories are conceptually independent of one another. Profitability measures the cost of producing things without regard to their physical production, while efficiency measures the physical production of things without regard to their cost. Production costs and output are thus treated as exogenous variables; the relation between them is established by the market price of the product. The price mechanism regulates the relation between supply and demand. Comparison of production costs and output with market price permits the rational calculation of the optimal allocation of production factors.

The New Economic History has an explicit positivist bias.[6] Its analytical techniques are regarded as value-neutral, and their use is presumed to allow ideological bias to be separated from the scientific analysis of facts. Quantitative data are taken to be objectively true.[7] However, the mechanical juxtaposition of fact and value fails to adequately address the problems that this perspective poses for historical analysis. Much of the methodological and theoretical justification for this approach is concerned with the nature of the data and its adequacy for mathematical or statistical manipulation, the techniques employed in their quantification, and the appropriateness and adequacy of the economic models applied to the data. The results of its procedures may be valid from the perspective of economic theory. However, the inferences drawn from them for the purposes of historical analysis merit scrutiny.[8] While they may have heuristic value, the results of such inquiry are much less certain than it may seem on first sight. This quantitative approach is no more or no less objective and value-free than other social scientific approaches. Its data are constructed in relation to the cognitive requirements of the theory. Its techniques of quantification depend upon what Carlo Ginzburg refers to as the "equalization of individuals".[9] They cognitively recognize only what is homogenous and comparable and disregard particulars. Here the "individuals" are the historically formed relations of human actors to one another and to nature.

In this approach, categories that refer to social, political and cultural or ideological relations are conceived as contingent factors that are external to "the economy" and are assigned a different theoretical status. Thus, social relations and, more particularly, social relations of production – that is, the relations through which human beings come together to produce society and transform nature – are excluded from consideration within the terms of the theory. The social relations of slavery are conceived simply as a juridical relation of property and are related to the categories of economic analysis only in a contingent, and external, manner. They are economically important only insofar as they affect the allocation and distribution of economic resources (production functions) and therefore the level and pattern of output in the economy.[10] Thus, neoclassical theory constructs the economy and factors of production by abstracting them from the institution of slavery, from social relations and from history and treating them in isolation as technical processes. By means of this logical operation, social relations and history, rather than being formative of economic processes, are transformed into "exogenous factors" that are contingent to universally valid economic categories.

By presuming the universal validity of abstract and timeless economic categories, neoclassical theory constructs and maintains a persistent dualism between economic analysis and historical process. Categories of economic analysis are treated as being independent of and external to history, while all social, political, cultural or ideological phenomena are regarded as contingent and are judged against universal categories of economic rationality. Such a conception eliminates from consideration the specificity of historical relations and the definite constellations of diverse relations and forces that determine particular historical conjunctures. The problem of the historical origins of economic relations disappears from view. Instead, history itself is construed as the progressive loosening of constraints on factor realities: the continual development of the division of labour in response to changes in price and productivity. The market and market rationality become at once the beginning and endpoint of historical change as well as the prime force behind it.

The New Economic History is premised upon an abstract and arbitrary conception of time and space. Its fundamental conceptions and formulations are formal categories that are outside of space and time or are at best oriented towards the very short term. The long term, fundamental to historical analysis, is the sum of virtually infinite short-term relations, or chains of events, that may be joined together or broken apart at any point. While neoclassical economic theory accounts for shifting patterns of output and distribution, it is unable to provide causal explanations for historical change. Instead, it must have recourse to factors that come from outside its explanatory framework to account for change. Within these assumptions, it is difficult to conceptualize structural transformations. Indeed, precisely those political, social or ideological elements that are relegated to secondary and contingent status are frequently mobilized to explain change. Often these take the form of exceptional events, individuals or movements that cannot be accounted for within the terms of the theory.

Perhaps an even graver danger is that economic analysis is constructed around events whose importance is presumed *a priori*. Williams emphasized the interdependence of the abolition of the slave trade, slave emancipation and free trade, and he sought to explain these events as part of a long-term transformation that created a free-trade regime. However, in much of the Williams debate, they are treated as sequence of distinct individual events. The abolition of the slave trade in 1807 is privileged as *the* important event to be explained, the first event in the chain. It is the fulcrum of the entire analysis, which is divided into periods before and after abolition, with the result that the termination of the slave trade itself is taken as the explanation for subsequent developments. But this choice simply reflects an unsubstantiated common-sense view that privileges short-term political, legal and ideological events at the expense of a deeper analytical appreciation of structural transformations. Here we risk an arbitrary and mechanical conception of historical change. Economic analysis is oriented towards illuminating the crucial event. The event becomes a kind of switching station: either the economic train proceeds through the station on the same track and continues towards its destination (in which case, the event is disqualified) or it switches tracks and proceeds towards a new destination (in which case, the event is presumed to be significant).

Aside from its contribution to economic theory, this quantitative approach to economic history has a heuristic value for historical analysis. It enables us to make a purely quantitative assessment of economic performance on the condition that we abstract from social relations, politics, ideology and ecological conditions that comprise the historical configuration under consideration. The danger is that, in making such abstractions, we disarticulate the historical configuration of forces and relations and then attempt to reintegrate the fragmented parts (unexplained exogenous factors) around our abstracted construction of the economy, rather than reversing the procedure and attempting to interpret our abstract and quantitative findings within the rich complex of relations forming the historical conjuncture.

Significantly, the major studies based on this approach have emphasized the positive performance of slavery according to these criteria and have attributed slave emancipation to the success of contingent "extra-economic factors", most notably politics and ideology, in undercutting the economic system.[11] Williams's most prominent and systematic critic, Seymour Drescher (1977), finds no correlation between either long-term or short-term economic trends and the abolition of the slave trade.[12] Therefore, in his view, the economic motive for abolishing the slave trade must be disqualified. Indeed, he finds that abolition of the slave trade was achieved by a mass popular movement with a humanitarian ideology. This act undermined an otherwise viable institution and set in motion a process of economic decline that led to the abolition of slavery itself in the 1830s. In subsequent work, Drescher has devoted himself to exploring the ideological, social and political sources of abolition, particularly popular religious and social networks.

Sugar and Slavery in the "Age of Revolution"

In *Capitalism and Slavery*, Williams seeks to understand the causal relationships among diverse processes of varying duration that occur in specific historical settings, and the ways in which these processes structure the possibilities and constraints for collective and individual action. He offers a historical conception of capitalism that is at once economic *and* political. The two decisive moments of Williams's account are the American and Haitian Revolutions. His fundamental concern is with the role of these two revolutions in provoking the crisis of Britain's colonial empire and undermining the conditions for mercantilism and slavery. The historical importance of mercantilism cannot be fully appreciated by treating it simply as an "economic" system within the framework of neoclassical theory. Nor does the Marxist conception of mercantilism as a national phenomenon that expresses the limitations and "immaturity" of commercial capitalism in Britain provide an adequate interpretation. Mercantilism is both a political and an economic system. If political power opened the way for trade, the rationale for trade was to enhance the wealth and power of the state. Mercantilism was an instrument not only for establishing control over colonies but also for political, diplomatic, military and economic competition. It finds its fullest expression in the rivalry between European states.

Both the British mercantile system and the French *exclusif* asserted control over the sources of tropical production and attempted to dictate circuits of trade in order to increase metropolitan wealth. But they were also instruments of political and maritime power in the Anglo-French contest for dominance over the Atlantic and world-economies from 1763 to 1815. Victory over France in the Seven Years' War (the Treaty of Paris, 1763) gave Britain a predominant position in the Americas and extended its maritime supremacy. These developments were intimately related to politics on the European continent. Britain was able to avoid direct involvement in European politics but manipulated the continental balance of power through control of the seas and overseas maritime trade.[13] However, the West Indies remained at the heart of the colonial empires of both England and France, and they were of strategic importance to Anglo-French rivalry on both sides of the Atlantic.

The period from 1764 to 1783 was the golden age of West Indian sugar production. The centre of production had shifted to the big islands – Jamaica for the British and Saint-Domingue for the French – at the expense of the smaller islands. Even though Britain returned Cuba to Spain after 1763, the brief British occupation stimulated the slow but steady growth of a regime of sugar and slavery there as well. France's loss of its North American colonies put its Caribbean colonies at a disadvantage, as Britain's North American colonies were able to provide its West Indian sugar colonies with cheap provisions.

As Williams demonstrated, the thirteen North American colonies destabilized the British mercantile system.[14] Despite imperial and mercantile restrictions, the West Indian provisioning trade enabled the thirteen North American colonies to build up their own shipping and commerce, including shipbuilding, and the slave trade. Cheap North American foodstuffs, livestock and timber reduced the costs of the West Indian plantation colonies. Britain had to modify the Navigation Acts and its monopoly of colonial trade in order to accommodate the North American provisioning trade. Further, the capacity of both the British and American slave trade surpassed the demand from the British West Indies, and both supplied significant numbers of slaves to Britain's rivals. Finally, the North American colonies became actively involved in the rum trade with French Saint-Domingue (which presented ample opportunities for contraband in sugar and other tropical staples). As the importance of North American merchants grew in the lucrative Saint-Domingue trade, they refused to extend credit to British planters and insisted on cash payments. They then took the cash and bought cheaper goods in Saint-Domingue. This practice drained currency from the British West Indies as it increased trade with Saint-Domingue.[15] Thus, North American commerce undermined the mercantile systems of both Britain and France by creating a pole of economic activity outside of each metropolis.

US independence in 1783 accelerated the destabilization of the British mercantile system and prejudiced the British West Indian colonies. British policy closed the West Indian trade to the newly independent republic, cutting the sugar colonies off from this crucial source of supplies, raising their production costs and creating hardship.[16] However, here it is important not to look just at the direct consequences of US independence for Britain's West Indian sugar colonies. Rather, it is more productive to look at the relationship between the United States and the British Empire from the perspective of the Atlantic, if not the world-economy. With independence, the United States became increasingly involved in the international slave trade, and it began to trade more actively with Saint-Domingue and Cuba, reinforcing the productivity of the British West Indies' two main competitors. Indeed, increased commerce with the United States contributed to the exceptionally rapid growth of the slave population and sugar production in Saint-Domingue between 1783 and 1791.[17]

In Williams's view, the Haitian Revolution was the second major turning point for West Indian slavery. What began as a conflict between white and free coloured elites over citizenship and the status of the colony in the new French republic was transformed into a revolutionary struggle against colonialism and slavery by mass slave resistance. The revolutionary forces in Saint-Domingue defeated, in turn, a French army, a British army and another French army, each sent to suppress them. The final outcome was the creation of the independent republic of Haiti. The struggle in Saint-Domingue was a turning point for slavery throughout the Americas. Williams argues compellingly that the attitude of William Pitt, prime minister and close associate of abolitionist William Wilberforce, towards the abolition of the slave trade turned on the success or failure of the British expeditionary force in Saint-Domingue and the outcome of the conflict there. In Williams's words, "Pitt could not have had Saint Domingue and abolition as well."[18] The successful revolution in Saint-Domingue overthrew slavery in Europe's most prosperous colony and resulted in the dramatic withdrawal of the world's largest sugar producer from the world market. Just as significantly, it removed Britain's chief rival for domination of the Atlantic and eroded the rationale for mercantilism in the Western Hemisphere. Defeat in Haiti crippled France's colonial system and ended its imperial ambitions in the Americas. Deprived of Haiti, Napoleon sold Louisiana to the United States. The combined effects of the Revolution and Britain's victory in the Napoleonic Wars led to the destruction of the French Navy and decline of the French port cities, leaving the United States as Britain's only potential challenger in the Atlantic.

The French and Haitian Revolutions, together with the Napoleonic Wars, brought an end the century-long struggle between Britain and France for domination over the European world-economy. The period from 1789 to 1815 was marked by revolution, war, blockades and embargoes that transformed economic and political relations throughout the Atlantic. Markets were irregular and prices were volatile. The movement of goods between the Americas, Britain and Europe was far from regular or secure. Neutral shipping was subject to interference, especially by Britain. The strategic political situation shifted rapidly and often in extreme directions, as Pitt's options over Haiti illustrate. The British West Indian sugar colonies enjoyed a considerable but relative advantage because of British control of the sea lanes and privileged access to the home market. But, even so, occupation and annexation of foreign sugar colonies made their position more precarious. The British slave trade was abolished in the midst of this turbulent period.

As we have seen, Seymour Drescher demonstrated that the British West

Indies were more valuable to Britain, both in relative and absolute terms, during this period than at any previous time. The sugar colonies increased their production in the fifty years preceding abolition of the slave trade. They were Britain's most important non-European trading partners from 1722 until 1822, and their share of British trade was increasing during the period from 1793–97 to 1808–12.[19] Drescher's contribution is salutary insofar as it compels us to rethink the relation between Britain and its West Indian colonies and to empirically ground our interpretations. However, to focus only on the bilateral relations between Britain and its colonies in a period when world sugar production was undergoing rapid restructuring, especially given the destruction of the plantation system in Saint-Domingue, limits the scope of analysis and creates a false sense of stability. I find Drescher's formulation of either economic factors or non-economic factors as the cause of the abolition of the slave trade less persuasive, and I am not convinced of the assumption that abolition of the slave trade was the watershed event for the destruction of slavery in the British West Indies, if not the wider Atlantic world. I also share David Beck Ryden's concern that subsequent scholarship has focused on social and cultural change in Britain and their relation to the reform movement.[20] The relational nexus between Britain, its colonies and the Atlantic economy has slipped from view.

Ryden regards dismissal of the decline thesis as premature.[21] Using West Indian rather than London price data, he argues that local prices are a better indicator of conditions in the colonies. The London data reflect rising shipping costs, largely due to the Seven Years' War, the American Revolution, the French Revolution and the Napoleonic Wars, as well as inflation throughout the economy caused by the war with France. They are not an accurate measure of planter revenues. Correcting for these factors, he finds a long-term decline in prices during the eighteenth century. This fall was particularly acute during the period of inflation following the brief rise in prices during the Haitian Revolution. Planters had to either obtain higher prices or sell more sugar in order to obtain the same real income. However, Ryden argues that the decline in the value of sugar is not in itself evidence of the decline of the sugar estates' viability, nor a confirmation of the Williams thesis. Rather, he locates the crisis of the British West Indian sugar industry in the increased production and reorganization of markets following the Haitian Revolution.

With the destruction of the Saint-Domingue plantation regime, British West Indian planters increased production and began to export more to continental Europe. Once they began to produce for a market outside of Britain, they were exposed to competition from more productive foreign regions (especially Cuba) that enjoyed lower transportation costs. British and continental prices became increasingly aligned with one another. Increase in the supply in the years before 1807 exceeded any increase in demand. Increased production had little impact on real revenue, and the rate of profit fell for West Indian planters in the year immediately preceding the abolition of the slave trade. Abolition occurred against the background of a rapid decline of the West Indian sugar economy – it was not its cause.

Aside from the substantive merits of his interpretation, Ryden's contribution is important because of the care with which he reconstructs the broad historical context of his economic analysis and the attention that he devotes to local conditions in the Caribbean. He raises important questions about the appropriateness of data and the kinds of inferences that can be drawn from them. Further, he points the way towards a possible reconciliation of quantitative and qualitative sources.

However, my purpose is not to interpret the abolition of the slave trade. It is rather to reframe the way we think about it and to extend the spatial and temporal parameters of the discussion. If the Haitian Revolution contributed to the crisis of the British West Indian sugar colonies, it stimulated new zones of slave production elsewhere in the Americas and helped to profoundly reshape the Atlantic political and social order in other ways as well. The outbreak of the revolt in Saint-Domingue provided the planter class of Havana with the occasion to put forth an aggressive programme to dominate world sugar production. Francisco Arango y Parreño's *Discurso sobre la agricultura de la Havana y medios de fomentarla* (1792) declared that Saint-Domingue's misfortune was Cuba's opportunity.[22] What planters required to achieve this goal was free trade in sugar, free trade in slaves and the systematic application of science and technology to sugar production.[23] This was effectively the blueprint for the astounding transformation of the Cuban sugar industry. Free trade in slaves was declared in 1797 and was extended until formal abolition in 1817. A massive illegal slave trade followed, which lasted into the 1850s. After a series of temporary licensing agreements that permitted trade with neutral countries, beginning in 1792 and 1793, Cuban planters secured free trade in 1818. Their chief market was the United States. Technological innovation and increasing scales of production became the hallmark of the Cuban industry, including the steam engine, the vacuum pan and the centrifuge, but also the railroad, the telegraph and the steamship. By the 1820s, Cuba emerged as the world's leading sugar producer, and it doubled its output every decade into the 1860s.

Although in no way a rival to England, the United States also consolidated its power politically and economically during the turbulent years between 1789 and 1815. It established itself as an independent commercial and naval power at sea and opened the way for expansion on its western frontier. The United States became the hub of a new wave of economic expansion that revitalized slavery, redefined the division of labour and restructured market relations in the Atlantic economy. Its presence as an independent state outside of the European state system imposed new conditions on the Atlantic political order and shaped British strategy after 1815. The United States became an important factor in the Atlantic carrying trade. It could build ships more cheaply than Britain and offered cheaper transportation costs. It was actively involved, directly or indirectly, in the international slave trade even after it abolished its own slave trade. With the destruction of the plantation regime in Saint-Domingue, the United States developed strong economic ties with Cuba. It was the primary market for Cuban sugar,[24] and according to historian Manuel Moreno Fraginals, Cuba was the only place where Britain could not undersell its competitor.[25] Equally important was US territorial expansion on the North American continent. As a consequence of the revolution in Saint-Domingue, the United States secured West Florida and Louisiana. The Battle of New Orleans (1814) consolidated American independence and gave it unimpeded access to the western frontier and navigation on the Mississippi River and southern rivers. After the forced removal of native peoples, the southern cotton frontier quickly took shape. The invention of the cotton gin in 1793 made commercial production of short-stapled, upland varieties of cotton feasible and broke Britain's dependence on traditional sources of supply. The unprecedented growth of cotton cultivation in the US South matched the expansion of cotton manufacture in Britain. By 1820, the South was the world's leading cotton producer and virtually monopolized the supply of cotton for British industry.[26] By 1831, cotton had supplanted sugar as Britain's leading import. Between 1815 and the Civil War, the United States supplied over three-fourths of the raw cotton consumed in Britain, and US production determined the price of cotton in world markets.[27]

With the definitive defeat of France in 1815, British control of overseas trade was to be more important than ever if it were to reorganize the balance of power in post-war, post-revolutionary Europe.[28] As the world's pre-eminent commercial, industrial and maritime power, Britain was in a position to economically dominate the Americas. However, to do so, it had to prevent the reassertion of a European colonial presence in the Americas as well as the formation of closed economic zones. But the new element was the presence of independent American states. First the United States and then the independent states of South America were outside of the European state system and balance of power. The Americas had been disarticulated from Europe. In the absence of colonial domination, the market was to provide the links between sovereign states. Britain was in position to dominate the markets but needed to secure the political conditions through which markets form and operate. The creation of a stable international political order among sovereign states would allow the British market economy to operate. British domination of the market would underwrite the organization and stability of the interstate system.

New Commodity Frontiers and the Crisis of the British West Indian Sugar Colonies

The new economic historians present a positive assessment of the British West Indian sugar industry after abolition of the slave trade, especially with the acquisition of Trinidad, Guyana and the other ceded islands after 1815. They emphasize the increasing imports, favourable prices and a growing share of British trade immediately after abolition. According to David Eltis, war and revolution put a greater share of the world's plantation produce in Britain's hands than ever before. Seymour Drescher differentiates between the British West Indies, which declined slightly in both value and tonnage after 1807, and imports from conquered and occupied territories, which increased by 86 per cent in value and nearly 150 per cent by weight. The aggregate figure, he argues, disguised the decline of the older British sugar colonies in the Caribbean. The real situation in the British West Indies only became apparent with the end of the conflict in 1814. Nonetheless, even with the return of some of the occupied territories at the end of hostilities, slave-produced sugar from the British colonies still accounted for over half of the world's supply.[29]

For both Drescher and Eltis, the acquisitions of Guyana and Trinidad were essential to the increase of British West Indian production after 1814. Together they brought more cultivated land into the empire than all of the cultivated land in the existing West Indian colonies.[30] According to Drescher, the British slave colonies were "still capable of vigorous growth and expansion",[31] while Eltis emphasizes that "the long-run economic data testify to the continuing vitality of the British West Indies well into the nineteenth century".[32] However, in their view, there was only one factor that prevented the British colonies from taking full advantage of the post-war boom: labour. Abolition of the slave trade undercut the potential prosperity of the British West Indian sugar colonies. In Drescher's well-known formulation, abolition of the slave trade was an act of *econocide* provoked by abolitionism in the form of a mass movement and a new liberal sensibility. It was the first step in an inevitable chain of events that dismantled slavery and culminated in slave emancipation.

This assessment of the long-term prospects of the British West Indian sugar industry is, in my view, overly optimistic. The quantitative economic historians show that there was considerable room to reorganize and expand productive activities in the British West Indies, with the colonies remaining productive and able to return a reasonable rate of profit. However, these findings are not incompatible with decline. By focusing on market and price competition between national units, their approach underestimates, if not ignores, the changing structure of the Atlantic economy. Foreign competitors only enter this analysis insofar as they affect conditions for British producers. Further, by treating land, labour and capital as independent factors of production, it disaggregates the historical relations through which production is organized. The result is an abstract and one-sided economic interpretation that juxtaposes economic to non-economic factors. Historical processes operating at the level of the world and Atlantic economies – the expansion and reorganization of production, the restructuring of markets, and the creation of a new division of labour – are eliminated from consideration. Similarly, the ways that particular ecologies, material processes of production, technologies, and forms and scales of collective labour are combined in specific historical circumstances are not regarded as analytically significant.

Put another way, what is missing from the neoclassical account is the historical and material geography of capital. The vitality of capitalism as a historical relation has less to do with profitability in an accounting sense than with its capacity to create new productive spaces on an expanding scale. It is here that Eric Williams offers rich insight and opens the way for new interpretation, provided that we shift the unit of analysis from the British Empire to the Atlantic or world-economy. From this latter perspective, the US South (cotton), Cuba (sugar) and Brazil (coffee) appear not as external factors that act upon the British West Indies from the outside but rather as new slave commodity frontiers[33] that formed as part of the same world-economic processes that resulted in the crisis of mercantilism and slavery in the British Empire. These new productive zones entailed the massive redeployment of slave labour under new conditions and the creation of new commodity circuits linking the Atlantic world. Slavery itself was reconfigured with increasing scales of production, growing pressure to increase the productivity of labour, new technologies of production and transport, and new modes of labour discipline and social control. The traffic in slaves – legal and illegal, or international and internal – was the motor of these developments, even as slave trading operated under new conditions in the face of British abolitionism. The economic and material expansion of the world-economy and the formation of these new slave commodity frontiers created the crisis of the old colonial spaces that were no longer able to compete under the new conditions, even though they remained substantial producers and brought profitable returns.

World sugar production and consumption expanded dramatically during the first half of the nineteenth century. Old producing regions increased their output and new regions emerged. British West Indian sugar production also expanded during this period, but it was unable to keep pace with the changing conditions of world production. From 1791 to 1815, British West Indian sugar production increased more rapidly than at any other time in its history. Peace in 1814 brought about a boom in sugar production as pent-up demand was released and planters throughout the Americas rushed to fill the void left by Saint-Domingue.[34] The British colonies were best positioned to take advantage of this situation. They had been least disrupted by war and revolution, had regular access to shipping and benefited from the acquisition of new territories, particularly Guyana. Their output fell below that of the previous period but between 1815 and 1819 they still accounted for nearly half of the world's supply, which had risen by 38 per cent despite the destruction of Saint-Domingue.[35]

By 1820, the post-war boom ended and prices fell. Markets became more stable and increasingly synchronized with one another. Competition between producing regions became more acute. This contraction disclosed consider-able geographical differentiation among the British West Indian colonies. After 1814–18, sugar production ceased to expand in the small islands, and they accounted for a progressively smaller share of British output. Jamaica remained an important centre of production, although it no longer attained pre-1807 levels. In 1820, it still produced nearly ninety-eight thousand metric tons of sugar. Afterwards, production gradually declined, and Jamaica was replaced by Cuba as the world's largest single supplier during the decade of the 1820s. Led by Demerara, British Guiana became a valuable addition to the empire and grew rapidly. Its production increased nearly fivefold between 1814–18 and 1829–33 and reached a pre-emancipation high of nearly sixty thousand metric tons in 1830. By the late 1820s and early 1830s, sugar pro-duction had stagnated and declined in the Lesser Antilles and Jamaica. The losses in these old colonies were offset by increases in Guiana, Mauritius and Trinidad, but the British colonies' share of world production fell from nearly 50 per cent in 1815–19 to just under 25 per cent in 1838–42. During the same period, sugar production also fell in the French West Indian colonies, where the slave trade remained active. In Brazil, land was available and the Atlantic slave trade continued to supply labour. Sugar cultivation spread to areas outside of the northeast. However, the expansion of sugar cultivation was extensive rather than intensive. Attempts at innovation were sporadic and production techniques were largely unchanged. Production tripled between 1820 and 1850 and then levelled off.[36]

Changes in sugar markets and sugar consumption also undermined the British West Indian colonies. British West Indian producers continued to enjoy a protected position in the British national market as long as the Navigation Acts remained in effect. However, British territorial expansion in the Caribbean ended in 1815 and planters there were faced with rising costs. With the end of the Napoleonic Wars, Britain gained command of the continental market. British refiners, shippers, warehousemen, and commercial and financial interests were becoming involved in trading large quantities of both British and foreign sugar in Europe. As cheaper Cuban and Brazilian sugar found markets in Europe, British West Indian sugar was excluded. Re-exports of British West Indian sugar had to be subsidized by government drawbacks and bounties in order for British West Indian planters to be competitive with countries that were customers for British manufactures. At the same time, Britain either warehoused cheap foreign sugar for resale on the continent by British merchants or carried it directly to Europe for sale in "spot markets".[37] British West Indian re-exports dropped from about one hundred thousand tons in 1802 to twenty-seven thousand tons in 1827. As British sugar producers became increasingly dependent on preferential duties and the home market, British domestic consumption doubled between 1815 and 1840. By the 1830s, the West Indian colonies were no longer able to supply British demand.[38]

Redefining the Atlantic Division of Labour

If the British West Indies remained significant centres of sugar production and continued to yield profits to those who invested in them into the 1830s and beyond, that does not mean that they did not decline. The condition of a capitalist market economy is not simply to make profit. Rather, it is to make profits on an ever-renewed and ever-increasing scale. This process of capital accumulation continually establishes new material and social conditions of production. The decline of the British West Indian sugar industry is apparent if we look beyond the British colonial economy to the dramatic rise of new producing zones, especially Cuba, and the restructuring of the Atlantic division of labour as a whole. (Here we may also include the emergence of the American cotton frontier and the Brazilian coffee frontier.) Sugar production in Jamaica and British Guiana, the two most important British West Indian sugar colonies, was eclipsed by production in Cuba (figure 6.1). Jamaican

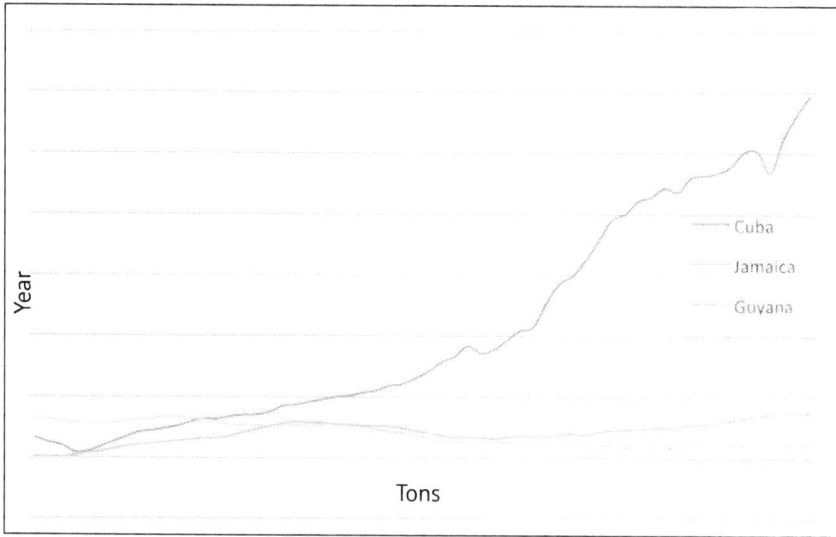

Figure 6.1. Comparative Sugar Production, 1807–1866 (5 Year Weighted Average)
Source: Noel Deerr, *A History of Sugar* (London: Chapman and Hall, 1949), 1:126, 131, 193–204.

production declined gradually after the post-war boom, while British Guiana's output increased sharply between 1807 and about 1827. Its production remained relatively stable until the abolition of slavery, after which it declined slowly until the 1840s, when indenture resolved the labour question – production climbed to a bit beyond its previous high levels after that. Cuban sugar production, in contrast, climbed steadily and sharply upward. It surpassed both Jamaica and British Guiana in the early 1820s to make Cuba the world's leading sugar producer, and it increased nearly eightfold between 1820 and 1860 to dominate world sugar production.

The production curves for Jamaica, British Guiana and Cuba attest to the creation of new conditions of sugar production during the first half of the nineteenth century. The expansion of sugar production entails the mobilization of labour and technology and the transformation of specific ecologies under given historical circumstances. The material processes of sugar require both agricultural and industrial operations. Land, labour and technology must be combined in the proper proportions in order to secure the optimal conditions of production. No more cane can be planted than can be milled, and no more syrup can be extracted than can be processed into crystallized sugar. Further, cane has to be processed within seventy-two hours after it is cut or fermentation impedes crystallization. Consequently, the material and economic requirements of sugar production impose a particular scale of activity and economy of time and space on producers. They involve the production of space and transformation of nature and, at the same time, are subject to specific physical-material limits. From this perspective, the specific geographies of sugar production in Jamaica, British Guiana and Cuba disclose the processes of expansion and differentiation that shaped the crisis of the British West Indian sugar industry and formed a new Atlantic division of labour.

Jamaica was a settled plantation zone in which the size and geography of the island as well as the existing pattern of land tenure and cultivation restricted possibilities for expansion and greater productivity. It had been the leading sugar producer in the British West Indies during the eighteenth century. The plantation zone was concentrated on the prime sugar lands in the southern coastal lowlands, the inland alluvial plains extending from St Thomas to Clarendon, across the north coast and into the Westmoreland plain. At the time of the Haitian Revolution, there was still room for new investment and territorial expansion. Jamaican sugar production nearly doubled between 1792 and 1805, and it surpassed the output of Saint-Domingue at its peak. New plantations were constructed, but these were often located in regions with less favourable soil and climatic conditions or in the interior of the island, where transportation costs were higher. Eighty-four new sugar estates were established between 1792 and 1799, over half of them in the northern districts of St Ann, St James and Trelawny. James Robertson's map, drawn in 1804 at the high point of Jamaican sugar production, documents 830 sugar estates for the entire island. These were densely concentrated on the northern and western coastal plains as well as the southern coastal lowlands. However, after the downturn of the sugar market in 1806, a quarter of Jamaica's new plantations were abandoned. By 1832, the number of estates had dropped to about 670. This contraction of productive land was especially pronounced in Portland, where climatic conditions were unfavourable, and among those estates that had been opened up in the interior of the island. Those parishes that were affected least by emancipation were those that had been occupied longest.[39]

Within the core plantation zone, the built environment itself was an obstacle to the amelioration of production. The dense occupation of the soil and the existence of contiguous properties made it difficult for estates to expand or to establish new properties. Production was organized on a scale adequate to eighteenth-century technical conditions – that is, to wind-, water- or animal-powered mills. However, expansion might have been possible within individual properties, as planters often occupied more land than they could cultivate, in order to limit competition. In such instances, it could be difficult to maintain the optimal proportions between the capacity of the slave gangs, the size of the cane fields and the factory. Further, planters with capital already sunk in slaves and equipment might be reluctant to invest in new plants that could offer only marginal increases in output. Nonetheless, Jamaica possessed large sugar estates that were capable of technical improvement. In 1830, 36 per cent of the slaves lived on units of over two hundred slaves.[40]

Jamaican planters were actively concerned with increasing their efficiency and with technological improvement of their operations. Beginning around 1800, they were quick to take advantage of new industrial technologies, including the horizontal three-roller mill and the steam engine. Before 1815, the majority of steam engines purchased in Jamaica were low-pressure engines of ten horsepower or less. Afterwards, Jamaican planters preferred to buy more efficient, high-powered engines of American manufacture. These ameliorations allowed Jamaican planters to maintain high levels of production and productivity. New steam-powered milling technologies could process more cane and could extract more juice from a given quantity of cane. However, they could only reach their full potential if the area under cultivation could be increased and more cane could be supplied to the mill. The possibilities for the extension of cane cultivation in Jamaica were limited. After the 1820s, productivity, like production, declined gradually from the high levels attained between 1796 and 1805, but remained above the pre-1796 levels.[41] However much the planters of Jamaica exhibited entrepreneurial behaviour and sought to maximize their opportunities, they could not go beyond the constraints of the physical environment.

British Guiana was the most important addition to Britain's West Indian colonies after the Napoleonic Wars. Attracted by the rich soil and favourable climatic conditions, English planters began moving to the Dutch colonies of Berbice, Demerara and Essequibo as early as the 1760s. By 1813, 95 per cent of the European settlers were British. British Guiana was late in developing compared to the rest of the Caribbean and, at the beginning of the nineteenth century, was still a new commodity frontier. It possessed large tracts of virgin land and excellent conditions for cotton, coffee and sugar cultivation. However, the colony's unusual ecology imposed distinctive conditions on the development of the plantation system there. The British Guianese plantation belt was restricted to the coastal plane, an area of 1,750 square miles. This land was at or below sea level and subject to alternating periods of heavy erosion and substantial accretion. The plantations were constructed on land reclaimed from the sea using Dutch techniques of polder construction. Plantation agriculture in British Guiana depended on an elaborate system of dams, canals and sluices for drainage, irrigation and transportation. The construction and maintenance of this infrastructure required an enormous amount of labour and capital. Walter Rodney estimates that the original construction of this hydraulic system required moving at least one hundred million tons of soil by hand.[42] Hence, a heavy capital investment was required even before sugar production was undertaken.

Poldering and the need to control the movement of both water and land created a particular agricultural landscape. Plantations in British Guiana were large, contiguous and relatively uniform in their internal organization. Flood and water control was centralized on each estate. Collectively, they safeguarded the plantation zone from the sea and backland flooding and controlled the water supply. They were connected with one another through the network of canals and waterways and the coastal road linking them with Georgetown.[43] Although sugar was grown under the Dutch, cotton and coffee predominated and much land remained uncultivated. Plantations were already large. Initial allotments along the coast were 250 acres, and planters had the right to a second grant extending into the interior. A limit of 1,000 acres was established for sugar plantations and 500 acres for coffee.[44]

British reconquest of Guiana in 1796 initiated a massive shift of British capital and slaves to the colony. The slave population doubled from 1792 to 1802, and between 1803 and 1805 twenty thousand slaves were imported from Africa. Cotton, sugar and coffee exports increased dramatically between 1789 and 1802.[45] After 1810, cotton and coffee, faced with foreign competition, began to gradually decline, while sugar production rose, particularly during the boom period between 1815 and the early 1820s. Many planters planted all three crops and shifted gradually to sugar. However, by the 1820s, the decline of cotton and coffee became more pronounced, while sugar production continued to increase. The need to invest in land, new steam technology and slaves made British Guianese sugar planters vulnerable to falling prices after 1820. Land was gradually concentrated in the hands of British merchants with enough capital to maintain production, and planters grew more cane and produced more sugar in order to offset falling prices. By 1830, most East Coast Demerara plantations had converted to sugar. Steam mills replaced the wind- and cattle-driven mills. Several plantations had merged, and many passed into the hands of British corporations.[46]

While land was abundant and there was room for expansion of the area under cultivation, British Guiana was chronically short of labour.[47] Plantations were already big in 1815. Of them, 8 per cent had more than 300 slaves, 40 per cent had between 200 and 300, and 46 per cent had between 100 and 200.[48] However, the expansion of sugar production and increased demand for labour coincided with the end of slave trade. High productivity of the soil, economies of scale and technological innovation compensated for the relative shortage of labour. The size of plantations, the amount of capital required to make them profitable and the shortage of labour all encouraged technological improvement. At the same time, the size of the estates and the scale of operations meant that planters could take full advantage of the increased capacity of new machinery. That estates were contiguous to one another and relatively uniform in their layout meant that consolidation of estates was a possibility, as new refining technologies required increased area under cultivation in order to achieve their maximum efficiency.

British Guianese planters innovated in both agricultural and manufacturing aspects of sugar production, and they invested heavily in machinery.[49] The firm of Bolton and Watt sold 114 steam engines to Guianese planters between 1803 and 1820. The number fell to 32 between 1820 and 1852, but by 1830 most estates had steam power. It is likely that after 1820 these were higher-capacity and more efficient high-pressure engines, not the Bolton and Watt engines. The other major innovation was the vacuum pan, which revolutionized sugar boiling. Various historians have complained that the vacuum pan was invented in 1813 but only deployed in the Caribbean decades later.[50] However, there is a great difference between the early models and the vacuum pans and multiple-effect boilers that appeared in the 1830s–1840s. The latter devices were extremely expensive. They could cost between £40,000 and £50,000. They increased both the quantity and quality of the sugar obtained from a given amount of syrup, but they required a far more extensive area of cane to be cultivated than was necessary for non-mechanized mills in order to make full use of their capacity and to compensate for the costs of purchase and maintenance. The first vacuum pans were successfully tried out in British Guiana in 1830, sixteen years before they were first installed in Jamaica. By 1832, vacuum pans were operating on six estates in British Guiana.[51] Shortage of skilled "pan boilers" slowed their adoption in the 1830s and early 1840s, but they became more common afterwards.[52]

British Guianese sugar plantations were larger and more capital-intensive than those in the rest of the British West Indies. The largest plantations had between four hundred and seven hundred slaves. John Gladstone had two thousand slaves on several plantations at the time of emancipation.[53] Production more than tripled between 1814–18 and 1829–33.[54] The trend towards consolidation of estates and corporate ownership continued after emancipation when Asian contract labour replaced slave labour.[55] In 1841, 239 plantations produced about 33,000 hogsheads of sugar. Of these, only 31 produced more than 250 hogsheads. Ten years later, 170 plantations produced a total of 460,000 hogsheads of sugar. Of these plantations, 86 produced more than 250 hogsheads, of which 23 employed the vacuum pan.[56]

In contrast to Jamaica and British Guiana, Cuba offered exceptional conditions for the development of sugar production from the 1790s onward. The Cuban sugar frontier encompassed approximately thirty thousand square miles. This zone was virgin prairie with ideal soils and climate for sugar production. But I am not making the case for geographical determinism. Rather, my concern is with the historical conditions under which land, labour and technology are combined in order to transform natural environments in accordance with the requirements of sugar production. Indeed, the extent of the Cuban frontier was an obstacle to its development until the problem of overland transportation was solved by the development of the railroad network beginning in 1837.

Slavery and sugar production expanded slowly in the region around

Havana from the time of the English occupation in 1763 until 1792. The outbreak of the Haitian Revolution and the destruction of the Saint-Domingue sugar industry provided the Havana planters with their great opportunity, and they took full advantage of it. Between 1792 and 1818, the Havana planters established the conditions necessary to develop the Cuban sugar industry. First, they freed themselves from the constraints of Spanish mercantilism and secured the right to free trade in sugar and the right to import slaves without restriction. They enjoyed exceptional access to the rapidly expanding US consumer market and to US goods and capital. The sugar boom also signalled an unprecedented expansion of the slave trade to Cuba. David Eltis estimates that over 780,000 slaves were imported to Cuba between 1791 and 1867.[57] Cuban planters were competing with protected sugars, especially in European markets. They were constantly concerned with the scale and productivity of production, and they sought to systematically promote technological innovation and the application of scientific methods to production. Finally, in 1818, they won the right to absolute private property in land, including the right to clear the forest, which had been the preserve of the Royal Navy.[58]

Between 1792 and 1800, the number of sugar mills increased from 237 to 350, with another 50 under construction in the regions around the ports of Havana and Matanzas. Total production increased from 14,500 tons in 1791 to 41,000 tons in 1807, while average production per mill rose from 60 tons in 1791 to 136 tons in 1804. There were no significant technological innovations during this period, but the first giant mills with over three hundred slaves and producing over 300 tons of sugar each made their appearance. By 1820, there were 625 plantations throughout the entire province of Havana, predominantly located near the coast to facilitate transport, and total production climbed to 55,000 tons. The 1827 census registered 1,000 sugar mills in Cuba. Only 2.5 per cent of these had steam power. Nonetheless, Cuba produced nearly 77,000 tons of sugar and surpassed Jamaica's peak year. Three years later, its output reached 105,000 tons and it became the world's leading producer.[59]

Initially, increased production owed more to the multiplication of sugar mills than to technological transformation. The majority of Cuban mills were still clustered around the ports of Havana and Matanzas. Transportation was the key obstacle to the full exploitation of Cuba's sugar frontier, particularly as the volume of sugar to be moved increased so dramatically. Havana's planter elite was increasingly concerned with road construction and developed a plan to build a canal from Havana to Güines. The key breakthrough was the construction of the Havana-Güines railroad in 1837. Rail transport provided cheap and efficient transportation that opened up Cuba's interior to sugar cultivation. As the rail network extended into the interior, the number of sugar mills multiplied.[60] Perhaps more importantly, the creation of the railroad coincided with a cycle of technological innovation in sugar manufacture. The steam engine, all-metal horizontal grinding mills, the vacuum pan and the centrifuge were introduced during the 1830s and 1840s, and each of these implements underwent improvement. After the establishment of the railroad, Cuban planters were able to extend the sugar frontier and to establish new plantations on a scale that made optimal use of each new technological innovation. By 1840, Cuba was producing over 160,000 tons of sugar (more than 19 per cent of the world sugar market). Ten years later, its output reached nearly 295,000 metric tons or one-quarter of the world's supply, and by 1868 Cuban production had climbed to 720,000 tons or 30 per cent of a growing world market.[61]

Carlos Rebello's 1860 enumeration of sugar production shows both the increasing scale of production and technological innovation on Cuba's sugar mills and the shift of the centre of production towards the interior of the island. There were 359 animal-powered mills with an average capacity of 113 tons, 889 semi-mechanized mills with an average output of 411 tons, and 64 fully mechanized mills with an average production capacity of 1,176 tons. (The latter accounted for 5 per cent of the plantations but 15 per cent of production.) The average size of an estate was 1,432 acres. The semi-mechanized mills, which combined steam power – frequently high-pressure engines of 100 horsepower or more – with iron horizontal grinding mills and multiple trains of open-kettle boilers, and the fully mechanized mills, which integrated the most advanced milling technology with multiple-effect vacuum pans, were concentrated in the new zones of the sugar frontier: Colón, and the current provinces of Villa Clara, Cienfuegos and Sancti Spíritus.[62] Cuba's domination of the world sugar market was achieved through the extensive development of its sugar frontier and significant increases in the productivity of individual plantations.

Conclusion: The Legacy of Eric Williams

Jamaica, British Guiana and Cuba represent three different trajectories of sugar plantation economies worked by slave labour. In each instance, the local ecology was transformed in strikingly different ways by the material and social requirements of slave sugar plantation production. At the same time, developments in each zone became increasingly interdependent through the expansion of the world-economy, the restructuring of markets and the reorganization of the Atlantic division of labour between 1783 and 1866. Each zone was capable of responding to the transformations of the world sugar market in different ways. While a more complete account of sugar and slavery during this period would necessarily address many other factors, these material conditions set the parameters of the history of the sugar economy. From this perspective, the "decline" of the British West Indian sugar industry is apparent. In both Jamaica and British Guiana, individual estates could adjust to market conditions and remain productive and profitable. Nonetheless, even as they did so, they fell further behind. Each colony and the British West Indies as a whole were eclipsed by the unprecedented growth of the slave sugar complex in Cuba. This "decline" is inseparable from the restructuring of the Atlantic division of labour and the increasing scale and productivity of world production. It is not reducible to a single event or series of events. Rather, it is a unified and long-term structural shift, like the movement of tectonic plates against one another. It is within this long-term movement that the social history, politics and ideology of slavery and emancipation need to be reinterpreted and reassessed. In such a rethinking, Eric Williams remains the fundamental reference, both for the questions he asked and the insight that he provides.

NOTES

1. Eric Williams, *Capitalism and Slavery* (1944; reprint, Chapel Hill: University of North Carolina Press, 1994), 113–14.
2. Ibid., 135, 136.
3. Maria Sylvia de Carvalho Franco, *Homens Livres na Ordem Escravocrata* (São Paulo:

Editora Ática, 1976), 9–16; Francisco de Oliveira, *A Economia Brasileira: Crítica á Razão Dualista* (Petrópolis: Editora Vozes, 1981), 9–13; Terence K. Hopkins, "World-Systems Analysis: Methodological Issues", in *World-Systems Analysis: Theory and Methodology*, ed. Terence K. Hopkins and Immanuel Wallerstein (Beverly Hills: Sage Publications, 1982), 151–52.

4.   William Darity, "Eric Williams and Slavery: A West Indian Viewpoint?" *Callaloo* 20, no. 4 (1997): 800–16; Barbara L. Solow, "Caribbean Slavery and British Economic Growth: The Eric Williams Hypothesis", *Journal of Development Economics* (1985): 99–115; Barbara L. Solow, "Capitalism and Slavery in the Exceedingly Long Run", in *British Capitalism and Caribbean Slavery: The Legacy of Eric Williams*, ed. Barbara L. Solow and Stanley L. Engerman (Cambridge: Cambridge University Press, 1987), 51–77.

5.   Seymour M. Drescher, *Econocide: British Slavery in the Era of Abolition* (Pittsburgh: University of Pittsburgh Press, 1977); David Eltis, *Economic Growth and the Ending of the Transatlantic Slave Trade* (New York: Oxford University Press, 1987), 5.

6.   Robert W. Fogel, *Without Consent or Contract: The Rise and Fall of American Slavery* (New York: W.W. Norton, 1989), 9–13; R.W. Fogel and Stanley L. Engerman, *Time on the Cross: The Economics of American Negro Slavery*, vol. 1 (Boston: Little Brown, 1974), 3–12; ibid., vol. 2, 3–19.

7.   Symptomatically, perhaps, those mounting the most effective challenge to Williams's positions have relied on a quantitative critique, while those defending him have largely relied on qualitative evidence (see Selwyn H.H. Carrington, *The Sugar Industry and the Abolition of the Slave Trade, 1750–1810* [Gainesville: University of Florida Press, 2002]). Quantitative historians have tended to be dismissive of qualitative evidence because of its alleged subjective bias. We have yet to satisfactorily reconcile these two kinds of approaches.

8.   Pierre Vilar, "Pour une meilleure compréhension entre economists et historiens: Histoire quantative ou économétrie rétrospective?" in *Une histoire en construction: Approche marxiste et problèmatiques conjoncturelles* (Paris: Éditions du Seuil, 1982), 295–313.

9.   Carlo Ginzburg, "Microhistory: Two or Three Things That I Know About It", *Critical Inquiry* 20, no. 1 (1993): 21.

10.   Stanley L. Engerman, "Some Considerations Relating to Property Rights in Man", *Journal of Economic History* 33, no. 1 (1973): 43–65.

11.   John H. Conrad and John R. Meyer, *The Economics of Slavery and Other Studies in Economic History* (Chicago: Aldine, 1964), 45, 47, 83–84; Fogel, *Without Consent or Contract*.

12.   Drescher argues that "the British West Indies were absolutely and relatively far more valuable to Britain during the period of intense debate on the imperial

slave trade (1788–1807) and on the world slave trade (1814–1820) than during the period when there had been no organized British pressure against the slave trade (1720–1775)". They accounted for a higher proportion of British trade, whether taken in the aggregate or measuring imports and exports separately, after 1773 than before. Further, they were Britain's most important non-European trading area from 1722 to 1822, and their share of British trade was increasing over their closest rivals during the period from 1793–97 to 1808–12 (Drescher, *Econocide*, 16–17).

13. Ludwig Dehio, *The Precarious Balance: Four Centuries of the European Power Struggle* (New York: Vintage, 1962).

14. Williams, *Capitalism and Slavery*, 108–25.

15. Ibid., 116.

16. R.B. Sheridan, "The Crisis of Slave Subsistence", *William and Mary Quarterly* 33, no. 4 (1976): 614–41; Carrington, *Sugar Industry*; David Beck Ryden, *West Indian Slavery and British Abolition, 1783–1807* (Cambridge: Cambridge University Press, 2009).

17. Williams, *Capitalism and Slavery*, 121–23; J.H. Coatesworth, "American Trade with European Colonies in the Caribbean and South America, 1790–1812", *William and Mary Quarterly* 24, no. 2 (1967): 243–66; J.A. Dun, " 'What Avenues of Commerce, Will You, Americans, Not Explore!': Commercial Philadelphia's Vantage onto the Early Haitian Revolution", *William and Mary Quarterly* 62, no. 3 (2005): 473–504.

18. Williams, *Capitalism and Slavery*, 147–50.

19. Drescher, *Econocide*, 16–17.

20. David Beck Ryden, "Does the Decline Thesis Make Sense? The West Indian Slave Economy and the Abolition of the British Slave Trade", *Journal of Interdisciplinary History* 31, no. 3 (2001): 347.

21. Ibid.; Ryden, *West Indian Slavery and British Abolition*.

22. Francisco Arango y Parreño, "Discurso sobre la agricultura de la Habana y medios de fomentarla" (1793), in *Obras*, vol. 1 (Havana: Dirección de la Cultura, 1952), 114–75.

23. Dale Tomich, "The Wealth of Empire: Francisco Arango y Parreño, Political Economy, and the Second Slavery in Cuba", *Comparative Studies in Society and History* 45, no. 1 (2003): 4–28.

24. As Rafael Marquese's chapter in this volume demonstrates, the United States played an analogous role in the development of Brazilian coffee production.

25. Manuel Moreno Fraginals, *El ingenio: Complejo económico social cubano del azúcar*, vol. 1 (Havana: Editorial de ciencias sociales, 1978), 15–36.

26. D.A. Farnie, *The English Cotton Industry and the World Market, 1815–1896* (Oxford:

Clarendon Press, 1979), 11–12; Stuart Bruchey, *Cotton and the Growth of the American Economy, 1790–1860* (New York: Harcourt, Brace, 1967), 47–48.

27. Farnie, *English Cotton Industry*, 15; L.C. Gray, *History of Agriculture in the Southern United States*, vol. 2 (Gloucester, MA: Peter Smith, 1958), 691.

28. Dehio, *Precarious Balance*.

29. Eltis, *Economic Growth*, 5–6; Drescher, *Econocide*, 147–48.

30. Eltis, *Economic Growth*, 5–6.

31. Drescher, *Econocide*, 160.

32. Eltis, *Economic Growth*, 5.

33. Jason Moore's concept of commodity frontiers ("Sugar and the Expansion of the Early-Modern World-Economy: Commodity Frontiers, Ecological Transformation, and Industrialization", *Review* 23, no. 3 [2000]: 409–33) calls attention to the ways that the production and distribution of specific primary products restructures geographic space at the margins of the world-economic system in such a way as to require further expansion. For Moore, a commodity frontier is a zone beyond which further expansion is possible as long as there is uncommodified land and, to a lesser extent, labour. The movement of population and the transformation of nature follow upon the demand for commodities. This concept calls attention to the transnational migratory character of primary production and of slave labour (Antônio Barros de Castro, *7 ensaios sobre a economia brasileira*, vol. 2 [Rio de Janeiro: Forense Universitaria, 1971], 48–83) and enables us to conceptualize the relation between specific ecologies, place and the geographical expansion of the capitalist economy. It contrasts Eric Williams's "law of slave production", which relies on soil exhaustion as the single explanatory factor for the decline of slave zones of production. This contrast allows us to differentiate old productive zones from new frontiers.

34. Levi Marrero, *Cuba: Economía y Sociedad*, vol. 12: *Azúcar, Ilustracion y Conciencia 1763–1868* (Madrid: Editorial Playor, 1985), 108.

35. Dale Tomich, *Slavery in the Circuit of Sugar: Martinique in the World Economy, 1830–1848* (Baltimore: Johns Hopkins University Press, 1990), 23.

36. Noel Deerr, *The History of Sugar*, vol. 1 (London: Chapman and Hall, 1949), 193–201; Moreno Fraginals, *El ingenio*, vol. 1, 40–42; ibid., vol. 2, 173.

37. If mercantilism was intended to secure sources of overseas production and trade for the metropolis, here it had become the means for West Indian planters to protect themselves from competition. Britain continued to pay higher prices for sugar without the benefits that mercantilism had provided for the national economy. This problem was especially acute in the re-export market. Williams's teleological association of industrial capital and the free market obscures the financial and commercial motives for removing the restrictions

on trade. Huskisson wanted to make London the "depot of the merchandise passing between the two worlds". In 1823, his Warehousing Bill allowed foreign goods, including sugar, to be re-exported free of duty. This policy was based on notions of "comparative advantage" and the allocative efficiency of the market system (Geoffrey Ingham, *Capitalism Divided? The City and Industry in British Social Development* [New York: Schocken Books, 1984], 113–15). Nonetheless, until the Corn Laws were repealed, Britain had a dual-market system: one that subsidized colonial producers and kept domestic prices high, and another that attempted to control continental markets by controlling the unrestricted flow of produce from American producers.

38. Marrero, *Cuba: Economía y Sociedad*, vol. 12, 108; Tomich, *Slavery in the Circuit of Sugar*, 28; Williams, *Capitalism and Slavery*, 133–54; Drescher, *Econocide*, 155–57; Moreno Fraginals, *El ingenio*, vol. 2, 157–61; Lowell Ragatz, *The Fall of the Planter Class in the British West Indies, 1763–1833* (New York: Octagon Books, 1971), 434–35.

39. Deerr, *History of Sugar*, 193–202; Drescher, *Econocide*, 93–103; Moreno Fraginals, *El ingenio*, vol. 2, 106–30, 156–65; Barry W. Higman, *Slave Population and Economy in Jamaica, 1801–1834* (Cambridge: Cambridge University Press, 1976), 14; Barry W. Higman, *Jamaica Surveyed* (Kingston: Institute of Jamaica Publications, 1988), 10–11; Veront Satchell, *Sugar, Slavery, and Technical Change: Jamaica, 1760–1830* (Saarbrücken: VDM Verlag Dr Müller GmbH, 2010), 102, 166.

40. Higman, *Slave Population and Economy in Jamaica*, 14.

41. Satchell, *Sugar, Slavery, and Technical Change*, 176–80.

42. Walter Rodney, *A History of the Guyanese Working People, 1881–1905* (Baltimore: Johns Hopkins University Press, 1981), 2–3; Emília Viotti da Costa, *Crowns of Glory, Tears of Blood: The Demerara Slave Rebellion of 1823* (New York: Oxford University Press, 1994), 9; Wazir Mohamed, "Frustrated Peasants, Marginalized Workers: Free African Villages in Guyana, 1838–1885" (PhD diss., Binghamton University, 2008), 93–110.

43. Mohamed, "Frustrated Peasants, Marginalized Workers", 9; Costa, *Crowns of Glory*, 44.

44. Costa, *Crowns of Glory*, 44; Mohamed, "Frustrated Peasants, Marginalized Workers", 93–110.

45. Costa, *Crowns of Glory*, 46–47; Alan H. Adamson, *Sugar without Slaves: The Political Economy of British Guiana, 1838–1904* (New Haven, CT: Yale University Press, 1972), 24.

46. Costa, *Crowns of Glory*, 46–47.

47. Mohamed, "Frustrated Peasants, Marginalized Workers", 133; Adamson, *Sugar without Slaves*, 24.

48. Costa, *Crowns of Glory*, 47; Adamson, *Sugar without Slaves*, 24–25.

49. Allyson Stoll, "Not for Want of Go-Aheadism in Field and Factory: The Technological Trajectory of the Guyana (British Guiana) Sugar Industry from 1800 to the 1930s" (PhD diss., Cornell University, 2011); Allyson Stoll, "Thoroughly Tested and Tried: Cane Culture, Technology, and Environmental Change in Nineteenth Century Guyana", *Journal of Caribbean History* 45, no. 1 (2011): 92–127.

50. Adamson, *Sugar without Slaves*, 26–27; Satchell, *Sugar, Slavery, and Technical Change*.

51. Stoll, "Not for Want of Go-Aheadism", 164; Mohamed, "Frustrated Peasants, Marginalized Workers", 127–33; Satchell, *Sugar, Slavery, and Technical Change*, 99.

52. Tomich, *Slavery in the Circuit of Sugar*, 195–97; Stoll, "Not for Want of Go-Aheadism", 162ff.

53. Costa, *Crowns of Glory*, 47–48; Mohamed, "Frustrated Peasants, Marginalized Workers", 116, 127–33.

54. Deerr, *History of Sugar*, vol. 1, 193–201; Moreno Fraginals, *El ingenio*, vol. 2, 106, 156–65.

55. Stoll, "Not for Want of Go-Aheadism", 21.

56. Adamson, *Sugar without Slaves*, 175.

57. Eltis, *Economic Growth*, 245.

58. Reinaldo Funes Monzote, *From Rainforest to Cane Field in Cuba: An Environmental History since 1492* (Chapel Hill: University of North Carolina Press, 2008).

59. Moreno Fraginals, *El ingenio*, vol. 1, 67–71; Reinaldo Funes Monzote and Dale Tomich, "Naturaleza, Tecnología y Esclavitud en Cuba: Frontera Azucarera y Revolución Industrial", in *Trabajo Libre y Coactivo en Sociedades de Plantación*, ed. José Antonio Piqueras (Mexico City: Siglo XXI, 2009), 75–117; Franklin W. Knight, *Slave Society in Cuba during the Nineteenth Century* (Madison: University of Wisconsin Press, 1970), 30–31.

60. Oscar Zanetti and Alejandro García, *Sugar and Railroads: A Cuban History, 1837–1959* (Chapel Hill: University of North Carolina Press, 1998).

61. Moreno Fraginals, *El ingenio*, vol. 1, 46–47, 67–71, 95–102, 167–255; ibid., vol. 2, 93–97, 106–174; ibid., vol. 3, 35–36; Knight, *Slave Society in Cuba*, 14–18, 40–41.

62. Moreno Fraginals, *El ingenio*, vol. 1, 170–73; Funes Monzote, *From Rainforest to Cane Field*, 129–31.

Chapter 7

The Triangular Trade from a Global Perspective

RONALD FINDLAY AND KEVIN HJORTSHØJ O'ROURKE

"The present study is an attempt to place in historical perspective the relationship between early capitalism, as exemplified by Great Britain, and the Negro slave trade, Negro slavery and the general colonial trade of the seventeenth and eighteenth centuries." These are the words with which Eric Williams opens his enduring classic, *Capitalism and Slavery*. In the next paragraph, he states, "It is strictly an economic study of the role of Negro slavery and the slave trade in providing the capital which financed the Industrial Revolution in England and of mature industrial capitalism in destroying the slave system."[1] He thus combines in one sentence the two distinct "Williams theses" associated with his name: first, that the profits of the slave trade "financed" the Industrial Revolution; and second, that the abolition of the slave trade in 1807 and of slavery itself (within the British Empire) in 1838 was a response to the "decline" of the earlier capitalism of the Commercial Revolution and its replacement by the later capitalism of the Industrial Revolution, the transition from what William Parker called the "Age of Adam Smith" to the "Age of Schumpeter".[2]

Whether intentionally or not on Williams's part, these two apparently distinct theses can be neatly linked together in Marxian terms by the argument that Negro slavery was a foundation for the earlier commercial stage of capitalism but had eventually become a "fetter" on the development of the later industrial stage, and that its abolition was therefore in the economic self-interest of the capitalist ruling class and not, as it superficially appeared to be, the result of benign, humanitarian intervention on the part of William Wilberforce and others. Just as medieval serfdom had been the basis of feudalism propelling the economic system forward from the collapse of the ancient world, but then became an obstacle to the free mobility of labour in response to wage differentials as required by capitalism, so also Negro slavery had to be abolished after it had fulfilled its specific historical role of providing the "primitive accumulation" required for the emergence of capitalism. We leave it to others, much better informed about Williams's intellectual formation, to discuss whatever validity this hypothesis of a Marxian link might have.

The logical difficulty that this unified thesis presents, however, is that Negro slavery was the essential labour force for the supply of raw cotton to the Lancashire cotton textile industry, the springboard of the Industrial Revolution itself. The industry was just getting underway in the 1790s and was still very underdeveloped in 1807, the year of the abolition of the British slave trade – in 1838, the year of the abolition of slavery in the British Empire, it had a long way to go before reaching maturity. Why shut down the supply of slave imports from Africa when the demand for cotton was growing by leaps and bounds, driven by technological progress in spinning and weaving? The only interest group with a credible incentive to do this would be slave owners in the New World, the price of whose existing human assets would immediately rise in response to the abolition of the trade across the Atlantic. In other words, did abolition represent protectionism on the part of the slave-supplying industry in the New World at the expense of the Lancashire cotton textile industry, which lost out because of the higher future prices of its essential intermediate input entailed by the restriction on the supply of the slave labour force? Again, this is a question that we would like to pose to others better qualified than ourselves – in this case, experts on abolition. In this connection, we note that no less than three major works on abolition have been published recently, namely, *Inhuman Bondage* by David Brion Davis, *Abolition* by Seymour Drescher and *The American Crucible* by Robin Blackburn. The last of these is sympathetic to the Williams thesis, while Davis is ambivalent because, while he acknowledges that the plantation system contributed to the growth of the metropolitan economies, he believes the strict thesis itself to have been "wholly disproved" by the economic historians. Drescher's book, surprisingly, does not mention the name of Eric Williams at all.[3]

It appears that Williams considered his research problem in *Capitalism and Slavery* to have been the role of the slave trade in this first commercial phase, lasting essentially until its abolition in 1807, rather than the subsequent industrial phase. Sugar was, therefore, the main commodity involved, rather than the comparative latecomer, cotton. This would explain the relatively narrow and more tenuous focus of the book on the role of slave trade *profits* in the *financing* of the initial phases of the Industrial Revolution, rather than on the stronger and more direct and sustained link between raw cotton as an essential intermediate *input* into the *production* of the cotton textile industry and all the ramifications thereof. This did not prevent Williams from making acute observations on the subject of cotton, as in his statement that "Manchester received a double stimulus from the colonial trade. If it supplied the goods needed on the slave coast and on the plantations, its manufacturers depended in turn on the supply of the raw material. Manchester's interest in the islands was twofold."[4] It also explains why the subject that Dale Tomich aptly calls the "second slavery" – the growing of cotton in the southern United States up until the Civil War and of sugar in Cuba and coffee in Brazil up to the 1880s, before emancipation and abolition – was not considered as part of his research agenda.[5]

General Equilibrium Model: Structure and Results

The complex web of relationships between Europe, Africa and America involved in the triangular trade can be depicted in various ways. In art, we have the famous 1796 engraving by William Blake, with the three naked ladies representing "Europe Supported by Africa and America". Not having Blake's artistic gifts, we are forced to rely on the more mundane alternative of a general equilibrium model, originally presented by Findlay, who in turn drew on a pioneering contribution by Darity.[6] The simplest version of this model has each "continent" completely specialized on a single commodity: Europe on manufactured goods, denoted M; America on raw material inputs for manufacturing, denoted R; and Africa on slaves, denoted S. Taking M as the *numeraire*, denote the relative price of the raw material R as p, and that of slaves S as v. The output of M is a function of capital K and labour L, as determined by a neoclassical production function exhibiting constant returns to scale and permitting substitution between these two inputs, provided that a constant quantity of R per unit of M is available. The supply of L is given, but there is a perfectly elastic long-run supply curve of capital at an interest rate r*, equal to the constant rate of time preference assumed for the agents in the economy. The output of R in America depends upon a fixed supply of land T and the input of slave labour S, with the marginal product of the slave labour R'(S) positive, but diminishing as S is increased. Slaves grow their own food, so the entire marginal product of a slave in terms of R accrues to the owner of the plantation on which he or she works. The flow supply of new slaves from Africa, provided by the coastal slave-raiding states such as Dahomey, is an increasing function of the relative price in terms of manufactures v. The slave population in America is not assumed to be able to reproduce itself – in other words, mortality exceeds fertility, at a constant rate n, which can therefore be regarded as the rate at which the slave owner's asset "depreciates". We assume that all legs of the triangular trade are bilaterally balanced – that is, there is no international lending or borrowing, although the same interest rate r* will prevail in both Europe and America. All markets are perfectly competitive. Given these individual building blocks, it now remains to be shown how the general equilibrium of the intercontinental system as a whole is determined in the long-run steady state.

In such a steady state, European manufacturers must be maximizing profits, so that the marginal value product of capital, net of the raw material cost, must be equal to r* plus the rate of depreciation of the capital stock. In America, slave owners must earn a marginal value product $pR'(S)$ of the slave just sufficient to cover interest r* plus "depreciation" n on the equilibrium asset price v* of the slave. If we denote the export of slaves from Africa as E(v), it must be the case that E(v*) is equal to nS*; that is, the supply of fresh slaves to the New World at the price v* must be just enough to leave S* unchanged. In Findlay,[7] it is shown that we can solve the system to obtain the equilibrium steady-state values S*, E*, R*, M*, K*, p* and v* of all the variables we have introduced so far, along with q* denoting the marginal value product $p*R'(T)$ of the fixed supply of land T in America. In words, we have determined the size of the slave population in America, the annual flow of slave exports from Africa to satisfy the replacement demand nS*, the output of raw materials (raw sugar, tobacco, cotton and so on) in America, the output of manufactures in Europe and the endogenous supply of capital used to produce it, as well as the relative prices of the slaves and the raw materials, in terms of the manufactured product as the *numeraire*. Import demand for manufactures by the plantation owners of the New World is readily obtainable also, with the net surplus of their exports to Europe covering the cost of the slave imports from Africa. Exports of manufactures by Europe to both Africa and America must cover the cost of the import of raw materials from America. The wealth of Europe will be equal to K^*, the capital stock, while the wealth of America will be equal to v^*S^*, the asset value of the slave population, plus q^*T, the asset value of the land on which the New World crops are grown. Africa is not obtaining any wealth beyond the consumption of manufactured imports of the slave-exporting states and is in fact running down its stock of human resources with all the associated disruption that this causes.

The impact of any change in parameters on all the equilibrium values can now be examined. Among the most interesting examples are population growth in Europe; technological progress in European manufacturing (that is, an "industrial revolution"); supply shocks in the New World arising from extensions of the land frontier or technical progress, such as Eli Whitney's invention of the cotton gin; or a restriction in slave exports from Africa, as resulting from the 1807 abolition of the (legal) trade in slaves.

An increase in the labour force L of Europe will increase the demand for the raw material exported by America and so raise the equilibrium relative price p^* in terms of manufactures, thus reducing the "value added" by capital and labour at any given capital-labour ratio. The marginal product of capital will therefore have to rise to maintain equality with r^*. Thus, because of constant returns to scale, K^* and therefore M^* will both rise less than proportionately to the increase in L, so that per capita real income and the real wage in Europe will both fall. The higher p^* and S^* in America will lead to higher export of slaves E^* from Africa at a higher price v^* in terms of manufactures, so that the terms of trade of both Africa and America improve at the expense of Europe.

An industrial revolution in Europe can be modelled as a Hicks-neutral shift in the manufacturing production function, which can be shown to lead to increases in M^*, K^*, R^* and S^*, as well as in p^* and v^*, so that once again we have Europe's terms of trade deteriorating, while America's and Africa's improve. It is possible that the terms of trade deterioration could be so great as to negate the positive effect of technological progress on real income at constant relative prices, so that we have a case of Edgeworth-Bhagwati "damnifying" or "immiserizing" growth.[8]

Positive supply shocks in America arising from more land or better technology would lead to a reduction in p^* and increases in R^*, M^* and K^*, so that the American terms of trade worsen, to the benefit of Europe in this case, leading similarly to the possibility of "damnification", but now in the opposite direction. The effect on v^* and the quantity of slave exports from Africa is ambiguous, because the increase in the volume of R^* may be partly or fully offset in its effect on the demand for new slaves by the increase in their productivity due to more land or better technology. Needless to say, the benefits of the improvement in productivity will all be appropriated by the owners rather than by the slaves.

The abolition of the international slave trade introduced by Britain in 1807 restricted the volume of slave traffic but did not eliminate it completely, since considerable smuggling still took place, despite the strenuous efforts of the Royal Navy. We mimic the effects of the abolition by treating it as analogous to the imposition of an export tax that shifts the supply curve of slaves from Africa $E(v)$ to the left, leading to a rise in v^* and a fall in S^*, causing in turn a fall in R^*, M^* and K^* and a rise in p^*. Clearly, the overall scale and volume of activity in the Atlantic economy as a whole is reduced. The terms of trade of America are worsened, but the rise in v^* means that the owners of the lower stock of slaves will experience an increase in the value of their human assets, though the value of the land T will fall. In Africa, the abolition will result in a fall of the price received by the exporters, since they will only obtain the "after-tax" price of v^* minus the "export tax".

An extended version of the model is also presented in Findlay,[9] where the main modification is to introduce an agricultural sector – the output of which is assumed to be non-tradable – into the "European" economy in order to increase its realism and make the manufacturing sector changes less dramatic, both at home and in the Atlantic economy as a whole. The *qualitative* effects of all the comparative static results reported above, however, remain largely unchanged.

The Historical Record

We can now confront the predictions of the model with the historical record of the Atlantic economy. According to Philip Curtin, what he calls the "sugar revolution" associated with the "plantation complex" did not fully emerge in the Caribbean until about 1640, spreading from the eastern islands of St Kitts and Nevis, Guadeloupe, Martinique, Antigua and especially Barbados to eventually reach the larger islands of Hispaniola and Jamaica. Small islands had an initial advantage of proximity to the sea, since transport costs on land were a serious obstacle before the introduction of railways.[10] These islands were originally intended for European settlement with indentured labour, but comparative mortality rates in the tropics decided the issue in favour of the importation of African slaves. According to Fogel and Engerman, "the great majority of the slaves brought into the British, French and Dutch Caribbean colonies were engaged, directly and indirectly, in the sugar industry".[11] They estimate that 40 per cent of slave imports in Brazil were engaged in sugar culture and, in Spanish America, somewhere between 30 and 50 per cent.

Over 12 million Africans were transported in the Middle Passage from the fifteenth century to the final end of the trade around 1870. The annual level of slave exports rose from an average of 18,756 in the seventeenth century to 64,946 in the eighteenth, with over 80,000 per annum being transported between 1780 and 1830 (aside from a dip between 1811 and 1820, in the wake of abolition).[12] Of the total transported over the entire period, 58 per cent were transported between 1700 and 1810. As the model predicts, therefore, the slave trade rose with the initial onset of the Industrial Revolution.

The British Caribbean, the French Caribbean and Spanish America imported 22 per cent, 11 per cent and 13 per cent, respectively, of total slave imports up to 1866. Brazil imported 44 per cent and the North American mainland a surprisingly small share of only 4 per cent (with the remainder going mostly to the Dutch and smaller European colonies).[13] The large subsequent African American population of the United States is due to the fact that it was the only slave-importing region that experienced a sustained excess of fertility over mortality, which in turn was due to the relatively restricted extent of sugar cultivation on the mainland that kept the death rate down, as well as the better climate.

The prediction that the Industrial Revolution would improve the terms of trade of Africa relative to Europe is also borne out by the finding of Eltis and Jennings that Britain's gross barter terms of trade with Africa rose from 100 in 1700 to 112 in 1750, before falling to 40 by 1800. For example, according to them, one slave was worth two muskets at the beginning of the eighteenth century, but fifteen at the end.[14] Curtin also reports that the terms of trade of the Senegambia region in West Africa rose from 100 in 1680 to 475 in 1780, during which period the share of slaves in total exports rose from 55 to 86 per cent.[15]

Turning now to the European corner of the triangle – more particularly, its most dynamic component, Great Britain – we learn from Deane, drawing on Davis, that the share of British exports to North America, the West Indies and Africa (the other two components of the triangle) rose from 12 per cent in 1700 to 60 per cent in 1798, while their share of imports into Great Britain rose from 20 per cent to 32 per cent. In other words, the share of the triangular trade to total British trade rose very substantially over the course of the eighteenth century.[16] Foreign trade itself, however, grew more than twice as fast as national income, so that the "colonial" trade was undoubtedly a major driving force of Britain's overall economic growth. The index of real national income grew from 100 to 251 in 1700–1800, while the output of the export sector grew from 100 to 544. Exports of manufactures to the New World and re-exports of colonial produce to the rest of the world clearly led the way forward for the British economy during this crucial century. France, the larger and, at this time, only slightly less dynamic European economy, experienced very similar trends in its foreign trade and economic growth, with colonial trade again being the main driving force.[17] Saint-Domingue was more fertile than the British islands of Barbados and Jamaica, its slave population doubling in a few decades to almost half a million in 1791, on the eve of the great slave revolt. Sugar was, of course, the key commodity over most of the eighteenth century, with per capita consumption in Britain rising from about four pounds per head in 1700–1710 to eighteen pounds per head in 1800–1809.[18] The slave population of the British West Indies rose from 100,000 to 600,000 in the course of the eighteenth century, while sugar production rose fivefold from 25,000 to 125,000 tons.[19] British sugar imports, nearly all from the West Indies, doubled between 1700 and 1748 and rose fourfold between 1748 and 1815. Sugar was the main import into Britain from the 1750s to the 1820s, when it was overtaken by cotton.[20]

Cotton appeared late in the triangular trade; in 1791, exports from the United States were only 189,000 pounds, but it then took off explosively to about 70 million pounds a year by the time of the War of 1812. Cotton exports continued to grow rapidly right up to the outbreak of the Civil War in 1861 as the main source of supplies for the Lancashire cotton textile industry, the spearhead of the Industrial Revolution. The terms of trade in the United States also improved sharply, again as predicted by the model. There is little doubt that, had it not been for the abolition of 1807, there would have been a substantial expansion in the slave traffic, and hence of raw materials and manufactures as well, across the Atlantic.

Despite the abolition of the slave trade, slavery itself continued until 1838 in the British West Indies, 1865 in the United States, and the 1880s in Cuba and Brazil, the so-called second slavery (by analogy with the "second serfdom" of eastern Europe) from the fourteenth to the sixteenth century. The next three sections will briefly explore this later "industrial" phase of slavery with respect to cotton in the United States, sugar in Cuba and coffee in Brazil.

The United States

The thirteen British colonies on the North American mainland, which later became the United States, straddled one side of the Atlantic triangle – that linking Europe to the New World. The northern colonies, including New England, were in many respects more like Old England than the New World, in that their economic systems were based on free labour, growing mostly grains and producing manufactured goods. The Southern colonies, like the British West Indies, had a substantial African slave population but with several significant differences, of which we have noted two already: sugar was not the main crop on which the slaves were engaged, and the slave population had a positive instead of a negative rate of natural increase. Despite its relative lack of participation in the Atlantic slave trade, the United States in 1800 had a slave population of over one million, which grew to 1.75 million by 1825, constituting 36 per cent of the slave population of the New World

– compared with 31 per cent for Brazil, which had imported vastly greater numbers of African slaves up to that time. By 1860, the slave population of the United States was around four million, the vast majority of them born in the United States itself.

Slave imports into the mainland British colonies were by no means negligible, however, and rose from about 1,600 a year in the first two decades of the eighteenth century to about 5,700 a year in the 1760s, before declining during the Revolutionary War and its aftermath. They then rose to over 8,700 a year in the first decade of the nineteenth century, as the model predicts, before collapsing to only 500 a year in the following decade, after the abolition of 1807, and finally vanishing altogether.[21]

Again, just as the model predicts, the terms of trade of the United States, with cotton as the leading export, sharply rose from 100 in 1790 to 162 by the end of the decade. The volume of cotton exports rose explosively from a mere 189,000 pounds in 1791 to about 40 million pounds a year by 1805, and then 93 million pounds in 1810, before falling as a result of the War of 1812, recovering to 82 million pounds by 1815.[22] The area under cotton spread rapidly from the original Southern colonies to Alabama, Mississippi, Louisiana, Arkansas, Texas and Florida, propelled in part by those precocious offspring of the Industrial Revolution, the railroad and the steamboat.

The division of the United States into two uneasily coexisting economic systems – the free labour farming and manufacturing economy of the North, and the plantation slave economy of the South – has been plausibly likened by Gavin Wright to a "cold war" scenario, with of course the difference that this one ended with an actual outbreak of hostilities and the military defeat of one side by the other.[23] As in the twentieth-century case, there was an active debate regarding the relative performance of the two economic systems. As Wright points out, the South did well in terms of the volume of production and per capita real income, since the rapid growth of world demand for cotton, as we have seen, generated more favourable terms of trade and export-led primary sector growth on the slave plantations. He argues, however, that this very same prosperity meant that the most important form of wealth accumulation in the South was in the asset value of the slaves themselves, rather than in land and manufacturing capital, as in the North. He also argues that the fact that slave property was literally *movable* meant that there was much less demand for public infrastructure such as railroads and canals to induce the westward movement of free immigrant labour, since the slaves could simply be bodily transported like cattle to more fertile western regions as the original soil of the Southern plantations deteriorated. The incentive to accumulate human capital in the slave population was absent, even though the returns could in principle have been captured by the owners, since the collective risk of resistance and rebellion that such accumulation posed was too high. Wright's entire argument is well summed up by a wonderful 1844 quotation from Ralph Waldo Emerson that he cites: "Slavery is no scholar, no improver; it does not love the whistle of the railroad; it does not love the newspaper, the mail-bag, a college, a book, or a preacher . . . it does not increase the white population; it does not improve the soil; everything goes to decay."[24]

Following Barbara Solow, we can fruitfully contrast the economies of the North and South in terms of the well-known Domar trilemma: only any two, but not all three, attributes of free labour, free land and a landowning aristocracy can be true of any economic and social system at any one time.[25] Thus, the North had the first two but not the third, while the South had the last two but not the first. After the Civil War, the United States had a unified economy, just like the North had earlier with the first two, but the third feature of a landowning aristocracy had disappeared from the post-bellum South.

The Southern slave owners, with their single-minded concentration on the asset value of their human property, had no interest in population increase of almost any sort, whether of slave imports or white immigrants. They were even ambivalent about territorial expansion, since more land under cotton would lower the price of cotton and hence that of the slaves themselves, the most valuable item in their portfolios. Needless to say, all these examples of rational, individual self-interest handicapped them fatally in the geopolitical competition between the two systems, with the North eagerly following Horace Greeley's injunction for young men to "go west and grow up with the country", with surges of infrastructure spending to make it easier for those young men, and women also, to undertake the journey. The number of free immigrants up to 1860 was about four million, the same as the total slave population at that date.

The impression left by Wright's analysis is that the antebellum South suffered a particularly severe and protracted case of the phenomenon we now call the "Dutch Disease", resulting from the combination of strong external demand for cotton and the institution of slavery. It undoubtedly experienced substantial prosperity of a sort, but only at the expense of undermining the possibility of sustained growth in the future on the basis of free labour. Wright's emphasis on the pernicious role of the endogenously determined high asset prices for the slave labour force is consistent with the long-run model of Dutch Disease presented in Findlay, in which high land prices during a natural resource boom "crowd out" capital formation in the manufacturing sector and, in this case, public infrastructure as well.

The North, on the other hand, was poised to exploit the advantages of the open western frontier on the basis of free immigration, in accordance with the famous thesis of Frederick Jackson Turner. This "frontier thesis" has been deployed in economic history by Guido di Tella in relation to Argentina and by Knick Harley in relation to North America. The argument is modelled in Findlay, where the extent of the frontier is endogenously determined, along with the influx of free labour from Europe, as a function of the rising demand for wheat and beef, which initially was mainly for the domestic market but eventually led to the "European Grain Invasion" after the fall in transport costs in the 1880s.[26]

Despite strenuous efforts at compromise, aimed at keeping slavery unchanged in its original habitat but restricted in its westward extension, the contradictions between the two economic systems were too pronounced to permit reconciliation. Fort Sumter was bombarded on 12 April 1861 and the "irrepressible conflict" broke out.[27]

Since it seems to be surprisingly little known, it may be useful to note here the astute analysis of Karl Marx on precisely why this conflict was irrepressible or irreconcilable. In a piece on "The North American Civil War" for the Vienna journal *Die Presse*, dated 25 October 1861, he says, "The cultivation of the Southern export crops cotton, tobacco, sugar etc. by slaves is only profitable so long as it is conducted on a mass scale by large gangs of slaves and in wide areas of naturally fertile soil requiring only simple labor."[28] As a consequence of this system, the soil was eroded and new fertile areas had to be found, to which the original slave population had to be transferred. Thus, the system had to expand in order to maintain itself, and the Republican formula of confining slavery to where it already existed and prohibiting its westward extension made secession inevitable after Lincoln's victory in the 1860 election.

Cuba

Despite its being one of the earliest of the Spanish colonies in the New World, sugar did not figure prominently in the economic history of Cuba until the British occupation of Havana in 1762 during the Seven Years' War, which did so much to ensure her primacy in the world economy. Previously, the island was just the hinterland for the natural harbour and fortress of Havana, the hub for ocean transport between Spain and its colonies in the New World, with tobacco as the main crop. The slave population was small, leavened by manumission of skilled artisans in the cities, and of increasingly mixed ethnicity. The British occupation opened the island up to the importation of new supplies of slaves and the production of sugar for export to Spain and the American mainland. Several traditional restrictions on trade and economic activity were removed, and an era of liberal Enlightenment reforms of social and economic life began, reflecting trends in the mother country itself. Among the most important, according to Franklin Knight, was the removal on the restriction on felling hardwood forests (placed earlier to preserve their use as a source of masts for the Spanish navy).[29] Once the felling of the forests was permitted, plantations could freely expand in extent and railroads could open up the interior, so that by the 1860s the island had become largely deforested. Freer trade meant not only freer trade in goods but in slaves as well, leading to a rapid expansion of the slave population by imports from Africa and Jamaica, where sugar production was declining.

American trading and financial interests developed strong links with a new class of merchants and entrepreneurs, both *criollos* and *peninsulares*. The connection to the southern United States was particularly strong, with a growing sentiment on both sides for some form of closer political integration. Jefferson expressed interest in a Louisiana-style outright purchase of the island from Spain, while others advocated an independent republic in line with the experience of the Spanish colonies on the mainland in the 1820s. The Haitian Revolution of the 1790s had a profound effect on Cuba. Withdrawal of that major producer from the world market opened the field for exports from Cuba, while several French planters and merchants fleeing the revolt of the Black Jacobins sought refuge in Cuba, bringing their capital, skills and technological knowledge with them.

As explained by the well-known Veblen-Gerschenkron notion of the "advantages of relative backwardness" associated with being a latecomer, the Cuban sugar industry soon became the most advanced in the world, with extensive use of the steam engine in the crushing of cane and the refining of sugar, so that the "value add" of the sugar industry's exports in Cuba was greater than that of the more traditional sugar exporters. Not content with even refined sugar, the next stage of Hirschman-type "forward linkage" was the distillation of rum, undertaken by a Catalan immigrant with whose name, Bacardi, we are all familiar today.[30] The railroad made it cheap to extend production of cane deep into the interior of the island and to increase the economies of scale in the sugar mills. Plantations grew in size and scale – in terms of the slave labour force employed, the area planted and the capacity of the mills or *ingenios*. In 1860, the largest mill in Cuba, in Matanzas Province, reportedly owned by the queen mother of Spain, employed eight hundred slaves on 1,000 acres and had an annual production of 2,670 tons a year. According to Knight,[31] the Cuban planters consciously sought to overcome the relative scarcity of slave labour on their island, in comparison with Barbados and Jamaica, by substituting capital in the form of machinery based on water or steam. Cuba therefore became not only the largest sugar producer and exporter in the world by the middle of the nineteenth century but the technological leader of the industry as well.

In 1860, Cuba produced 450,000 tons of sugar a year, one-quarter of the world's output (easily outstripping Jamaica, which had less than a third of that level), most of it being exported to the United States.[32] The growth of sugar production was accompanied by a corresponding increase in the slave labour force, which increased from only about 38,000 in 1774 to over 436,000 in 1841, 43 per cent of a total population of just over one million. Together with another 15 per cent of the population who were free coloured, they formed a substantial non-white majority.[33]

The defeat of the South in the American Civil War ended any thought of annexation to the United States as a means of preserving the viability of slavery in Cuba. Tensions with Spain became more intense, especially in the less developed eastern parts of the island. In 1868, a rebellion led by a small sugar planter from Oriente Province, Carlos Manuel de Céspedes, broke out. He declared independence from Spain in the famous *Grito de Yara*, freeing his own slaves and calling for the abolition of slavery in the new independent republic the rebels wished to establish. Eric Williams makes an interesting argument that the high capital-labour ratio on the large estates of the monster *ingenios* had raised the productivity, and hence the price of slaves, to such an extent that the small planters could no longer afford them, and so they were likely to prefer a free labour market as a more level playing field against the large planters.[34] Spain itself was undergoing a liberal transformation and so was not averse to eventual abolition, the main support for the continuation of slavery coming from the large *criollo* planters of the western section of Cuba. The Spanish government was also aware that the entire international community, including the United States, would side with the rebels if moves towards ending slavery were not made. The rebellion of 1868 led to a bloody Ten Years' War that suppressed the rebellion, but in 1880 slavery was effectively ended, without much disruption to the sugar industry or the economy as a whole. As Franklin Knight says, "Slavery in Cuba was partly the victim of the steam engine."[35]

In an interesting contribution, Roger Betancourt traces the long delay in independence for Cuba, by comparison with other colonies in Spanish America, to the legacy of slavery, and he claims that it has distorted the sociopolitical evolution of the country to this very day.[36]

Brazil

Slavery in Brazil has a long history going back to the period of discovery, and it was intimately involved not only with sugar cultivation but with gold mining as well. Our concern here, however, is with its role in the extension of coffee production, beginning in the early nineteenth century with the opportunity created by the withdrawal of Haiti from the world market and continuing until the abolition of slavery in the 1880s, by which time Brazil had long been the world's leading supplier of this indispensable beverage.

"Brazil is coffee and coffee is the Negro" is a saying that Boris Fausto reports as being common among the elite in the first half of the nineteenth century. Slaves were imported at a rate of thirty-two thousand per year during 1811–20, rising to forty-three thousand per year during 1821–30.[37] Most of them either remained in Rio de Janeiro, the main port of entry, or were sent to the coffee estates of the nearby Paraíba Valley. The technology of coffee cultivation was very simple, not requiring any equipment more sophisticated than a sickle and a hoe. Land had to be cleared and the seeds planted, taking four years to yield a return. After picking, the crop was transported to Rio by mule trains, which brought supplies and tools on the return journey. Coffee already constituted about 18 per cent of Brazil's exports from 1821 to 1830, rising to 40 per cent by 1850, 53 per cent by 1860 and 61 per cent by the 1880s. The United States and Europe were the main markets, with Britain devoted to tea and relying on her own colonies for her limited coffee consumption. Britain, which dominated Brazil financially during this period, made several attempts to ban the slave trade, largely succeeding by 1851. Coffee producers subsequently had to rely on drawing their slaves from other sectors where production was declining, particularly in the sugar-growing regions of the northeast. Up to two hundred thousand slaves may have been reallocated from the sugar areas of the northeast to the coffee regions of the centre-south. An active internal slave trade developed to facilitate this process. Coffee cultivation outgrew the Paraíba Valley and expanded into the vast flat stretches of the Oeste Paulista region, where people spoke of a "sea of coffee" as far as the eye could see. Planters in this region were more "bourgeois" in orientation than the original "aristocratic" planters of the Paraíba Valley and more inclined to introduce capital-intensive new technology on larger estates, replacing the hoe and sickle with ploughs and hulling machines, and mule trains with railroads.

The virtual end of slave imports in the 1850s resulted in both rising prices for the existing stock and its gradual ageing because of the negative rate of natural growth. Mechanization and the use of free immigrant labour, mainly Italians and Portuguese, could not substantially rectify the problem. Public opinion came to feel increasingly that the continued presence of the institution was a national embarrassment, with even the army feeling that it was beneath their dignity to hunt runaway slaves. Despite this, the coffee planters continued to resist, but they were losing influence and ultimately gave way in 1888, when a law abolishing slavery without compensation was finally enacted, at long last ending slavery in the Western Hemisphere.[38]

According to Celso Furtado, "abolition was a measure more of a political than of an economic nature", since slavery was "more important as the basis of a regional system of power than as a form of organization of production", but it had nevertheless acted as "a stifling influence on the economic development of the country".[39]

The Williams Theses

As noted above, there are two Williams theses: one on the positive link between the slave trade and the Industrial Revolution, and the other on the role of economic interests rather than humanitarian concerns in the abolition of the slave trade. Our own work, previously and in the present brief essay, has been almost exclusively on the former, but we shall nevertheless offer some comments on the latter as well.

The evidence cited in *Capitalism and Slavery* on the first thesis is qualitative and largely anecdotal, lacking the quantitative base of measurement in "pounds sterling or pounds avoirdupois" that Williams himself regarded as so important, whenever available. It fell to Stanley Engerman to present the first estimate of slave trade profits for the year 1770 at an upper bound of 0.54 per cent of national income, 7 to 8 per cent of total investment and 38.9 per cent of commercial and industrial investment. Taking profits of sugar plantations as a whole, the estimates rise to 5 per cent of national income, while the share of total investment in national income was 7 per cent. So are these numbers high or low? Engerman found them low, but Barbara Solow and Findlay both found them high, so it is up to the reader to decide. Findlay also argued that dividing almost any magnitude in economics by national income can make it look irrelevant.[40] The Industrial Revolution itself could be reduced to a myth by observing that manufacturing output in Britain at the time was less than 10 per cent of national income.

Another very influential early estimate was by Patrick O'Brien, who put colonial profits in 1784–86 at 5.66 million pounds sterling compared with the total investment of 10.30 million pounds, or more than 50 per cent. He also gives an estimate for 1824–26 at slightly less than 50 per cent. He then stated, however, that the Williams hypothesis "founders on the numbers" and then made the famously quoted quip that "the periphery was peripheral".[41] We have given in Findlay and in Findlay and O'Rourke much argument and quantitative evidence to the contrary, as has Joseph Inikori in his comprehensive study on *Africans and the Industrial Revolution in England,* while Richardson is tough on the narrow profits version of the thesis but much less critical of the broader statement of the connection between plantation slavery and metropolitan growth within the British Empire. More importantly however, O'Brien's claim that "a hypothetical British edict abolishing the slave trade in 1607, rather than two centuries late, could not have made that much difference to the levels of wealth and income achieved in Western Europe in 1807" is directly contradicted by statements in O'Brien and Engerman that "without the enforced and cheap labor of Africans, the rate of growth of transnational commerce between 1660 and the abolition of the slave trade in 1808 would have been far slower", and that "it is difficult to envisage an alternative path of development that might have carried both international and British trade to the level attained by the early nineteenth century". O'Brien and Engerman also say that "the significance of exports is derogated by using national income as the sole point of reference". Unfortunately, these generous acknowledgements of the alternative view have not been generally noticed in the literature, which keeps on citing the "periphery was peripheral" quip as a pithy summary of received doctrine driving a stake through the heart of the Williams thesis.[42]

A persistent error in the long, drawn-out debate has been the notion that the Williams thesis requires the Industrial Revolution, or eighteenth-century British economic growth, more generally, to have been "caused" by slavery and the plantation economy. Thus, in his otherwise utterly admirable article, Richard Sheridan feels that he is supporting the Williams thesis when he says that "the economic growth of Great Britain was chiefly from without inwards", propelled forward by the expansion of the sugar plantations in the Caribbean.[43] This statement was promptly pounced on, in the very same volume, by David Richardson, who has no difficulty showing that "these relationships were more complex than Williams had suggested" when he argued that "profits from the slave trade and the slave-based plantation regime of the West Indies" were providing "a powerful exogenous input into British industrial growth" – that is, they were "chiefly from without inwards".[44] One has only to ask where the demand for the sugar exports of the Caribbean was coming from to see how indefensible the Sheridan statement is. But does that disprove or destroy the Williams thesis, properly understood? In our view, it does not do so in any way at all.

As stated in Findlay, "slavery was an integral part of a complex intercontinental system of trade in goods and factors within which the Industrial Revolution, as we know it, emerged. Within this system of interdependence it would make as much or as little sense to draw a causal arrow from slavery to British industrialization as the other way around."[45] Those who argue that African slavery was irrelevant or unimportant would have to specify some plausible counterfactual scenario to replace it, such as free labour (but at what price and amount?) or enslavement of some elements of the European population itself, to mention two ideas that have been floated by Robin Blackburn and David Eltis respectively.[46]

Williams himself clearly stated that "it must not be inferred that the triangular trade was solely and entirely responsible for the economic development. The growth of the internal market in England, the plowing-in of the profits from industry to generate still further capital and achieve still greater expansion, played a large part. But this industrial development, stimulated by mercantilism, later outgrew mercantilism and destroyed it."[47] It is interesting to see that, in this last sentence, he apparently considers the 1807 abolition of the slave trade as part of the general dismantling of mercantilist institutions and their replacement by a regime more oriented to laissez-faireism in the nineteenth century.

What now of the second, or "decline", thesis? In principle, one can imagine a labour system or institution such as slavery first being a boost or stimulus to the birth of industrial capitalism and then a hindrance or a fetter on its further development, requiring it to be abolished, as in the quotation about mercantilism above. Such a view might be plausible if slave labour were used only with crops such as sugar, tobacco and coffee, requiring only relatively slight processing or "value added" at later stages of production before being sold to the final consumer. Cotton, however, was a different case altogether. It was best grown under tropical conditions by slave labour, but it was also an intermediate input in a much longer chain of production requiring the spinning of the raw cotton into yarn and the weaving of the yarn into cloth, both of them activities that had become highly mechanized as a result of the technical innovations that launched the Industrial Revolution itself. If the plantation system was only a creature of the earlier commercial phase of capitalism, then what was it doing being so egregiously present at the creation of the new industrial world, the dawning of the "Age of Schumpeter", the full-blown capitalism based on "wage-slavery" that Karl Marx both celebrated and condemned in the *Communist Manifesto*? In 1848, there were over six million chattel slaves in the New World, more than four million of them in the United States alone.

Marx, of course, was not unaware of the apparent contradiction and – skilled Hegelian dialectician as he was – neatly turned it to his own advantage in the famous statement that "in fact, the veiled slavery of the wage-workers in Europe needed, for its pedestal, slavery pure and simple in the new world".[48] Marx saw the African slavery that emerged from the fifteenth century as part of the process of "The So-Called Primitive Accumulation", which generated the separation of the future wage-worker from the land or tools that could sustain him as an independent producer, by such means as the enclosure movement within Europe itself or by the "turning of Africa into a warren for the commercial hunting of black skins" that "signalized the rosy dawn of the era of capitalist production".[49] But when did primitive accumulation turn into just plain old regular capital accumulation? As far as we are aware, Marx himself does not say. In this connection, it is interesting that a Marxist like Eugene Genovese should consider the Southern slaveholders as a sort of "feudal remnant", with a fake cult of chivalry and other pseudo-aristocratic trappings, and seem unwilling to view them as rationally calculating profit-maximizers, as Fogel and Engerman do (and rightly so, in our opinion).[50]

The case of cotton thus seems to put the two Williams theses on the horns of a dilemma. The stronger and more viable the slave-based production of that commodity, the stronger is the case for the first thesis, but the weaker it is for the second and, of course, vice versa. We therefore agree with the position of Seymour Drescher and David Eltis that the 1807 abolition put a serious crimp into the Atlantic slave trade itself, the cotton-growing sector in the United States and the Lancashire cotton textile industry – in other words, all three corners or sides of the Triangular Trade. Indeed, this conclusion follows strictly from the model as outlined earlier, with abolition treated as analogous to an export tax on the slave trade. If abolition is therefore not to be regarded as simply a triumph of humanitarian morality, what interest groups might conceivably have benefited, if only as an unintended consequence of the benevolence of Wilberforce and his followers?

As noted already, there is only one group we can readily think of, namely, the slave owners themselves. The British West Indian sugar planters might have been afraid of losing out to more efficient producers in Cuba and elsewhere, and so sought a form of indirect protection, raising the prices of the stock of human assets that they held, as a consequence of abolition, instead of trying to get tariffs or other preferences for their sugar in the home market of the empire. This seems to be consistent with what Ryden, Darity and other recent defenders of the "decline" thesis are arguing.[51] Gavin Wright, in his illuminating "Lesson from the Mainland", notes that, despite the many differences, his observations on the attitudes of the American slaveholders find many parallels in the West Indies. Chief among these is the importance of, and the attention paid to, the asset value of the slaves held in their portfolios as a concern, taking precedence over land and output in calculating where their interests lay. "As slave prices began to rise above the African supply price, some slaveholders were tempted by the appeal of restricting new imports as a way of raising prices further or protecting themselves against price declines. There are indications that many planters on the older islands were ambivalent about the slave trade by the late eighteenth century, and this has to be considered a factor in the abolition movement."[52]

J.R. Ward offers a balanced appraisal of abolition and the decline thesis. He finds that "although the relative importance to Britain of slave-grown Caribbean produce was declining, Williams overstated his case by implying that by the time of abolition the West Indian colonies were regarded as moribund, redundant and due for liquidation", even though they were still of considerable importance in shipping, banking and imperial revenue. He goes on to say, however, that "the view which prevailed was that, although established investments had to be maintained, this no longer required continued slave trading". On the humanitarian agitation in Britain, he says that "the fact remains that the decision to end the slave trade had to be taken by Parliament, where evangelicalism was only a minority sentiment and where practical, strategic considerations were paramount". He sums up by saying that "British abolition was not merely cynical and self-interested, but neither did its authors believe that they were making a significant economic sacrifice".[53]

Abolition might have meant that American cotton planters would own fewer slaves, but it also implied higher slave prices, suggesting that planters might gain from this source. It might have implied lower cotton production, but again at a higher price, so profits might have risen if total output were pushed down towards the maximum monopoly profit level, in line with the "optimum tariff" solution for an open economy with some degree of monopoly power. These results are all purely conjectural and speculative, but might possibly be worth some further exploration. The "decline" thesis may therefore not be entirely without merit, after all, but would need considerably more research to be fully revived.

We hope that we have said enough in this brief chapter, however, to demonstrate that the legacy of Eric Williams that we celebrate in this volume is alive and well. We do so not just as an act of piety towards a creative researcher and stalwart fighter on behalf of the oppressed people of the Caribbean, who overcame incredible odds of racial prejudice and blatant discrimination, but in appreciation of the author of an enduring masterpiece in the historiography of the British Industrial Revolution and its relationship to the fateful trade across the Atlantic in capital, goods and, above all, people: the twelve million or so souls who endured the Middle Passage and their descendants, who are now transforming the world on both sides of the great ocean that they traversed from the fifteenth to the nineteenth century.

NOTES

1.   Eric Williams, *Capitalism and Slavery* (Chapel Hill: University of North Carolina Press, 1944), ix.

2.   See Gavin Wright, "Capitalism and Slavery in the Islands: A Lesson from the Mainland", in *British Capitalism and Caribbean Slavery: The Legacy of Eric Williams*, ed. B.L. Solow and S.L. Engerman (Cambridge: Cambridge University Press, 1987), 301.

3.   See Seymour Drescher, *Abolition: A History of Slavery and Antislavery* (Cambridge: Cambridge University Press, 2009); David Brion Davis, *Inhuman Bondage: The*

Rise and Fall of Slavery in the New World (Oxford: Oxford University Press, 2007); Robin Blackburn, *The American Crucible: Slavery, Emancipation and Human Rights* (London: Verso, 2011).

4.   Williams, *Capitalism and Slavery*, 71.

5.   See Dale Tomich, "The Second Slavery: Bonded Labor and the Transformation of the Nineteenth Century World Economy", in *Rethinking the Nineteenth Century Contradictions and Movements*, ed. F.O. Ramirez (Westport, CT: Greenwood, 1988), 103–18.

6.   William Darity, "A General Equilibrium Model of the 18th Century Atlantic Slave Trade", in *Research in Economic History*, vol. 7, ed. Paul Uselding (Greenwich, CT: JAI Press, 1982); Ronald Findlay, "The Triangular Trade and the Atlantic Economy of the Eighteenth Century: A General Equilibrium Model", in *Essays in International Finance*, no. 177 (Princeton, NJ: Princeton University Press, 1990).

7.   Findlay, "The Triangular Trade".

8.   Jagdish Bhagwati, "Immiserizing Growth: A Geometrical Note", *Review of Economic Studies* 25, no. 3 (1958): 201–5.

9.   Findlay, "The Triangular Trade".

10. Philip Curtin, *The Rise and Fall of the Plantation Complex: Essays in Atlantic History* (Cambridge: Cambridge University Press, 1990).

11. Robert Fogel and Stanley Engerman, *Time on the Cross: The Economics of American Negro Slavery* (Boston: Little Brown, 1974), 20.

12. "The Trans-Atlantic Slave Trade Database", Emory University, accessed 2 July 2015, http://slavevoyages.org/tast/assessment/estimates.faces?yearFrom=1501 &yearTo=1866.

13. Ibid.

14. David Eltis and L.C. Jennings, "Trade between Western Africa and the Atlantic World in the Pre-Colonial Era", *American Historical Review* 93, no. 4 (October 1988): 936–59.

15. Philip Curtin, *Economic Change in Pre-colonial Senegambia in the Era of the Slave Trade* (Madison: University of Wisconsin Press, 1975).

16. Phyllis Deane, *The First Industrial Revolution* (Cambridge: Cambridge University Press, 1965).

17. François Crouzet, "England and France in the Eighteenth Century: A Comparative Analysis of Two Economic Growths", in *The Causes of the Industrial Revolution*, ed. R.M. Hartwell (London: Methuen, 1967), 139–75.

18. Sidney Mintz, *Sweetness and Power: The Place of Sugar in Modern History* (London: Penguin, 1985), 67.

19. Michael Craton, *Sinews of Empire: A Short History of British Slavery* (New York: Anchor Books, 1974), 139.

20. J.R. Ward, "The British West Indies in the Age of Abolition, 1748–1815", in *The Oxford History of the British Empire*, vol. 2: *The Eighteenth Century*, ed. P.J. Marshall (Oxford: Oxford University Press, 1978), 421.

21. "Trans-Atlantic Slave Trade Database".

22. Douglass North, *The Economic Growth of the United States, 1790–1860* (New York: W.W. Norton, 1966), 229, 231.

23. Gavin Wright, *Slavery and American Economic Development* (Baton Rouge: Louisiana State University Press, 2006).

24. Quoted in Wright, "Capitalism and Slavery", 289.

25. See Barbara Solow, "Capitalism and Slavery in the Exceedingly Long Run", in *Slavery: The Legacy of Eric Williams*, ed. B.L. Solow and S.L. Engerman (Cambridge: Cambridge University Press, 1987), 51–77; Barbara L. Solow, "Slavery and Colonization", in *Slavery and the Rise of the Atlantic System* (Cambridge: Cambridge University Press, 1991), 25–46; Evsey Domar, "The Causes of Slavery or Serfdom: A Hypothesis", *Journal of Economic History* 30 (February 1970): 18–32.

26. Kevin H. O'Rourke, "The European Grain Invasion 1877–1913" *Journal of Economic History* 57 (1997): 775–801.

27. Bruce Levine, *Half Slave and Half Free: The Roots of Civil War* (New York: Hill and Wang, 1992).

28. Quoted in Robin Blackburn, *An Unfinished Revolution: Karl Marx and Abraham Lincoln* (London: Verso, 2011), 127–38.

29. Franklin Knight, *Slave Society in Cuba during the Nineteenth Century* (Madison: University of Wisconsin Press, 1970), 17.

30. Hugh Thomas, "Cuba c. 1750–c. 1860", in *Cuba: A Short History*, ed. L. Bethell (Cambridge: Cambridge University Press, 1993), 15.

31. Knight, *Slave Society*, 20–21.

32. Ibid.

33. Ibid., 22.

34. Eric Williams, *From Columbus to Castro: The History of the Caribbean, 1492–1969* (reprint, New York: Vintage, 1984).

35. Knight, *Slave Society*, 178.

36. Roger Betancourt, "Cuba's First Attempt at Democracy and Its Long-Term Consequences" (unpublished mimeograph, University of Maryland, 2011).

37. Boris Fausto, *A Concise History of Brazil* (Cambridge: Cambridge University Press, 1999), 107–8.

38. Emília Viotti da Costa, "Empire 1870–1889", in *Brazil: Empire Republic, 1822–1930*, ed. L. Bethell (Cambridge: Cambridge University Press, 1989), 203.

39. Celso Furtado, *The Economic Growth of Brazil: A Survey from Colonial to Modern Times* (Berkeley: University of California Press, 1963), 154.

40. For a discussion of the findings, see Stanley Engerman, "The Slave Trade and British Capital Formation in the Eighteenth Century: A Comment on the Williams Thesis", *Business History Review* 46 (Winter 1972): 430–43; Solow, "Caribbean Slavery"; Findlay, "The Triangular Trade", 27.

41. Patrick O'Brien, "European Economic Development: The Contribution of the Periphery", *Economic History Review* 35, no. 1 (1982): 1–18.

42. See Findlay, "The Triangular Trade"; Ronald Findlay and Kevin H. O' Rourke, *Power and Plenty: Trade, War, and the World Economy in the Second Millennium* (Princeton, NJ: Princeton University Press, 2007); Joseph Inikori, *Africans and the Industrial Revolution in England* (Cambridge: Cambridge University Press, 2002); David Richardson, "The British Empire and the Atlantic Slave Trade, 1660–1807", in *The Oxford History of the British Empire*, vol. 2: *The Eighteenth Century*, ed. P.J. Marshall (Oxford: Oxford University Press, 1988), 440–64; O'Brien, "European Economic Development", 9; Patrick O'Brien and Stanley Engerman, "Exports and the Growth of the British Economy from the Glorious Revolution to the Peace of Amiens", in *Slavery and the Rise of the Atlantic System*, ed. B.L. Solow (Cambridge: Cambridge University Press, 1991), 181–82, 187.

43. Richard Sheridan, "Eric Williams and Capitalism and Slavery: A Biographical and Historiographical Essay", in *British Capitalism and Caribbean Slavery*, 232.

44. David Richardson, "The Slave Trade and British Economic Growth, 1748–1776", in *British Capitalism and Caribbean Slavery*, 132.

45. Findlay, "The Triangular Trade", 28.

46. Eltis, *Rise of African Slavery*; Blackburn, *American Crucible*.

47. Williams, *Capitalism and Slavery*, 105.

48. Karl Marx, *Capital*, vol. 1 (reprint, New York: International Publishers, 1967), 759.

49. Ibid., 751.

50. Eugene Genovese, *The World the Slaveholders Made* (New York: Vintage, 1989).

51. David Ryden, "Planters, Slaves, and Decline", in *Capitalism and Slavery: Fifty Years Later*, ed. H. Cateau and S.H.H. Carrington (New York: Peter Lang, 2000), 155–70; William Darity, "Economic Aspects of the British Trade in Slaves: A Fresh Look at the Evidence from the 1789 Report of the Lords of Trade", in *Capitalism and Slavery: Fifty Years Later*, 137–53.

52. Wright, "Capitalism and Slavery", 299.

53. Ward, "The British West Indies", 427.

Chapter 8

Capitalism, Slavery and the Brazilian Coffee Economy

Eric Williams and the Historiography of Brazilian Slavery

RAFAEL MARQUESE

Two years before the publication of *Capitalism and Slavery*, Brazilian historian Caio Prado Jr published his groundbreaking *Colonial Roots of Modern Brazil*. Despite their differences, both books had several common themes, including the centrality of New World slave economies to the making of European capitalism and the negative legacies of slavery in the Caribbean and Latin America. The convergence of their perspectives can be found in the pioneering work of Alice P. Canabrava on the Caribbean sugar industry in the first half of the eighteenth century. The arguments developed in her 1945 dissertation (and it seems unlikely that she had been aware of *Capitalism and Slavery* at the time) were very similar to those put forward by Williams, a consequence of the influence of Caio Prado Jr and economic historians of the first generation of the *Annales* School.[1]

It is not surprising therefore that Eric Williams was positively received by Brazilian social scientists after the late 1950s. *Capitalism and Slavery* influenced not only Celso Furtado, an economist affiliated with the Economic Commission for Latin America and the Caribbean's project, but also the group of sociologists from the University of São Paulo associated with Florestan Fernandes and Roger Bastide, who used it to review and criticize perspectives related to an alleged Brazilian racial democracy.[2] Williams's analytical perspective was warmly received, to a large extent because of the emergence of the so-called Dependency Theory in Brazil and other parts of Latin America.[3] The best example of this association can be found in the doctoral dissertation of Fernando Henrique Cardoso, a former student of Florestan Fernandes. The framework employed by Cardoso to analyse the transition from slavery to the capitalist cattle-raising economy of Rio Grande do Sul (the starting point of his analysis of the problem of dependence in Latin America) was completely inspired by the arguments of Eric Williams's book.[4]

Especially inspired by Williams's interpretation were two historians also coming from the University of São Paulo. Their works quickly became fundamental references in their respective fields and in Brazilian historiography. The first was Emília Viotti da Costa's doctoral dissertation, finished in 1964, which addressed the crisis of slavery in the coffee zones of centre-south Brazil. The second was Fernando Novais, who examined the crisis of Portuguese colonialism in America at the turn of the nineteenth century in his 1973 doctoral dissertation.[5]

Emília Viotti da Costa's work is based on extensive research on slavery in the coffee provinces of Rio de Janeiro, Minas Gerais and São Paulo during the nineteenth century. Viotti da Costa offered a sophisticated analysis of the abolition of slavery in Brazil, assessing its economic, social, political and ideological dimensions. She considered the event "a result of a long process involving structural changes, situations, and a series of events that culminated in the Golden Law". From this perspective, the study of abolitionism and slave resistance – and their centrality in ending the institution – was accompanied by an analysis of the structural transformations that made abolition possible in 1888. These transformations included the end of the transatlantic slave trade in 1850 and the beginning of the interprovincial slave trade; experiments with free labour; the demographic and cultural creolization of the slave population; the movement of coffee production into the new frontier of western São Paulo; the impact of railroads on the coffee economy (which improved the transportation system, stimulated new economic activities and urbanization, and created new opportunities for free labourers); and the growing split between planters from the oldest areas of the Paraíba Valley (deeply attached to slavery) and their counterparts from the new frontier areas (less committed to it). Thus, Viotti da Costa shared Williams's interpretative framework on the "contradiction between capitalist development and slavery".[6]

The interpretation offered by Emília Viotti da Costa in *Da Senzala à Colô-nia* had a great impact during the 1970s. Her comparison between planters from the Paraíba Valley and the New West, for instance, appeared in Eugene Genovese's comparative analysis of New World slave systems, in Robert Top-lin's book on the abolition of slavery in Brazil and in Warren Dean's mono-graph on the coffee county of Rio Claro. João Manoel Cardoso de Mello's essay on Brazilian "late capitalism" also employed Eric Williams's argument, albeit in different ways. Even those historians and social scientists who defended the existence of a colonial slave mode of production, and who were critical of Williams's book, did not fail to recognize the significance of not only *Capitalism and Slavery* but also of those historians who closely followed him, such as Novais and Viotti.[7]

With the growth of New Economic History, the kind of analysis offered by Eric Williams in 1944 gradually lost ground. Moreover, in the second half of the 1970s, the innovative works of Pedro Carvalho de Mello and Robert Slenes revised many of the assumptions of the historiography on nineteenth-century Brazilian slavery inspired by *Capitalism and Slavery*. Focusing on the period after the abolition of the transatlantic slave trade, Mello and Slenes demonstrate the economic rationality behind the purchases of slaves to work in the coffee plantations of centre-south Brazil until the 1880s. They note the similarities between the entrepreneurial mindset of slaveholders in the Paraíba Valley and western São Paulo. One of their main arguments is that the roots of the crisis of slavery in Brazil could not be found in the progress of capitalist productive forces, but rather in the destruction of the political legitimacy of slavery caused by abolitionist pressure.[8]

In order to measure the impact of abolitionism, historians sharing the theoretical and methodological assumptions of the New Economic History treat the movement as an "exogenous factor" to the economic sphere, separat-ing the elements of a historical process that in the studies of Eric Williams and Emília Viotti da Costa appeared as a contradictory unity. Viotti replied to these historiographical revisions in a lengthy preface to the second edition of her book.[9] The issue was nonetheless seen as settled by the 1980s. The view that the findings of the New Economic History represented the last and final word on the role of economic forces in the crisis of Brazilian slavery has become paradigmatic.[10] It is somewhat ironic that, precisely when economic

history was losing ground to the social and the cultural history in international academia, the economic history of the crisis of Brazilian slavery led
to the development of its social and cultural history. Described by Robert
Slenes as "a new 'paradigm,' or theoretical language", this "historiographical
revolution" has based itself "on the substitution of an 'economicist' vision,
according to which slavery withers with the rise of capitalism, for a 'political'
one; economically vigorous, slavery is now destroyed by a struggle between
historically constituted agents".[11]

The concept of capitalism, taken by this "new 'paradigm,' or theoretical
language" as an abstract category unable to give intelligibility to processes
experienced by real subjects of flesh and bone, was simply thrown away by
historians of Brazilian slavery.[12] Themes such as the cultural patterns of
slaves and their descendants, slave resistance, the national and the immigrant
worker, and the legal and political struggles over the legitimacy of slavery
came to the fore. Despite the undeniable merits of this historiography – its
contribution to a better understanding of the history of slavery in Brazil is well
established – it neglects the long-term historical processes and the broader
global contexts within which the Brazilian slave system was inscribed. View-
ing history as a wide space of indetermination whose outcome stems from
multiple and equivalent local actions, social and cultural historians of the
crisis of slavery in Brazil eventually came to share – perhaps inadvertently –
some of the theoretical assumptions of the New Economic History, its methodological individualism in particular.[13]

Going back to the original proposal put forward by Eric Williams and by
those who shared his theoretical assumptions can still be fruitful. But the
limits of his work should be taken into account, particularly the gap it presents
between, on the one hand, a conceptualization of capitalism as a national phenomenon confined to the advance of industrialization, free labour and free
trade in Britain; and, on the other, a broader conception (that his own book
suggests) of the capitalist economy as a transnational phenomenon.[14] Indeed,
throughout the second part of *Capitalism and Slavery*, Williams emphasizes
the strict relationship between the British industrial economy and the North
American slave cotton economy, a connection that can be extended (with
certain modifications) to the slave economies of Cuba and Brazil. If, on
the one hand, the forces of industrialization had destroyed slavery in the

British possessions, on the other hand they stimulated the growth of African slavery in these other spaces. According to Williams, "British capitalism had destroyed West Indian slavery, but it continued to thrive on Brazilian, Cuban and American slavery."[15]

The aim of this chapter is to explore the discontinuities in the relationship between the capitalist world economy and slavery in the Americas through an examination of the coffee economy in the nineteenth century. The focus of debates on the "Williams thesis" has always been on the British Empire and the sugar economy. This approach continues to prevail. David Beck Ryden's more recent book on the abolition of the British transatlantic slave trade shows the general validity of Williams's second thesis, with a close examination of the British economy. Joseph Inikori, who broadens the scope of the discussion by considering the entire European international trade between the sixteenth and the nineteenth centuries, centres his main attentions on trade and production inside the English circuits.[16]

There are two reasons to shift the focus to coffee and, by extension, to Brazil. First, it is a theme and an area largely ignored in the major international debates on the Williams thesis. Second, and more important, the coffee economy was absolutely central to Brazilian slavery and the Atlantic world in the nineteenth century. The coffee world market had gone through a great transformation by the end of that century. Starting as a beverage with a relatively restricted market, coffee became a primary stimulant of the industrial urban societies – almost an input of the working classes, we could say. Brazil and the United States were at the forefront of this transformation. At the end of the eighteenth century, the world's largest producer was the French colony of Saint-Domingue, responsible in 1790 for 50 per cent of a global offer of approximately 70,000 tons. From the beginning of the Saint-Domingue revolution to the abolition of slavery in Brazil, global coffee production increased almost tenfold, reaching 663,600 tons, 56 per cent of which were produced by the South American country. Moreover, in 1888, 60 per cent of all Brazilian coffee was sent to a single market, the United States, which had become responsible for a third of global consumption. In the first decade after abolition, the commodity chain became tighter. In 1900, Brazilian plantations produced 76 per cent of the world's coffee. The United States bought 41 per cent of what was offered on the world market, with 49 per cent of those purchases coming from Brazil.[17] It is also noteworthy that the transition from Saint-Domingue to Brazil was accompanied by substantive changes in the patterns of slave labour. In 1790, 158,000 slaves worked on Saint-Domingue coffee plantations, producing 34,500 metric tons of coffee that year.[18] Almost one hundred years later, the Dutch agronomist C.F. van Delden Laërne estimated that 284,000 slaves were working in the coffee plantations of Rio de Janeiro, São Paulo and Minas Gerais, producing, however, close to 350,000 metric tons.[19] A rough calculation of the slave labour's productivity shows 0.22 metric tons per slave in Saint-Domingue and 1.23 in Brazil – almost six times higher.

It is possible to identify three distinct moments in the relation between the capitalist world economy and slave-grown coffee between 1790 and 1888, when interactions between the global forces and the local forces underwent substantial changes. The first one (1790s–1820s) was marked by the crisis of the coffee economy built in the Caribbean basin during the eighteenth century. The second phase (1830s–70s) saw the making of a new coffee economy in Brazil, directly connected to the rise of a new industrial order in the North Atlantic. The third moment was framed by the crisis of the Brazilian slave coffee economy as a result of the American Civil War (1861–65) and the reorganization of the capitalist world economy during the so-called Great Depression (1873–96).

In this chapter, I will focus on phases two and three, since authors critical of the use of Eric William's arguments to understand the crisis of Brazilian slavery have generally focused on the second half of the nineteenth century. In order to do so, I will follow Antônio Barros de Castro's suggestion that we should situate the Brazilian coffee economy "in three phases and three spaces", in a formulation that was also directly inspired by Eric Williams's remarks on the "law of slave production". According to Castro,

> the characteristic that deeply distinguishes not only the so-called coffee cycle but that is also key to interpret the meaning of this crop in Brazilian economic history is its striking "mobility". Coffee was among us [in Brazil] an "itinerant culture". In its expansion as in its crisis, we must analyze it as an activity in motion. Given this characteristic, a booming crop comprised a pioneer zone, where the coffee is penetrating; a zone where it is consolidated and fully productive; and a decadent zone where the culture is in decline.[20]

In each phase, we can grasp specific relations between pioneer, mature and declining zones in the world arena that greatly illuminate the contradictory interplay between the capitalist world economy and slave-grown coffee. My central aim is to recover usefulness of the concept of capitalism to properly understand slavery in Brazil and its link to global flows of goods and people. The objective is to highlight the perennial contribution of Eric Williams and his Brazilian readers.

The Brazilian Slave System and the Making of the Coffee World Market

Brazilian control over the global supply of coffee was attained in the 1830s, largely because of slavery (in 1833, the country produced 67,230 tons of coffee, roughly the same amount as the world's total production in 1790). Britain's strong pressure for the abolition of the transatlantic slave trade to Brazil, a condition for the recognition of the country's political independence (reached in 1822), led the first Brazilian emperor to sign a treaty in 1826 establishing the end of the slave trade in May 1830. In 1831, D. Pedro I was forced to resign the throne. The Brazilian parliament, empowered by the fall of the monarch, approved a draconian law against the slave trade in November 1831, aiming to shut it down once and for all. Its practical effect was short-lived, however. In the mid-1830s, the volume of the illegal transatlantic trade quickly recovered in response to the growing demand for labour in the coffee plantations of the river valley of Paraíba do Sul, a hitherto sparsely populated region relatively close to the city and port of Rio de Janeiro, the country's capital. In fifteen years (1835–50), more than half a million enslaved Africans were landed at the ports of south-central Brazil, the highest numbers of the nefarious trade in its entire history. With ideal conditions for coffee growing, during the following half-century (c. 1830–80) the Paraíba Valley would be the core of the Brazilian Empire's coffee economy and also the strongest bastion of slave power in the country.[21]

From the beginning, the Brazilian coffee production was articulated to the American economy. On the one hand, in 1832 the US Congress made coffee a duty-free product, a decision that lasted virtually for the entire nineteenth century. With this measure – approved because of pressures from Southern slaveholding interests – the growth of the Brazilian production became inter-connected to the growth of the American consumer market.[22] On the other hand, the US shipbuilding industry provided, during the 1830s and 1840s, the vessels that moved almost 60 per cent of all the slaves illegally imported into Brazil. When not directly engaged in the business, the US companies that sold the slave ships to the Portuguese and Brazilian enslavers based in Rio de Janeiro were the very same that controlled the bulk of coffee exports from Brazil to the United States. In other words, the take-off of the Brazilian coffee economy (based on the illegal slave trade) was part of the gears of the US antebellum economic growth.[23]

The social costs of the success of coffee production in Brazil went hand in hand with its environmental costs. The strategies of landscape and labour management adopted in the Paraíba Valley plantations followed some of the standards previously established by European colonial powers in the Indian Ocean and the Caribbean, but with a few key and substantial modifications. The coffee trees were planted in the mountainous topography of the Paraíba Valley in parallel vertical lines that ran from the base to the top of the hills. The difference from the former practices of the British, Dutch and French lay in the distance between those lines. In the West Indies, the coffee trees were planted in quincunx with small spaces between the bushes, and one *alqueire de terra* (a Brazilian unit of land equivalent to 48,400 square metres) contained on average about 15,700 bushes. In the Paraíba Valley, the quincunx formation was not followed, and the vertically aligned rows were planted at a 3-metre distance, each *alqueire de terra* containing just 5,100 bushes. This apparent waste of land (an elastic factor of production in Brazil) was directly related to the organization of the slave labour process. Coffee culture in the Caribbean was time-intensive: it required slow weeding, the use of manure and was based on a classic task system for the crop. Each slave was in charge of 2,000 bushes and, during the harvest, he was forced to carefully pick a barrel of beans (the equivalent to three Brazilian *alqueires* as a unit of volume; an *alqueire de café* has 50 litres), after which he would have free time at his disposal. In the Brazilian plantations, slave labourers were divided into gangs made up of twenty to twenty-five members and kept under the direct super-vision of an overseer. Their main activity during the crop-growing season was weeding, done two to three times a year. Each slave was put into a row, and, with the large spaces between the lines of coffee bushes, the overseer at the base of the hill could easily supervise the pace of labour and therefore accelerate it when it seemed to be too slow. For the harvest, Paraíba Valley planters adopted a peculiar variation of the task system, rewarding slaves with monetary gains – never with free time – proportional to the extra amount of beans collected, or applying harsh physical punishment if the minimal task was not accomplished. In Brazil, the coffee yields varied greatly from year to year along with the amount of beans to be harvested. The planter or his general overseer set the tasks of the harvest according to the progress of the agricultural cycle. In bad years, the minimum task was settled at three *alqueires de café* (the maximum amount established for the West Indies plantations). In good years, it ranged from five to seven *alqueires de café*, sometimes reaching nine *alqueires de café*. Under this labour regime, Brazilian slaves were forced to cultivate twice as many trees as their West Indies counterparts, which meant 4,000 bushes.[24]

Due to geo-ecological conditions, the productivity of coffee trees in Brazil was higher than in the Caribbean, but as the practices of landscape and labour management described brought an astonishingly fast rate of soil depletion (in two decades, the areas planted with coffee trees in vertical alignment always became completely unproductive), planters had to continually plant new bushes on virgin lands. The constant movement into new areas of exploitation was a structural feature of the coffee economy in Brazil. Insofar as the coffee frontier began to move to the eastern Paraíba Valley, to the Zona da Mata in Minas Gerais and to the so-called Old West of São Paulo (an old sugar zone) in the mid-nineteenth century, transportation costs became a key issue. The making of the Brazilian coffee economy had depended on a transportation system based on mules, a legacy of the eighteenth-century gold mining economy. Mules were very effective for carrying the coffee production from the western Paraíba Valley to the Rio de Janeiro harbour between the 1820s and 1840s. With coffee and slave prices soaring after 1850 and with the extension of the commodity frontier, the mule system turned into an obstacle to the territorial expansion of the coffee economy, since distances longer than two hundred kilometres from the coastal ports made freight costs on mules prohibitive.[25]

Railroads were the only possible solution to the transportation bottleneck.

Before the 1850s, the lack of capital and technical know-how to overcome the barrier presented by the Serra do Mar prevented their construction in the centre-south of Brazil. The end of the transatlantic slave trade, with the consequent release of its capital, plus the formation of a sound banking system, the global capital flows and the development (in the United States and Europe) of appropriate technologies for mountainous topographies allowed the accumulation of the financial and technical resources required for the construction of the first railroads in Brazil. Founded in the mid-1850s, the railways departing from Rio de Janeiro (D. Pedro II) and Santos (São Paulo Railway) would reach the coffee areas in the middle of the following decade.[26]

The closing of the frontier of African enslavement in 1850, an outcome of the escalation of British pressure against the transatlantic slave trade to Brazil, meant that the acquisition of new enslaved labourers to the coffee frontier could only occur within the territorial borders of the Brazilian Empire. The US South provided a vivid example of the viability of such a path, with the large flows of slaves from the less economically dynamic areas of the South to the cotton frontiers of the Gulf States, all based on the natural reproduction of the slave population. Both ways (internal slave trade and natural reproduction) were tried in the coffee-growing regions of Brazil, the first with more success than the second. But above all, the US South served as a sort of political and ideological wall of contention for the Brazilian slave system. The economic success of the slave power of the North Atlantic – the largest consumer market for Brazilian coffee – showed to Brazilian politicians and the public opinion that it was possible to maintain their slave power intact in the South Atlantic within a hostile global interstate system.[27]

The World Crisis of Slavery and the New Brazilian Coffee Frontier

Hence the deep impact that the American Civil War had over the destinies of Brazilian slavery. The war directly stimulated the debates around a Free Womb Law project, converted into imperial law in 1871. The Free Womb Law represented the turning point of Brazilian slavery, since it initiated the chain of events that in less than two decades would end a secular institution. But, in the short run, the Civil War had positive effects for the Brazilian coffee economy. During the conflict, US demand for coffee decreased, but this was compensated by the failure of harvests in Brazil caused by a moth pest during 1861–62. With the naval blockade, New Orleans, the main entrance for Brazilian coffee into the United States, lost her position to New York. Two years after the Union victory, the prices paid for coffee in the New York market exploded and remained in a strong uptrend until 1878. These positive circumstances were related to the substantial increase in the demand from northern and midwestern states, a direct consequence of the growing population and the per capita consumption.[28]

Precisely when the international coffee prices took off, the tracks of the D. Pedro II and the São Paulo Railway reached the Paraíba Valley and São Paulo's "Old West". In the following years, different railroads expanded deeper into the coffee zones of centre-south Brazil. After being taken over by the imperial government, the D. Pedro II quickly covered the western Paraíba Valley (a mature zone of the coffee economy on the verge of economic collapse due to environmental decline) and advanced towards the Zona da Mata region in Minas Gerais (a former pioneer zone, now on its way to becoming a consolidated zone). The Estrada de Ferro Cantagalo linking Niterói to the eastern Paraíba Valley (still a pioneer zone) was built between 1860 and 1873 with the money of slaveholders. The same model was used in the creation of railroad companies in the province of São Paulo after the tracks of the São Paulo Railway (a British company) arrived in the highlands. The Paulista (1869) and the Mogiana (1872) railways were assembled with capital raised by frontier planters, both being the two main arteries of coffee expansion in the state of São Paulo until the first decades of the twentieth century.[29]

The confluence of rising international prices and the arrival of the railroad to pioneer and consolidated zones brought a renewed impetus to the expansion of the Brazilian coffee economy. However, under the new conditions produced by the approval of the Free Womb Law, this confluence set in motion a range of forces that would push slavery in the different coffee areas (decaying, mature and pioneer) to its ecological, social and political limits, thus accelerating the crisis of the institution nationwide.

The Free Womb Law was approved in September 1871 against the vote of representatives from the coffee provinces of the centre-south.[30] In reaction to this clear political defeat, the coffee planters from Rio de Janeiro, Minas Gerais and São Paulo tried, in the following year, to recover from the setback, curbing any advance of the anti-slavery platform that had threatened to expand during 1869–71. The strategy was temporarily successful. As in the aftermath of the abolition of the transatlantic slave trade in 1850, the abolitionist potential contained in the debates on the free womb as a gradual way to end slavery was gagged. It is not surprising, therefore, that the 1871 legislative measure had not been able to break the high prices of slaves. These were inflated by the positive trend in coffee prices that started in 1848, which got stronger after 1868, and the lower costs of transportation, since railroads were able to carry larger volumes of coffee beans from the more distant and productive zones.

The years from 1872 to 1881 marked the peak of the internal slave trade in Brazil, with almost one hundred thousand slaves transported to the coffee provinces of the centre-south. The regional distribution of these slaves was not uniform.[31] All coffee planters bought them, but the main buyers were in the frontier zones that recently saw the arrival of railroads. This was the case of Cantagalo: between 1873 (the year the railroad got there) and 1882, its slave population rose from 17,562 to 21,621. An analogous pattern can be observed in all counties of the "New West" of São Paulo (that is, beyond the Campinas region) covered by the railroad companies Paulista and Mogiana. From 1874 to 1882, the number of slaves in these places increased from 26,282 to 38,242. During this exact same period, the slave population in the older coffee counties of the western Paraíba Valley stagnated (Valença and Barra Mansa in Rio de Janeiro) or decreased (Vassouras and Piraí in Rio de Janeiro; Bananal in São Paulo).[32]

These numbers show the uneven impact of railroads and the Free Womb Law over the "three spaces" of the Brazilian coffee economy during the 1870s. The western Paraíba Valley, a region that had dominated the world coffee market since the 1830s, had at that time a stabilized slave population with a moderate tendency towards natural growth. However, in this whole area, the profits from coffee production were diminishing. The arrival of the D. Pedro II railroad in the positive phase of the early 1870s stimulated the acceleration of the exploitation of its natural and human resources. A greater number of coffee bushes were allocated for each field slave and the remaining forest reserves were torn down to replace the greater quantity of unproductive shrubs.[33]

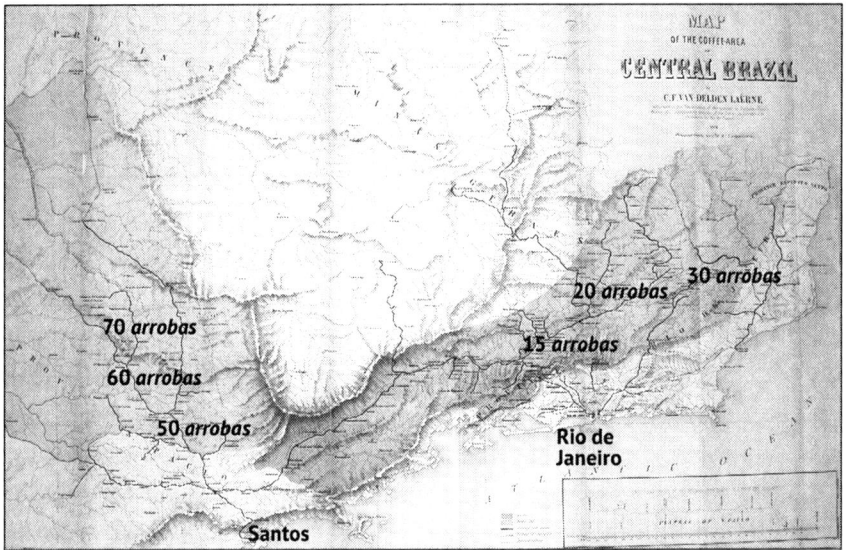

Figure 8.1. **Source:** C.F. van Delden Laërne, *Brazil and Java: Report on Coffee-Culture in America, Asia, and Africa* (London: W.H. Allen, 1885), 328–35. 15 *arrobas*: estimates from Vassouras/Valença plantations (RJ); 20 *arrobas*: estimates from Juiz de Fora (MG); 30 *arrobas*: estimates from Cantagalo (RJ); 50 *arrobas*: estimates from Campinas plantations (SP); 60 *arrobas*: estimates from Limeira/Rio Claro (SP); 70 *arrobas*: estimates from Araras (SP).

Planters in the frontier areas dealt with a quite different situation. During his tour through centre-south Brazil between September 1883 and April 1884, aiming to investigate the secrets of the coffee giant of South America (Java's greatest rival), the Dutch agronomist C.F. van Delden Laërne collected detailed information about forty-four coffee plantations, gathering data on their labour force, machinery, area and land productivity. Rearranging the data concerning the productivity of coffee bushes and projecting it on Laërne's book's beautiful map (figure 8.1), which highlights the areas that exported coffee through the port of Rio de Janeiro (the western Paraíba Valley: the region from Vassouras to Bananal; Zona da Mata: the region of Juiz de Fora; the eastern Paraíba Valley: the Cantagalo region) and the areas that exported their production through the port of Santos (the "Old West": Campinas region; the "New West": the region served by the Paulista and Mogiana rails), we can clearly see the contrast between the three spaces of the Brazilian coffee economy (the pioneer, mature and decaying zones) and to what extent the western Paraíba Valley was now in the position of a decaying zone.

In the pioneer zone of the New West, soil productivity and land prices stimulated the migration of planters by the late 1870s and early 1880s. A newspaper article published in Resende (a county of the western Paraíba Valley) reported on 9 February 1878 that "in São Simão [a county north of Araras, New West of the São Paulo province] just a few areas have been cultivated and the whole county is still covered with splendid and exuberant forests . . . frost-free lands for coffee are still moderately priced – the alqueire has been sold at an average of R$40,000 [forty thousand *réis*]".[34] In Resende, one *alqueire* of increasingly scarce virgin land was quoted in 1878 at R$400,000 (four hundred thousand *réis*). Coffee productivity was even more frustrating, with only 16 *arrobas*[35] per thousand bushes. In São Simão, it was 100 *arrobas* per thousand bushes. In 1878, the Mogiana railroad reached Casa Branca, a city about sixty kilometres distant from São Simão.[36] The prospect of an arriving railroad promoted an intense land speculation and a subsequent rise in their prices. The extension of the railway to Ribeirão Preto, the first station after São Simão, made the average price of an *alqueire* rise to R$115,000 in 1884, nearly three times its price from six years earlier. Land prices in the Ribeirão Preto coffee frontier were nevertheless well below the prices of virgin soils in Vassouras, being equivalent to the value of its already – or nearly – exhausted lands.[37]

In sum, by promoting the maximum exploitation of the decaying areas of the Paraíba Valley and stimulating the upsurge in land values in the frontier zones of western São Paulo, the railroads deepened the separation between them. Labour demand was determinant in this increasing discrepancy.[38] In order to realize capital gains in the plantations built in the frontier areas, the need for labour became more pronounced. During the 1870s, demand had been met by the interprovincial slave trade, but in 1883 – the year Laërne collected data on coffee productivity and rail trails coming to the "Potosi of coffee" (as contemporaries called the Ribeirão Preto area) – this was no longer possible because of the effects railroads had had on the coffee economy and, consequently, on the internal flows of slaves in the Brazilian Empire.

The purchases in the post-1871 internal slave market had different characteristics from those in its US counterpart of the antebellum period. The provinces that, between 1872 and 1881, lost their slaves to the coffee zones were those that had prospered with cotton during the Civil War in the United States. With the recovery of the southern economy during Reconstruction, the cotton farmers and the small foodstuff producers in northeastern Brazil found themselves compelled to sell their slaves to the centre-south (the regional sugar plantations could not buy because of the crisis generated by Cuban competition), especially after the great drought of 1877–80 hit them hard.[39] A similar process happened in the south: the competitiveness of River Plate cattle ranchers, served by an expanding railway system, led cattle ranchers and *charqueadores* in Rio Grande do Sul to sell their slaves to the coffee provinces.

Without the prospect of maintaining the slave system based on natural reproduction, the post-1871 interprovincial slave trade focused on young men born in Brazil, detached from their family networks and coming from regions where labour patterns were different from the harsh realities of the centre-south coffee plantations.[40] After their arrival, they were forced to obey strict disciplinary protocols they had not experienced before, to meet an astonishing workload and to live in militarized, collective slave barracks. It is no coincidence, therefore, that the zones that had acquired more slaves in the interprovincial trade were the ones that saw the largest increase in slave resistance. The observation highlights an important difference between the western Paraíba Valley and the frontier areas of the eastern Paraíba Valley and the (Old and New) West of São Paulo. Cases of overseers being murdered by slaves (one of the more serious expressions of slave unrest) who had been bought in the interprovincial slave trade were not rare in these regions during the 1870s, but the perception of the risks posed by the introduction of big groups of uprooted slaves was more acute in the areas that depended more on them for the expansion of their coffee production.[41] Indeed, the over-exploitation of labour in the western Paraíba Valley (where slaves lived in relatively cohesive communities) did not produce the kind of tensions that galvanized the pioneer zones of the coffee economy.[42]

Between the late 1870s and the early 1880s, the strategy to stop the anti-slavery platform, employed right after the approval of the Free Womb Law, sank with the articulation of the Brazilian abolitionist movement on a national basis and, above all, with the new modes of collective slave resistance in the frontier zones. The first victory came with the provincial laws passed in local assemblies in São Paulo, Minas Gerais and Rio de Janeiro in 1881, banning the interprovincial slave trade through the imposition of taxes that made it unaffordable. Three main arguments were the basis of the law presented to the São Paulo assembly in 1878: (1) the Free Womb Law had a harmful effect on slave discipline, given the general perception that the institution lost its legitimacy as it could not reproduce it over time; (2) the interprovincial slave trade dangerously disturbed master-slave relationships with the constant introduction of uprooted slaves from northern Brazil in the plantations of São Paulo; (3) the polarization between a free north and a slave-owning south foreshadowed the previous experience of the American Civil War, making it necessary to maintain the national commitment to the institution so that a similar outcome in Brazil could be prevented. Also important was, in 1881, the apprehension over the effects that abolitionist agitation could have on plantation discipline.[43] In other words, the political actors who endorsed the law against the interprovincial slave trade in the São Paulo assembly showed their awareness of all the social and political tensions generated by coffee expansion in the centre-south during the 1870s.

Contrary to their expectations, the tensions of slavery only increased. The signs could be seen already in 1882 with the spread of rumours about connections between plantation slaves and abolitionists, which became more threatening after 1885 with the intersection between the anti-slavery movement and the collective action of slaves calling for immediate abolition. During 1887 and 1888, Brazil was shaken by an abolitionist revolution that had precisely the coffee frontier of São Paulo as one of its epicentres.[44]

The Abolition of Slavery and the International Labour Market

As we have seen, the revisionist historiography of the 1980s and 1990s questioned the opposition between planters from the Paraíba Valley and those from western São Paulo as an analytical tool capable of explaining the political future of slavery in its final crisis. The previous generation of historians argued that, in a context of growing contradictions between the development of capitalist productive forces and the social relations of slave production, progressive planters of western São Paulo, looking for appropriate conditions for employing free labour or searching for wage labourers more attuned to an economic rationality than they already had, found an innovative solution to the problem of slavery in mass immigration, an option that was always unavailable to the more traditional planters of the Paraíba Valley. Critics of this view argued that these two groups of planters were attached to slavery until the eve of abolition, responding to market forces that were virtually the same in both places. The decision of western planters to invest in immigration was the product of escalating social and political conflicts after 1886 (and not a pre-existing project attuned to modern capitalist rationality). Thus, the end of the institution would have been mainly the result of the actions of the subaltern agents (slaves, freedmen, urban labourers, abolitionists) that had risen against it, but whose agency would have burdened unevenly the planters from the Paraíba Valley and western São Paulo.

Despite its undeniable relevance, the revisionist model (now predominant in the historiography dealing with Brazilian slavery) does not offer a complete account of how the expansion of the commodity frontier under the particular historical conditions of the late nineteenth-century world economy *forced* planters from the "pioneer zone" to address, in a very innovative way, the problem of labour supply – an argument that was originally put forward by, among others, Emília Viotti da Costa, Alice Piffer Canabrava, Paula Beiguelman, João Manuel Cardoso de Mello and Flávio Saes, all of them following in Eric Williams's footsteps.[45]

Coffee exports from the "Rio zone" (according to the distinction placed by Laërne's map) showed a clear downward trend after the peak of the 1881–82 harvests.[46] In the following years (1883–90), the overall volume remained high, but was increasingly based on the expansion of coffee plantations in the Zona da Mata region of Minas Gerais, an area that took advantage of the expanding railway network that had the port of Rio de Janeiro as its axis. Having a significant demographic basis and large reserves of unexplored virgin forests, planters in the Zona da Mata passed through the crisis of slavery without major disruptions or the need for additional external manpower. Coffee production continued to expand at the turn of the century by employing free national labourers (many of them former slaves) in multiple variations of the sharecropping system.[47]

The "Santos zone", which included the Old West and the New West of São

Paulo (the latter being a region of very low demographic density), experienced a completely different situation. The growth in exports after 1881 (the product of coffee bushes planted in the new expansion areas during the height of the interprovincial slave trade) intensified the pressure for more workers. Another noticeable increase in shipments from Santos occurred in 1887 with the product of coffee trees planted after 1883, when the interprovincial slave trade had already been closed and the only alternative to frontier planters of São Paulo was the intra-provincial slave trade.[48] The New West planters, well served by the Paulista and Mogiana railways, were following market incentives. Between 1878 and 1885, the prices paid in US dollars in New York sharply dropped, but were counterbalanced by the devaluation of the Brazilian currency. Between 1886 and 1892, prices in US dollars doubled in an exchange market that remained favourable to Brazilian exporters. Those price movements demonstrate once again the close ties between the two ends of the coffee commodity chain in the era of mass consumption.[49] The reaction of New West planters was immediate: in 1889–90, 112,000 tons were shipped from Santos; in 1890–91, 176,700; in 1891–92, 222,000. The increase came from coffee trees planted between 1886 and 1888, precisely at the height of the abolitionist movement and slave revolts. How do we explain the business behaviour of the frontier coffee planters in such a critical situation, when their expectations of the permanence of slavery for more than five years were virtually non-existent?[50]

To find an answer, we must go back to the debates opened in the provincial assembly of São Paulo in 1878, which culminated in the 1881 approval of the law forbidding the interprovincial slave trade. Here, the key actor was the Republican politician and slave owner Martinho Prado Jr, the chief proponent of the bill against the internal slave trade and a very active entrepreneur in the pioneer zone. In 1877, he began to invest his capital on land in the Ribeirão Preto area, constituting in a few years the territorial funds of the famous – and huge – Guatapará plantation. In 1878, the year the press in the western Paraíba Valley reported on the potential of the New West, he did the same in the pages of *A Província de São Paulo*. Also in 1878, the Mogiana Company got permission to extend its rails from Casa Branca to Ribeirão Preto, getting into a competition with the Paulista (Martinho Prado was one of its founders) for the rights over that area. Therefore, between 1878 and 1881, the new scale that coffee production could assume in the New West frontier had already been designed – depending, of course, on whether the crucial problem of labour supply could be solved. Laërne clearly understood the plans of those investing in the region: "in that country coffee-planting is passing through a crisis, which, as everybody knows, is threatening its very existence. But it is not the system of coffee-planting that has occasioned this crisis: it is exclusively the more and more urgent necessity of labourers. If this demand could be supplied, Brazil could send more than tenfold the amount of her present produce to the various emporiums of the world."[51]

Martinho Prado Jr belonged to a new group of planters who, from the late 1870s, articulated schemes for mass migration, in a preparation that ran parallel and in mutual reinforcement to the crisis of slavery, and gained from the accumulated experiences of the failed *sistema de parceria*. At the height of British pressure for the abolition of the transatlantic slave trade in the second half of the 1840s, planters of the Old West of São Paulo and the Paraíba Valley sought an alternative to slave labour by hiring immigrants. According to the scheme, colonization companies were going to recruit rural families in Europe by advancing the payments for transportation to the Brazilian plantations, their initial maintenance and the tools required for agricultural labour. The planters would determine which and how many coffee trees were in the charge of each immigrant (weeding and harvesting), allowing them to grow food on small plots of land. The money advanced would be paid through a sharecropping system: half the coffee harvested and processed (whose marketing was the responsibility of the planter, who also was going to charge interest on all loans made) would be reserved for the abatement of debt incurred for the voyage to the plantation. The debt had no deadline for its end before it was fully paid. After it was paid, the system would work as a classic model of sharecropping (half of the harvest went to the landowner, half to the worker).[52]

Between the beginning of the *sistema de parceria* in 1847 and its abandonment after the second half of the 1850s, a relatively small number of German and Portuguese immigrants (fewer than ten thousand labourers) were mobilized. The causes of its failure were many: from the perspective of the immigrant, the enormous weight of the original debt was an insurmountable burden; from the perspective of the planter, the inability to compel immigrants to work as slaves was disappointing (European labourers in this sharecropping system never cultivated more than one thousand coffee trees each; slaves cultivated four times more). In the 1850s, it was clear to the frontier planters that the only way to mobilize labour on a large scale for the expansion of their coffee plantations would be through the internal slave trade.[53]

Yet those efforts to reshape labour relations produced an accumulation of experiences that would lead, in the course of the 1870s, to a new model for the engagement of free labour. Tested with the small number of foreigners that continued to live in the coffee plantations of western São Paulo after the failure of the *parceria* system, the new system, called *colonato*, combined three distinct forms of remuneration. Based on family units whose head was in charge of negotiating the terms of labour directly with the planter, the *colonato* system provided (1) a fixed payment per family for the cultivation of a given amount of coffee trees (the basic unit of calculation was a "hoe", the equivalent to the capacity of an adult worker to work a day; women and youngsters under sixteen were classified as "half-hoes"; a "hoe" in general was in charge of weeding two thousand coffee trees); (2) varying payments during the harvest according to the amount of coffee individually picked by the family members; (3) permission for growing food between the rows of young coffee trees (that is, under four years after planting), or on marginal plantation lands specially allocated for that (the income from the eventual sale of foodstuff would belong entirely to the *colono*).[54] But if on the one hand the *colonato* system fitted perfectly with the coffee agronomic cycle, on the other the labourer was still missing. On the frontier of western São Paulo, precisely where this arrangement was born, the low demographic density required the attraction of foreign labourers, wherever they came from.

The potential of European or Asian immigration to supply the demand for labour in coffee plantations was an important variable throughout the crisis of slavery in Brazil. At the turn of the 1880s, the possibility of solving the problem through the introduction of indentured coolies from the Indian subcontinent or China was seriously debated in the country. The project was defeated by the decisive actions of the abolitionist movement in Brazil, which was well-informed about the real exploitative conditions of these labourers on the Cuban sugar plantations.[55] On the other hand, if the frontier planters could not envision the alternative represented by the Italians (by that point

Italy had very few people in transoceanic migration flows), like other contemporary actors in Brazil they had been watching closely, and for a long time, the huge influx of Europeans into the United States.

In 1878, the Paulista planter Queiroz Telles visited, on a semi-official mission, eight countries in western Europe to check which ones offered the best prospects for the recruitment of labourers. He reported to his class comrades back in Brazil that the deep and growing poverty of North Italy pointed to a possible solution.[56] In other words, the attention of the frontier planters turned to the Italians at the exact moment that Martinho Prado Jr – cousin of Queiroz Telles – was buying land in Ribeirão Preto, promoting the expansion of the Paulista railway and calling for the end of the interprovincial slave trade in the São Paulo assembly. After the approval of the latter, Martinho Prado Jr and his brother, Antonio da Silva Prado, began to prepare an institutional framework for mass migration: fully subsidized transportation for the families of rural European workers, approved by the São Paulo provincial assembly in 1884 (the previous experience of the *parceria* system had shown that, without full coverage of the costs of the transatlantic voyage, Brazil could not attract a large flow of voluntary migration); the requirement for immigrants to pass through an official hostel in São Paulo (Hospedaria dos Imigrantes, 1885 provincial law), from where they would be directly sent – also with subsidized passage – to the coffee plantations; the creation in 1886 of a Society for the Promotion of Immigration (Sociedade Promotora da Imigração) to coordinate the recruitment, transportation and distribution of immigrant labourers. In the year of its inception, the Sociedade Promotora da Imigração publicized with brochures in Northern Italy the immigration model for the coffee areas that would be adopted by the São Paulo State until the global crisis of the 1930s.[57]

In short, the making of mass immigration was an essential, constituent part of the crisis of slavery in Brazil and in multiplying the possible outcomes available to contemporaries. But how should we assess the commitment of frontier planters to slavery until 1888? Besides a sort of solidarity with their former class comrades, the behaviour reflected an attempt to manage the end of slavery, postponing abolition to the maximum to ensure a smooth transition to a new labour regime. For planters of the decaying zones, now completely depleted, there was no other option but to cling to the institution and hope for an eventual indemnity – as in the British model – for the compulsory emancipation of their slaves. At the breaking point of the 1888 revolution, the frontier planters were able to change clothes in an attitude typical of "political chameleons", in the precise expression employed by the historian Robert Toplin. Putting into practice between 1886 and 1892 the immigration project they had designed, 192,000 Italian labourers went to the coffee plantations in western São Paulo. If we take into account the volume of the interprovincial trade in slaves from 1872 to 1881 (one hundred thousand slaves for all the coffee provinces of centre-south Brazil), we can grasp how the labour supply provided by mass immigration promptly satisfied the pre-existing demand, bringing a solution to the crisis of slavery in the *"pioneer zone"* and establishing the basis to the spectacular expansion of its coffee production in the years after abolition.

Historians who explore the crisis of slavery in Brazil usually explain the problem of immigration from the perspective of demand – that is, they emphasize the factors of attraction. I have done the same so far. Scholars who work on migration, however, stress the importance of supply, or the push factors, in the specific case of the mass displacement of Italians to Brazil. Compared to the migratory flows of other Europeans, the phenomenon of the mass emigration of Italians to the Americas was relatively late. The movement took shape only after the Italian unification. Until 1886, the main destination was the United States. In the following ten years, however, Brazil became the prime receiver of Italians – mostly from Veneto – displacing the two other major New World destinations, the United States and Argentina.[58]

We can now see the other side of the reshaping of the global circuits of labour and commodities that were at the origins of the crisis of slavery in Brazil. The proletarianization of smallholders and tenants from the Italian Veneto and the impoverishment of its *braccianti*[59] were caused by the economic and agrarian transformations that marked Northern Italy after unification. The elimination of collective holdings, the abolition of the communal use of land, the advancing drainage of the plains – in other words, the forces that promoted the "capitalist transformation of the countryside" in Veneto – pushed the rural workers out of their traditional lands. Where rural properties were too divided, misery was common not only among the *braccianti* and the wage labourers but also for the ranks of smallholders and sharecroppers.

Nonetheless, the negative impacts of the institutional changes that followed unification were heightened by what Emilio Franzina and other scholars consider to be the central variable of the Italian agrarian crisis: "the dramatic fall in the international prices of wheat, whose first victims were not the poor peasants, but the small tenant farmers, smallholders, i.e., the small producers able to enter the market by themselves, but unable – because of their fragile position – to resist the violence of the cyclical crisis".[60] In the mid-1880s, with the deepening of the crisis caused by the continuous decrease in wheat prices, the major capitalist holders reduced the demand for labourers and the scarce earnings of the *braccianti* became even more reduced. One of the few ways to get out of this desperate situation was to emigrate. These rural workers, with large families and without any material resources, were easily regimented after 1886 by the São Paulo government policy of free transatlantic passages to the emigrants who were going to coffee plantations. The profile of the foreign immigrant desired by the planters who were facing the crisis of slavery in Brazil was a rural labourer on the move with his family and disciplined by Catholic preaching, exactly what their emissaries found in Veneto in 1878.

These developments require that we shift focus for a moment to the transformations that occurred in the last third of the nineteenth century in the world wheat market, since the agrarian transformations in Northern Italy were closely related to the "European grain invasion"[61] after the 1870s, a consequence of the rise in the production of the US Midwest and, after the 1880s, of the Russian steppes.

The reconfiguration of the global wheat market was being prepared since before the American Civil War. It included, at both ends of the commodity chain, the opening of the British market to the US product (with the overthrow of the Corn Laws in 1846) and the rise of Chicago as the nodal point for all the Midwest agriculture. The infrastructure composed of railroads, grain elevators, systems of grading and inspecting the grains, and the wheat futures market that made the agricultural complex of the Great West globally renowned was completed in 1861.[62] At the same time, it was in the states of Indiana, Illinois, Michigan, Wisconsin and Ohio that the new Republican Party found its stronger bases. In the 1856 presidential run, the party had established itself as a national political force, although still lacking supporters in the South. Since its inception, the Republican Party turned the Free

Soil programme into its electoral platform, advocating the necessity to open the western territories to the settlement of East Coast workers and European immigrants, a platform that merged well with the complex of economic interests rooted in Chicago. The Free Homestead became one of the chief slogans of the Republican Party and a reason for the spread of its electoral base in the major cities of the East Coast. Given its anti-slavery content, which sought to eliminate slavery from the western territories, the Free Homestead collided with the expansionist project advocated by Southern cotton planters. It was in the territorial issue and in its intersections with the problem of slavery that the sources of the collapse of the Second Party System lay, which led to the presidential election of Abraham Lincoln in 1860 and the outbreak of the Civil War – a conflict that can be read as a clash between two great expansionisms, the free wheat against the slave cotton.[63] The political conditions created by the secession of the Confederate States allowed the Federal Congress to easily approve the Homestead Act in 1862.[64] The Union victory accelerated the consolidation of the US domestic market, offering vast areas to the family farmers lured by the promise of free land on the prairies in the new states of Kansas, Nebraska, Minnesota, South Dakota and North Dakota, thus providing the take-off of the grain complex controlled from Chicago.[65]

Given the amount of product shipped from the United States to Europe, "in 1894 the price of wheat was only a little more than a third of what it had been in 1867". Based on this finding, Eric Hobsbawm argues that the so-called Great Depression (1873–96) should not be conceived as a period of decline in the overall volume of industrial and agricultural production, but rather as a moment of diminishing returns – and adds that "agriculture was the most spectacular victim of this decline in profits".[66] In this conjuncture, there was a major change in the composition of US agricultural firms, which allowed US farmers to simultaneously cope with the adversity they had created with the increase in volume of their output and establish the conditions for a new expansion. The mechanization of reaping and mowing allowed nuclear family units to successfully grow wheat in estates with up to three hundred acres, henceforth turned into the basic model of agricultural productive units throughout the Midwest.[67]

On the European side of the world economy, the US wheat market also rearranged the positions of buyers and sellers. Until the mid-nineteenth century, Russia was the major supplier of wheat to the British market. The combined effects of the abolition of the Corn Laws and the rise of the Midwest grain complex turned the British market into a dependent of US wheat, with the consequent exclusion of the Russian product. The changing structure of the wheat economy in Russia that followed the abolition of serfdom and the building of a large railroad network (with the inflow of British capital) connecting new areas of Ukraine with the Black Sea stimulated the Russian producers to search for new markets where they could compete with the US wheat. Northern Italy was exactly one of the new markets flooded with wheat from the Midwest plains and the Ukrainian steppes.[68]

In sum: the spread of global commodity frontiers was made possible by new means of transportation (railroads, steamboats). British financial expansion and the increasingly important role of the United States in the world economy after the Civil War unified the trajectories of two economic and human spaces – Brazil and Italy – that had hitherto been separated. Since the 1830s, the main market for Brazilian coffee was the United States, which had, between 1840 and 1860, been the mainstay of the defence of Brazilian slavery in the interstate system. As we have seen, the result of the American Civil War had a dual effect on the institution in Brazil. On the one hand, the exponential growth of the US population and their income levels enlarged the market for Brazilian coffee. During the same years that the railroad system was expanding in the new states of the Midwest (an integral part of the process of rising income and population growth), the Brazilian railroad system reached the coffee frontier, which allowed Brazilian planters to respond to rising prices but also deepened their pressure for labour. On the other hand, slavery in Brazil entered a crisis as another direct result of the American Civil War. In a global economic context that saw the emergence of new cotton, sugar and meat producers, market forces weakened the national commitment to slavery in Brazil as it gave impetus to a huge flow of slaves through an internal trade to the coffee-growing zone, the most competitive in the new international division of labour. The legitimacy of slavery in Brazil was permanently damaged after the approval of the Free Womb Law in 1871, paving the way for the gradual erosion of the power of slaveholders, the emergence of a national abolitionist movement and the political role of slaves themselves. Therefore, the same processes of the capitalist world economy that led to the expansion of the coffee market and placed increasing pressure on the social and political relations of slavery in the Brazilian Empire gave rise, at the other end of the commodity chain, to the expansion of the grain frontiers that had a devastating impact on Northern Italy. Changes in the world wheat market disrupted a region that, until then, had been outside the global flows of mass migration.

The thousands of Italian families that arrived at the port of Santos after 1886 were sent to plantations that, while following the same agronomic pattern created in the Paraíba Valley half a century earlier, greatly expanded their spatial scale of production. The coffee units that appeared on the pioneer fringes of the New West after 1888 abandoned the former plants of the Paraíba Valley, the same that hitherto had prevailed in the Old West of São Paulo. The new plantations gave innovative responses to handling huge amounts of bean and the coordination of labour forces that could easily exceed the thousands. The *colonato* system, with its complex mix of fixed payment on the weeding of coffee trees, payment per piece during the harvests and permission to grow foodstuffs, allowed the planters to extract a great amount of labour from the Italian immigrants.[69] However, they never extracted as much as they did with slaves before 1888. A good example is the Santa Gertrudes plantation, located at the current city of Cordeirópolis, São Paulo. Nowadays surrounded by a huge sea of sugar cane fields, the plantation was founded in the 1850s, employing slave labour until the collapse of the institution. At the time of the super-crop of 1906, which yielded 1,573 tons of coffee, its more than one million coffee trees were cultivated by 170 families (a total of 1,076 individuals), most of them Italians. Each "hoe" (an adult worker, or a woman plus a youth of sixteen years or younger) took care of two thousand coffee trees on average. Twenty years earlier, the Santa Gertrudes plantation had been visited by C.F. van Delden Laërne. At the time, 140 field slaves cultivated its 615,000 coffee bushes. The proportion, therefore, was almost 4,400 coffee trees of coffee per enslaved worker.[70]

Despite the drop in the levels of labour exploitation, it is possible to identify the legacies of slavery in the *colonato* labour relations and the practices of landscape management employed in the post-1888 Paulista frontier. Under slavery or *colonato*, the main goal of the labour process during the crop season was to collect the largest quantity of beans in the shortest possible time: without the whip, the payment method per number of beans picked (*colonato*) structurally resembled the monetary reward system for beans picked above the minimum task (slavery). The wide spacing between the rows, an early creation of the Brazilian coffee economy to increase the supervision of gang labour in weeding, was turned, under the *colonato* system, into a mechanism to lower the wages with non-monetary payments, by allowing the cultivation of food crops between the rows during the formation of new coffee grounds. In the Paraíba Valley, this agronomical technique, which completely depleted the soil every two decades, spurred the movement towards new frontiers. In the less hilly topography of western São Paulo, soil erosion was not as serious as it was in the Paraíba Valley, but we can also see the movement to the frontier as a consequence of the spaces between the rows. Driven by dreams of land ownership, the Italian immigrants always chose to work on the newly open coffee plantations when they could, since planters allowed them to cultivate their own crops between the rows of young coffee trees. As they were weeding for the planter, they were also working for themselves and, therefore, maximizing their own time. Besides the planter's search for more fertile land (soil productivity decrease continued, even in western São Paulo), the decisions of immigrants were an important vector of the continuous expansion of the frontier and the increasing Brazilian coffee production.

After the first decade of the twentieth century, with the chronic problem of coffee overproduction on a global scale, Italian immigration to Brazil lost momentum and the world coffee market profoundly changed. While this is another story, its foundations lie in the experience of the mass enslavement of Africans and their descendants. Just like our coffee-drinking habits.

NOTES

1. Eric Williams, *Capitalism and Slavery* (1944; reprint, Chapel Hill: University of North Carolina Press, 1994); Caio Prado Jr, *Formação do Brasil Contemporâneo* (1942; reprint, São Paulo: Brasiliense, 1987); Alice P. Canabrava, *O açúcar nas Antilhas (1697–1755)* (1946; reprint, São Paulo: IPE/USP, 1981).
2. Celso Furtado, *Formação Econômica do Brasil* (1959; reprint, São Paulo: Companhia

das Letras, 2009); Florestan Fernandes and Roger Bastide, *Relações raciais entre negro e brancos em São Paulo* (São Paulo: UNESCO/Anhembi, 1955).

3. Gerald R. Bosch Jr, "Eric Williams and the Moral Rhetoric of Dependency Theory", *Callaloo* 20, no. 4 (Autumn 1997): 817–27; Richard B. Sheridan, "Eric Williams and *Capitalism and Slavery:* A Biographical and Historiographical Essay", in *British Capitalism and Caribbean Slavery: The Legacy of Eric Williams*, ed. Barbara Solow and Stanley Engerman (Cambridge: Cambridge University Press, 1987), 323–29.

4. Fernando Henrique Cardoso, *Capitalismo e escravidão no Brasil meridional: O negro na sociedade escravocrata do Rio Grande do Sul* (São Paulo: Difusão Européia do Livro, 1962); Fernando Henrique Cardoso and Enzo Faletto, *Dependencia y Desarollo en América Latina* (Mexico City: Siglo XXI, 1969).

5. Emília Viotti da Costa, *Da Senzala à Colônia* (1966; reprint, São Paulo: Brasiliense, 1989); Fernando A. Novais, *Portugal e Brasil na crise do Antigo Sistema Colonial (1777–1808)* (São Paulo: Hucitec, 1979).

6. Costa, *Da Senzala à Colônia*, 28–30.

7. Eugene Genovese, *O mundo dos senhores de escravos: Dois ensaios de interpretação* (Portuguese translation; Rio de Janeiro: Paz and Terra, 1979); Robert Toplin, *The Abolition of Slavery in Brazil* (New York: Atheneum, 1975); Warren Dean, *Rio Claro: Um sistema brasileiro de grande lavoura, 1820–1920* (Portuguese translation; Rio de Janeiro: Paz and Terra, 1977); João Manoel Cardoso de Mello, *O Capitalismo Tardio* (1978; reprint, Campinas: Edições Facamp, 2009); Ciro Flamarion Santana Cardoso, "O modo de produção escravista colonial na América", in *América Colonial*, ed. Théo Santiago (Rio de Janeiro: Pallas, 1975); Ciro Flamarion Santana Cardoso, *Agricultura, escravidão e capitalismo* (Rio de Janeiro: Vozes, 1979); Jacob Gorender, *O escravismo colonial* (1978; reprint, São Paulo: Ática, 1985); José Roberto do Amaral Lapa (ed.), *Modos de produção e realidade brasileira* (Petrópolis: Vozes, 1980).

8. Robert W. Slenes, "The Demography and Economics of Brazilian Slavery" (PhD diss., Stanford University, 1976); Robert W. Slenes, "Grandeza ou Decadência? O mercado de escravos e a economia cafeeira da Província do Rio de Janeiro, 1850–1888", in *Brasil: história econômica e demográfica*, ed. Iraci del Nero da Costa (São Paulo: IPE-USP, 1986); Pedro Carvalho de Mello, "The Economics of Labor in Brazilian Coffee Plantations, 1850–1888" (PhD diss., University of Chicago, 1977); Pedro Carvalho de Mello, "Expectations of Abolition and Sanguinity of Coffee Planters in Brazil, 1871–1888", in *Without Consent or Contract: The Rise and Fall of American Slavery – Conditions of Slave Life and the Transition to Freedom*, vol. 2: *Technical Papers*, ed. Robert William Fogel and Stanley L. Engerman (New York: W.W. Norton, 1992), 629–46; Pedro Carvalho de Mello and Robert

W. Slenes, "Análise econômica da escravidão no Brasil", in *Economia brasileira: uma visão histórica*, ed. Paulo Neuhaus (Rio de Janeiro: Campus, 1980), 89–122.

9. The expression belongs to Pedro Carvalho de Mello, "Aspectos econômicos da organização do trabalho da economia cafeeira do Rio de Janeiro, 1850–1888", *Revista Brasileira de Economia* 32, no. 1 (1978): 26–28. For Viotti da Costa's response, see *Da Senzala à Colônia*, 25–54.

10. See, for instance, a synthesis of this historiography by Robert W. Slenes, "Brazil", in *Oxford Handbook of Slavery in the Americas*, ed. Robert L. Paquette and Mark M. Smith (New York: Oxford University Press, 2010), 124.

11. Robert W. Slenes, "O escravismo por um fio?", preface to Flávio dos Santos Gomes, *A Hidra e os Pântanos: Mocambos, quilombos e comunidades de fugitivos no Brasil (séculos XVII–XIX)* (São Paulo: Ed. Unesp, 2005), 17–18.

12. Slenes, "Grandeza ou Decadência?" 142; Silvia Hunold Lara, " '*Blowin' in the Wind*': Thompson e a experiência negra no Brasil", *Projeto História* 12 (1995): 43–56; Sidney Chalhoub and Fernando Teixeira da Silva, "Sujeitos *no* imaginário acadêmico: escravos e trabalhadores na historiografia brasileira desde os anos 1980", *Cadernos AEL* 14, no. 26 (2009): 13–45.

13. José Antonio Piqueras, "El Dilema de Robison y las Tribulaciones de los Historiadores Sociales", *Historia Social* 60 (2008): 59–89; Walter Johnson, "On Agency", *Journal of Social History* 37, no. 1 (2003): 113–24; Dale Tomich, *Through the Prism of Slavery: Labor, Capital, and World Economy* (Boulder: Rowman and Littlefield, 2004), 3–31; Barbara Weinstein, "The Decline of the Progressive Planter and the Rise of Subaltern Agency: Shifting Narratives of Slave Emancipation in Brazil", in *Reclaiming the Political in Latin American History: Essays from the North*, ed. Gilbert M. Joseph (Durham, NC: Duke University Press, 2001), 81–85.

14. Dale Tomich, "Econocide? From Abolition to Emancipation in the British and French Caribbean", in *The Caribbean: A History of the Region and Its Peoples*, ed. Stephan Palmié and Francisco Scarano (Chicago: University of Chicago Press, 2011), 303–16.

15. Williams, *Capitalism and Slavery*, 176.

16. David Beck Ryden, *West Indian Slavery and British Abolition, 1783–1807* (Cambridge: Cambridge University Press, 2009); Joseph E. Inikori, *Africans and the Industrial Revolution in England: A Study in International Trade and Economic Development* (Cambridge: Cambridge University Press, 2002).

17. Mauro Rodrigues da Cunha, "Apêndice Estatístico", in *150 anos de café*, ed. Edmar Bacha and Robert Greenhill (Rio de Janeiro: Marcellino Martins and E. Johnston, 1992), 283–391; Mario Samper and Radin Fernando, "Appendix: Historical Statistics of Coffee Production and Trade from 1700 to 1960", in *The Global Coffee Economy in Africa, Asia, and Latin América, 1500–1989*, ed. William

Gervase Clarence-Smith and Steven Topik (Cambridge: Cambridge University Press, 2003), 411–62.

18. For those estimates, see Laurent Dubois, *Avengers of the New World: The Story of the Haitian Revolution* (Cambridge, MA: Harvard University Press, 2004), 24–28; and David Geggus, "Sugar and Coffee Cultivation in Saint Domingue and the Shaping of the Slave Labor Force", in *Cultivation and Culture: Labor and the Shaping of Slave Life in the Americas*, ed. Ira Berlin and Philip Morgan (Charlottesville: University Press of Virginia, 1993), 76.

19. C.F. van Delden Laërne, *Brazil and Java: Report on Coffee-Culture in America, Asia, and Africa* (London: W.H. Allen, 1885), 119–24.

20. Antônio Barros de Castro, *Sete ensaios sobre a economia brasileira*, vol. 2 (Rio de Janeiro: Forense, 1971), 60–61. By the same author, see also " 'As mãos e os pés do senhor de engenho': dinâmica do escravismo colonial", in *Trabalho escravo, economia e sociedade*, ed. Paulo Sérgio Pinheiro (Rio de Janeiro: Paz and Terra, 1984), 46.

21. Tâmis Parron, *A política da escravidão no Império do Brasil, 1826–1865* (Rio de Janeiro: Civilização Brasileira, 2011); Rafael Marquese and Dale Tomich, "O Vale do Paraíba escravista e a formação do mercado mundial do café no século XIX", in *O Brasil Imperial*, vol. 2: *1831–1870*, ed. Keila Grinberg and Ricardo Salles (Rio de Janeiro: Civilização Brasileira, 2009), 339–83.

22. Steven Topik, "The Integration of the World Coffee Market", in *The Global Coffee Economy in Africa, Asia, and Latin América, 1500–1989*, ed. William Gervase Clarence-Smith and Steven Topik (Cambridge: Cambridge University Press, 2003), 21–49; Rafael Marquese, "Estados Unidos, Segunda Escravidão e a Economia Cafeeira do Império do Brasil", *Almanack* 5 (May 2013): 51–60.

23. Leonardo Marques, "Aiding and Abetting the Slave Trade: The United States and the Transatlantic Slave Trade to Brazil", paper presented to the conference "New Frontiers in the Economic, Cultural, and Digital History of the Atlantic Slave Trade: A Festschrift in Honor of David Eltis", 21–23 March 2013, Emory University, Atlanta, GA.

24. Rafael de Bivar Marquese, "African Diaspora, Slavery, and the Paraíba Valley Coffee Plantation Landscape: Nineteenth-Century Brazil", *Review: Fernand Braudel Center* 32, no. 2 (2008): 195–216.

25. Rogério de Oliveira Ribas, *Tropeirismo e escravidão: um estudo das tropas de café das lavouras de Vassouras, 1840–1888* (Curitiba: UFPR, 1989), 170–97; Herbert S. Klein, "The Supply of Mules to Central Brazil: The Sorocaba Market, 1825–1880", *Agricultural History* 64, no. 4 (1990): 1–25.

26. Almir Chaiban E-Kareh, *Filha branca de mãe preta: a Companhia da Estrada de Ferro D. Pedro II, 1855–1865* (Petrópolis: Vozes, 1982); Odilon Nogueira de Matos,

Café e ferrovias: A evolução ferroviária de São Paulo e o desenvolvimento da cultura cafeeira (São Paulo: Pontes, 1990), 65–68; Flávio Azevedo Marques de Saes, *As ferrovias de São Paulo, 1870–1940* (São Paulo: Hucitec – INL/MEC, 1981), 38–41.

27. Rafael Marquese and Tâmis Parron, "Internacional Escravista: A Política da Segunda Escravidão", *Topoi* 12, no. 23 (July–December 2011): 97–117.

28. Edmar Bacha and Robert Greenhill, *150 anos de café* (Rio de Janeiro: Marcellino Martins and E. Johnston, 1992), 20–21, 157; Antonio Delfim Netto, *O problema do café no Brasil* (São Paulo: IPE/USP, 1981), 16; Francis Beatty Thurber, *Coffee, from Plantation to Cup* (New York: American Grocer, 1884), 130.

29. Pierre Monbeig, *Pioneiros e fazendeiros de São Paulo* (São Paulo: Hucitec, 1984), 174–76; Nogueira de Matos, *Café e ferrovias*, 78–90.

30. Robert Conrad, *Os últimos anos da escravatura no Brasil, 1850–1888* (Portuguese translation; Rio de Janeiro: Civilização Brasileira, 1977), 362.

31. Robert W. Slenes, "The Brazilian Internal Slave Trade, 1850–1888: Regional Economies, Slave Experience, and the Politics of a Peculiar Market", in *The Chattel Principle: Internal Slave Trades in the Americas*, ed. Walter Johnson (New Haven, CT: Yale University Press, 2004), 331.

32. Ricardo Salles, *E o Vale era o escravo: Vassouras, século XIX: Senhores e escravos no coração do Império* (Rio de Janeiro: Civilização Brasileira, 2008), 258–59.

33. Marquese, "African Diaspora"; Stanley J. Stein, *Vassouras: Um município brasileiro do café, 1850–1900* (Portuguese translation; Rio de Janeiro: Nova Fronteira, 1990), 264–65; Slenes, "Grandeza ou Decadência?", 139–40; João Luis Ribeiro Fragoso, *Sistemas agrários em Paraíba do Sul (1850–1920): Um estudo de relações não-capitalistas de produção* (Rio de Janeiro: UFRJ, 1983).

34. *O Itatiaia*, 9 February 1878, in Maria Celina Whately, *O café em Resende no século XIX* (Rio de Janeiro: José Olympio, 1987), 52.

35. One *arroba* equals 32 pounds (14.7 kilograms).

36. Nogueira de Matos, *Café e ferrovias*, 91.

37. On land value in Ribeirão Preto, see Carlos de Almeida Prado Bacellar, "Uma rede fundiária em transição", in *Na Estrada do Anhangüera: Uma visão regional da história paulista*, ed. Carlos de Almeida Brado Bacellar and Lucíla Reis Brioschi (São Paulo: CERU-Humanitas, 1999), 111; on land value in Vassouras, see Stein, *Vassouras*, 264.

38. Cardoso de Mello, *O Capitalismo Tardio*, 68.

39. Slenes, "Brazilian Internal Slave Trade", 338–40; Michael Tadman, *Speculators and Slaves: Masters, Traders, and Slaves in the Old South* (Madison: University of Wisconsin Press, 1989).

40. José Flávio Motta, *Escravos daqui, dali e de mais além: O tráfico interno de cativos na expansão cafeeira paulista (Areias, Guaratinguetá, Constituição/Piracicaba e*

Casa Branca, 1861–1887) (São Paulo: FEA/USP, 2010), 147–50, 351–52; Richard Graham, "Another Middle Passage? The Internal Slave Trade in Brazil", in *The Chattel Principle: Internal Slave Trades in the Americas*, ed. Walter Johnson (New Haven, CT: Yale University Press, 2004), 311; Slenes, "Brazilian Internal Slave Trade", 351.

41. Eloy de Andrade, *O Vale do Paraíba* (Rio de Janeiro: Real Gráfica, 1989), 87–88; Hebe Maria Mattos de Castro, *Das Cores do Silêncio: Os significados da liberdade no Sudeste escravista – Brasil, século XIX* (Rio de Janeiro: Arquivo Nacional, 1995), 137–88.

42. Marquese, "African Diaspora"; Maria Helena P.T. Machado, *Crime e escravidão: Trabalho, luta e resistência nas lavouras paulistas, 1830–1888* (São Paulo: Brasiliense, 1987); Dean, *Rio Claro*, 135; Flávio dos Santos Gomes, *Histórias de quilombolas: mocambos e comunidades de senzalas no Rio de Janeiro, século XIX* (São Paulo: Companhia das Letras, 2006), 257.

43. Celia Maria Marinho Azevedo, *Onda Negra, Medo Branco: O negro no imaginário das elites, século XIX* (Rio de Janeiro: Paz and Terra, 1987), 114–58.

44. Jacob Gorender, *A escravidão reabilitada* (São Paulo: Ática, 1990), 133–88; Maria Helena Machado, *O Plano e o Pânico: Os movimentos sociais na década da abolição* (São Paulo: Edusp-Ed. UFRJ, 1994).

45. Costa, *Da Senzala à Colônia*; Alice Piffer Canabrava, "A grande lavoura" (1971), in *História Econômica: estudos e perspectivas* (São Paulo: ABPHE-Hucitec-Ed. Unesp, 2005); Paula Beiguelman, *A formação do povo no complexo cafeeiro: aspectos políticos* (São Paulo: Pioneira, 1977); Cardoso de Mello, *Capitalismo Tardio*; Flávio Saes, "Estradas de ferro e diversificação da atividade econômica na expansão cafeeira em São Paulo, 1870–1900", in *História Econômica da Independência e do Império*, ed. Tamás Szmerecsánsyi and José Roberto do Amaral Lapa (São Paulo: Hucitec-Edusp, 1996).

46. Mello, "Aspectos Econômicos da organização do trabalho", 29.

47. Anna Lucia Duarte Lana, *A transformação do trabalho* (Campinas: Ed. Unicamp, 1988); Anderson Pires, *Capital agrário, investimento e crise da cafeicultura de Juiz de Fora (1870–1930)* (Niterói: Universidade Federal Fluminense, 1993); Elione Guimarães, *Terra de Preto: Usos e ocupação da terra por escravos e libertos (Vale do Paraíba mineiro, 1850–1920)* (Niterói: Editora da UFF, 2009); on the general context, see Anderson Pires, *Café, Finanças e Indústria: Juiz de Fora, 1889–1930* (Juiz de Fora: Funalfa, 2009).

48. Motta, *Escravos daqui, dali e de mais além*, 274–345.

49. Bacha, "Política Brasileira do Café", 334, 341; Delfim Netto, *O problema do café*, 21; Topik, "Integration of the World Coffee Market", 31.

50. Mello, "Aspectos econômicos da organização do trabalho", 57.

51.   Laërne, *Brazil and Java*, 272–73.

52.   Verena Stockle and Michael Hall, "A introdução do trabalho livre nas fazendas de café de São Paulo", *Revista Brasileira de História* 6 (September 1983): 80–120.

53.   Costa, *Da Senzala à Colônia*, 158–61.

54.   Stockle and Hall, "A introdução do trabalho livre".

55.   Robert Conrad, "The Planter Class and the Debate over Chinese Immigration to Brazil, 1850–1893", *International Migration Review* 9, no. 1 (Spring 1975): 41–55. See also Peter Eisenberg, "A mentalidade dos fazendeiros no Congresso Agrícola de 1878", in *Homens Esquecidos: Escravos e trabalhadores livres no Brasil – séculos XVIII e XIX* (Campinas: Editora Unicamp, 1989), 150–59.

56.   Zuleika M.F. Alvim, *Brava Gente! Os italianos em São Paulo, 1870–1920* (São Paulo: Brasiliense, 1986), 47.

57.   Thomas H. Holloway, *Imigrantes para o café: Café e sociedade em São Paulo, 1886–1934* (Portuguese translation; Rio de Janeiro: Paz and Terra, 1984), 64–116.

58.   Holloway, *Imigrantes para o café*, 60–102.

59.   "This category, the most exploited of all menial workers, had a subtle difference between the obliged or fixed *braccianti*, who were linked to the property through an annual contract, and the temporary *braccianti* who worked only in times of great need for manpower, earning by day or task." Alvim, *Brava Gente*, 29.

60.   Emilio Franzina, *A Grande Emigração: O êxodo dos italianos do Vêneto para o Brasil* (Campinas: Editora Unicamp, 2006), 39, 144–45, 217, 264.

61.   Kevin H. O'Rourke, "The European Grain Invasion, 1870–1913", *Journal of Economic History* 57, no. 4 (December 1997): 775–801.

62.   Morton Rothstein, "America in the International Rivalry for the British Wheat Market, 1860–1914", *Mississippi Valley Historical Review* 47, no. 3 (December 1960): 401–18; D.W. Meinig, *The Shaping of America: A Geographical Perspective on 500 Years of History*, vol. 2: *Continental America, 1800–1867* (New Haven, CT: Yale University Press, 1993), 323–34; William Cronon, *Nature's Metropolis: Chicago and the Great West* (New York: W.W. Norton, 1991), 65–70.

63.   John Ashworth, *Slavery, Capitalism and Politics in the Antebellum Republic*, vol. 2: *The Coming of the Civil War, 1850–1861* (Cambridge: Cambridge University Press, 2008); Seymour Drescher, *Abolition: A History of Slavery and Antislavery* (Cambridge: Cambridge University Press, 2009), 317–25; Robert William Fogel, *Without Consent or Contract: The Rise and Fall of American Slavery* (New York: Norton, 1989), 302–52; Brian Schoen, *The Fragile Fabric of Union: Cotton, Federal Politics, and the Global Origins of the Civil War* (Baltimore: Johns Hopkins University Press, 2009), 237–59.

64.   Emília Viotti da Costa, "Política de terras no Brasil e nos Estados Unidos", in *Da Monarquia à República: Momentos Decisivos* (São Paulo: Brasiliense, 1987), 153.

65. Cronon, *Nature's Metropolis*; Eric Wolf, *A Europa e os Povos sem História* (Portuguese translation; São Paulo: Edusp, 2009), 378–83; Giovanni Arrighi, *O longo século XX: dinheiro, poder e as origens de nosso tempo* (Portuguese translation; Rio de Janeiro: Contraponto/Ed. Unesp, 1996), 300.

66. Eric Hobsbawm, *A Era dos Impérios 1875–1914* (Portuguese translation; Rio de Janeiro: Paz and Terra, 1988), 60–61.

67. Harriet Friedmann, "World Market, State, and Family Farm: Social Bases of Household Production in the Era of Wage Labor", *Comparative Studies in Society and History* 20, no. 4 (October 1978): 572–74.

68. Rothstein, "America in the International Rivalry"; M.E. Falkus, "Russia and the International Wheat Trade, 1861–1914", *Economica*, new ser., 33, no. 132 (November 1966): 416–29.

69. Wladimir Benicasa, *Fazenda paulista: Arquitetura rural no ciclo cafeeiro* (São Carlos: Escola de Engenharia de São Carlos – Universidade de São Paulo, 2007), 277–312; José de Souza Martins, *O Cativeiro da Terra* (São Paulo: Contexto, 2010), 76.

70. Maria Silvia C. Beozzo Bassanezi, "Fazenda Santa Gertrudes: uma abordagem quantitativa das relações de trabalho, em uma propriedade rural paulista, 1895–1930" (PhD diss., Faculdade de Filosofia, Ciência e Letras, Rio Claro, 1973), 182; Laërne, *Brazil and Java*, 334–35.

Chapter 9

The Industrial Revolution in Atlantic Perspective

County History and National History

JOSEPH E. INIKORI

Economic historians have debated the historical origins of the Industrial Revolution in England for decades. Over these decades, the competing explanations can be classified broadly, in terms of their emphasis, as inward-looking and outward-looking explanations. The inward-looking explanations emphasize internal factors, such as cultural elements (belief systems and the like), social structure and natural resource endowment (coal, land quality and so on), while outward-looking explanations place emphasis on trade (overseas trade, in particular). Neither of these two sets of explanations is mono-causal. The real bone of contention is the relative weights to attach to the contending factors in the analysis. The solution to the problem has remained elusive, because the unit of analysis has been overly national. Excessive focus on national history makes it difficult to observe the real weight of each contending factor in the long-run process of economic development. This is particularly so because an integrated national economy developed in England after the Industrial Revolution and not before. Economic historians have long been aware of the differences in the performance of England's regions during the critical period, 1650–1850. But the implication of these differences for the weighting of the contending factors in historians' explanations is not generally well understood.

This chapter attempts to spell out the implication more clearly to make it easier to comprehend. It contends that a comparative study of England's counties from the late medieval period to the mid-nineteenth century provides unambiguous evidence that allows us to give the pride of place to Atlantic trade in explaining the origin of the Industrial Revolution. We analyse evidence from recent research to show that the Industrial Revolution and its new technologies developed first and foremost in northwest England (Lancashire and the West Riding of Yorkshire, the former in particular), while East Anglia, which showed great promise earlier on, declined. The question this chapter poses is: what made the difference? The chapter attempts to demonstrate that it was Atlantic trade. We extend a challenge to inward-looking analysts, who emphasize cultural factors, social structure and natural resource endowment, to explain why the Industrial Revolution and its new technologies developed in northwest England and not in East Anglia or other southern regions of England.

To avoid the misunderstandings that often arise when issues are not clearly articulated, we need to separate two issues, often mixed up in debates on the Industrial Revolution, that are not necessarily compatible: *national average* short-term per capita income growth; and long-term structural transformation and technological development. Development economic historians and economists generally agree that it was the latter that gave rise to sustained per capita income growth in England – what they characterize as the beginning of modern economic growth. Historically, empirical evidence shows some instances of short-term growth leading to sustained per capita income growth; but more often, the evidence shows the contrary. That is why we have many ephemeral growth miracles ending up in a cul-de-sac. Historically, only short-term growths that gave rise to structural transformation and technological development have led to sustained per capita income growth – that is, modern economic development.

It is important to note that structural transformation and technological development are not necessarily accompanied simultaneously with per-capita income growth, *measured as a national average.* On the contrary, national average per capita income growth may stagnate or even decline, in the short run, at the very moment when structural transformation and technological development are occurring. This is even more so if structural transformation and technological development were concentrated initially in a few small, backwards regions, as, we propose to argue, was the case in England. The main reason for this is that, even if structural change and technological development were accompanied simultaneously with per capita income growth in the small, leading regions where they occurred, the growth would have been swamped in the national aggregate statistics by what happened in the other regions. Hence, it would not show up in the national aggregate measurements in the short run. The positive impact of the structural change and technological development on per capita income would have to spread to many more regions before it would show up in the national aggregate statistics. Clearly, we should not be surprised that this took a long time. This is why all static-growth models are not helpful in explaining the historical origins of the Industrial Revolution. Scholars involved in the debates must, therefore, be sure that their arguments ultimately focus on the historical origins of structural transformation and technological development, rather than short-term growth.

The chapter is organized into four sections. The first section comparatively reviews the more recent literature on the sources of structural transformation and technological development in early American industrialization and during the Industrial Revolution in England. The comparative literature review is intended to establish a causal pattern that would contribute to our determination of the relative weights to attach to the contending factors in our analysis. The identified unresolved issues in the literature set up the context for the comparative analysis of the long-run development experiences of selected English counties. Taken along with the causal pattern revealed in the literature, the comparative county study enables us to demonstrate unambiguously the critical role of Atlantic trade in the Industrial Revolution, which makes up the third section. But before that exercise, which is the main focus of the chapter, some issues concerning the concepts, import-substitution industrialization and export-led growth, are discussed in the second section for purposes of a clear understanding of the chapter's main arguments. The conclusion constitutes the last section.

The Sources of Structural Transformation and Technological Development

Economic historians generally agree that, before the twentieth century, market-based industrialization was a long, drawn-out process, with observable major changes in the organization and technology of production. The factory system was the most significant change in the organization of production; and mechanization and the adoption of steam power were the fundamental changes in technology. The movement from peasant craft to factory production was a critical element in the structural transformation process, culminating in the separation of manufacturing from agriculture, its concentration in urban centres and its ultimate predominance over agriculture in employment and contribution to the national product. Explaining the historical origins of the factory system seems to be of little concern to economic historians in recent years. Not too long ago, the lively discussion of proto-industrialization provided a forum for a serious examination of the long-run historical process that transformed independent producers of manufactures into legally free wage-workers, virtually dependent on the sale of their labour power to the owners of industrial capital.[1]

There was a consensus on the initial source of the transformation – the expansion of markets for manufactures. As Peter Kriedte noted in the 1980s, "The world market which was slowly coming into existence acted as the engine of proto-industrial growth."[2] The growth of markets for manufactures provided the scale of business, which made it economic for merchants to specialize in the supply of raw materials, tools (in some instances), the organization of production and quality specification, and the sale of the finished product in particular industries. While proto-industrialization created the necessary conditions for the rise of the factory system and mechanized manufacturing, it did not lead automatically to successful industrialization in all cases. Hence, the debate on proto-industrialization was inconclusive.[3]

The more recent literature has focused primarily on explaining the historical origins of the technological developments that changed the world, starting with the Industrial Revolution. As recent as 2004, a writer noted:

> Technological change was a central component in the industrialisation process
> of the late eighteenth and early nineteenth centuries, and thus in the making

of the modern world economy. Nevertheless, more than two centuries after the beginnings of industrialisation, our understanding of the factors that impelled and shaped the development, diffusion and impact of the new technologies of early industrialisation remains far from complete. As a consequence, important questions concerning the place and interpretation of technological change in industrialization remain unresolved.[4]

However, there is a rich literature on the subject, much of it from the 1990s, concentrated largely on the Industrial Revolution and early American industrialization.[5] The studies more directly relevant to the main focus of this chapter are those based on patent records.

Patent records have been effectively employed by Kenneth Sokoloff to demonstrate the sources of invention and innovation during early industrialization in the United States.[6] As a point of departure, Sokoloff notes the weakness in earlier attempts to trace the sources of invention and innovation by historians of business and technology, whose work provides a wealth of information on the development of technique in individual industries, but whose "typical mode of investigation has been to illustrate theories with individual cases, rather than to explore their consistency with a large body of evidence".[7] To avoid the pitfalls of arguments based on example, Sokoloff has employed a sample of about forty-five hundred patent records (about 30 per cent of the total) filed in the United States between 1790 and 1846, "randomly drawn from several indexes prepared by the commissioner of patents".[8]

The records contain a description of the invention or discovery patented, its industrial classification, the name and residence of the patentee, and the date the patent was granted.[9] More information on the patentees from other sources is added, including information showing "their occupation, degree of specialization in invention, and long-term commitment to patenting", on the basis of which inferences are drawn "about the knowledge they had and about other individual attributes relevant to their inventive activity".[10] Also added is a sample of "great inventors" comprising "160 individuals credited with at least one important invention between 1790 and 1846 by biographical dictionaries and histories of technology". The sample contains complete patent histories up to 1865, including "information on place and date of birth, schooling, occupation before and after major inventions, efforts to extract income from their discoveries, and other variables".[11]

The analysis of all this information shows important patterns: variation in overall inventive activity over time; geographical distribution of inventions; changes over time in the contribution of patentees in five specified occupational groups; and important attributes of the "great inventors", their careers and the regional distribution of their activities. The patterns revealed by the analysis of the evidence make it possible to draw inferences concerning the sources of invention and innovation during early industrialization in the United States.

Changes in inventive activity over time show that the bulk of the inventions between 1790 and 1846 occurred in two periods: from the late 1790s to 1812; and from the early 1820s to July 1836. Two significant developments preceding the first upswing should be noted. There was a span of prosperity followed by disruption of overseas trade by British naval interference with shipping lanes and the Embargo Act of 1807.[12] Sokoloff implies that the span of prosperity in 1790–1812 was broken temporarily by a brief disruption of foreign trade. From that, we may infer that foreign trade was the main source of the prosperity. The work of Douglass North leaves no doubt about that.[13] Again, Sokoloff does not show explicitly the role played by the disruption of foreign trade: "Patenting . . . began to grow rapidly with the interruption in foreign trade that preceded the War of 1812."[14] We may deduce from this a sort of import-substitution mechanism induced by the interruption of foreign trade after the creation of a domestic market for manufactures by imports from overseas. The second upswing in inventive activity occurred during the economic revival that extended from the early 1820s to 1836.[15]

The regional distribution shows a clear domination by the northeast, within which southern New England was the leader, followed by New York, Pennsylvania, the southern mid-Atlantic and northern New England, in that order.[16] Taking all the sectors of the economy together, annual patent rates per one million residents in southern New England increased from 7.2 per cent in 1791–98 to 65.2 per cent in 1805–11, and from 60.4 per cent in 1823–29 to 106.4 per cent in 1830–36.[17] The rates for New York were quite close to those of southern New England; those of the other three subregions of the northeast were closer together, but somewhat distant from the two leaders. All the other regions of the United States together were in a world of their own, with rates in the single digits – except for 1823–29 and 1830–36, when they recorded 10.4 per cent and 13.2 per cent, respectively. Within the regions, the geographical distribution also shows a strong association between patenting and proximity to navigable waterways,[18] again pointing to the importance of access to large and growing markets.

From these patterns revealed by the analysis of the evidence, Sokoloff concludes:

> Notwithstanding the obvious significance of factors such as slowly evolving, location-specific conditions, changes in the stock of knowledge, and learning-by-doing, *this analysis has highlighted the role of the expansion of markets in industrialization*. . . . The findings suggest that the growth of markets during the early stages of industrialization diffused a powerful and long-term inducement to inventive activity, and in so doing, helped raise the realization of economic gains into a self-sustaining process.[19]

This conclusion is further strengthened by the patterns from the analysis of information about the patentees. As mentioned earlier, the analysis shows changes over time in the contribution of patentees in five specified occupational groups. At the beginning of the rapid growth in inventive activity, most patented inventions were by a broad segment of the population, "men with relatively common skills and knowledge" – merchants, doctors, gentlemen, carpenters, shoemakers and so on.[20] Their contribution to urban patents declined from 65.4 per cent in 1790–1804 to 48.8 per cent in 1823–36, and 36.4 per cent in 1836–46. The comparable percentages for groups with possibly relevant special skills and knowledge – machinists, toolmakers and other producers/dealers of metal products – during the same periods are 11.6, 30.9 and 38.5.[21] From this, Sokoloff and Khan conclude that "the skills and knowledge necessary for patentable invention at the beginning of industrialization were widely dispersed among the population". Special technical skills or knowledge acquired through training in technical occupations were not a requirement. They add, "the new evidence makes it more difficult to maintain that exogenous advances in technical knowledge, or in its diffusion drove the beginning of the process . . . the greater sensitivity of this key group of patentees to economic conditions provides further evidence that the expansion of markets was a powerful inducement to the increase of inventive activity during early American industrialization".[22]

Analysis of information on the 160 "great inventors" leads, similarly, to a further strengthening of the markets-expansion argument. One important piece of information is their level of formal education. Almost one-half of them had little or no formal schooling; less than 25 per cent attended college. In terms of age, less than a third of them had their first major invention before thirty; the "macro-inventions" were largely by middle-aged and older men, for whom the main factor was experience rather than youthful genius. And the geographical distribution and temporal variation were similar to those of the general patents. What is more, the "great inventors" were highly entrepreneurial and geographically mobile, moving from regions of low to those of high market opportunities, leading Sokoloff and Khan to observe: "If successful invention were driven by randomly distributed factors like genius or luck, one would not expect the manifest extent of geographic concentration."[23] They sum up their findings thus:

> Analysis of biographical and complete patent histories through 1865 indicates that these "great inventors" were entrepreneurial and responded systematically to market demand. Their inventions were procyclical and originated disproportionately from localities linked with extensive markets. Although unexceptional in terms of schooling or technical skills, they vigorously pursued the returns to their inventions, redirected their inventive activity to meet emerging needs, and were distinguished by high geographical mobility toward districts conducive to invention and its commercialization.[24]

The patent records in England between the mid-seventeenth and the mid-nineteenth centuries have also been employed to show the nature and sources of invention and innovation during the Industrial Revolution.[25] A comparison of the revealed patterns with those of the American patents just examined may be helpful in establishing a generalizable pattern for the eighteenth- and early nineteenth-century inventions and technological innovations.

However, there are historiographical problems that are rather unique to the English system. O'Brien and his collaborators have pointed out common difficulties in the use of patent statistics to measure the flow of invention and innovation over time: "national series incorporate innovations of varying significance and do not differentiate between fundamental breakthroughs that transformed manufacturing techniques and those improvements operating at the margins of production". In addition, "a significant and shifting proportion of patented invention was never exploited commercially".[26] Using patent records alone may, therefore, present a distorted view of the flow over time and the geographical distribution of the inventions and innovations that were truly transformative, economically and socially. But there are other problems specific to the English system. Unlike the American system, "awards were made without any evaluation of originality or technical merit", for which reason "insignificant and derivative patents proliferated".[27] Furthermore, in England, there were other ways of deriving material benefits and social esteem from invention apart from the monopoly granted by patents. Private bodies, such as the Society for the Encouragement of Arts, Manufactures and Commerce (active in London from 1754), offered material and other incentives to inventors, making it unnecessary to incur the expense of taking a patent. Many important inventions, therefore, went without patents. Thus, between 1700 and 1800, out of 174 recorded textile inventions traced, only 77 were patented.[28]

These weaknesses notwithstanding, economic historians believe the patterns revealed are important.[29] O'Brien's more detailed study of invention and innovation in the textile industry provides a helpful reference point. In general, the patterns revealed by the English patent records are consistent with those of the United States studied by Sokoloff. Of particular importance, the changes over time show a strong association with economic conditions. As MacLeod put it, "The purchase of a patent was a commercial transaction. Patents were expensive to obtain, and nobody sought them without an economic end in view."[30]

Perhaps, given the weaknesses noted earlier, patents for capital goods are more reflective of the over-time flow of the transformative innovations. Their share of the total increased from 35 per cent in 1750–59 to 45.2 per cent in 1790–99. Of the 666 such patents granted between 1750 and 1799, 204 (30.63 per cent) were granted in the thirty-one-year period from 1750 to 1780; 168 (25.23 per cent) in the following ten years, 1780–89; and 294 (44.14 per cent) in the last decade, 1790–99. Textile machinery made up 15.9 per cent of the total, 50 per cent of which were in 1790–99; power sources made up 25.4 per cent, 43.8 per cent of which were in 1790–99.[31] It is thus clear that the pace of transformative invention and innovation accelerated in the last decade of the eighteenth century, an upswing that began in the 1780s. This is consistent with O'Brien's point that England's "Age of Invention" did not begin in the 1760s; it was in the 1790s that "an important technological discontinuity" occurred.[32] As MacLeod explains, a major factor that induced inventive activity in the capital-goods sector was the expansion of industries that employed such equipment in production:

> One might see this increase in numbers merely as further testimony to the burgeoning consumer goods industries and requirements of a growing population. But that was not all. For, during the period 1790–1830, if not earlier, the balance of investment shifted towards higher fixed-capital ratios. Cotton led the way (and was the only industry in which fixed capital represented over half the investment); the other textile industries followed. . . . With the growing investment there emerged a separate, specialist capital-goods sector.[33]

Sullivan's figures for the annual growth rate of producers' durable equipment (industrial machinery and equipment, ships, railway rolling stock, producer carriages and coaches, and farm machinery) show a continuing acceleration in the growth of fixed-capital investment in the first half of the nineteenth century, increasing from 1.67 in 1800–1830 to 2.65 in 1830–60.[34]

Taking all the patents together, two annual peaks in patenting in the eighteenth century, one in the 1780s (1783) and the other in the 1790s (1792), stand out.[35] According to MacLeod, the 1783 boom in patenting (64 in total) was dominated by consumer goods, while capital goods were more in the boom of 1792 (85 in all). On the whole, manufacturers helped to sustain the upward trend in the last two decades of the eighteenth century, in contrast to the pre-1760 fluctuations: "against a background of widening markets and crumbling controls, manufacturers and craftsmen kept one eye on their commercial opportunities, the other on their competitors. They responded in waves, whose occasional coincidence produced peaks in the patent totals. This happened in 1783 and 1792."[36]

Two elements in the English patent records distort the geographical distribution they present. According to MacLeod, it is often difficult to know whether or not the names and addresses stated are those of the actual inventors or their agents or financial backers. Even when the names are those of the inventors, the addresses may be where they were temporarily in London at the time the patent was being sought and not their permanent, provincial ones. This may help explain the prevalence of London addresses.[37] The other element is the proliferation of "insignificant and derivative patents" mentioned earlier. No separate sample of "great inventors", comparable to Sokoloff's sample of 160 such inventors in the United States, has been compiled for England during our period. The nearest to it is the ambitious research of O'Brien and his collaborators, aimed at gathering, from various sources, patent and biographical details on textile inventors, great and small, over the period 1688–1851.[38] The intention was to create two databases: "one designed to provide some sort of empirical foundation for an analysis of the pace and pattern of technological change, the other to explore the social, religious, educational, and cultural milieux of nearly 2,500 inventors". In the end, the second database could not be created, because "biographical details were hard to compile systematically".[39]

These difficulties notwithstanding, the patent records, in combination with other sources, show geographical distributions that are consistent with a decisive role of market extent and rate of expansion. From her detailed study of the English patent records, MacLeod reports, "Lancashire, Yorkshire and Warwickshire were prominent in the first half of the eighteenth century, and they remained so . . . *East Anglia's pattern, with no heed to the region's old industrial activity, is closer to that of the low-patenting arable counties of the East Midlands and South.*"[40] O'Brien's findings on the textile industry are in agreement: "there was a predictable tendency for inventive activity to emanate from the new and rising regions of cloth production in the midlands and north of England. Although the addresses of agents and businessmen 'representing' genuine inventors complicate the geographical picture, *the relative decline of London, East Anglia, and the southern counties as centres of inventive activity becomes transparent, especially after the turn of the century.*"[41]

The causal pattern revealed by the patent records is consistent with the endogenous theories of technological development which began in the mid-1980s, with emphasis on market size and its rate of growth.[42] What is more, it is also consistent with Adam Smith's dynamic theory of development.[43] What is fashionably characterized as Smithian growth, derived entirely from the division of labour without technological development, is an incomplete reading of Smith's theory.[44] Smith did include technological development in his vent-for-surplus theory of international trade:

> This great increase of the quantity of work, which in consequence of the division of labour, the same number of people are capable of performing, is owing to three different circumstances; first to the increase of dexterity in every particular workman; secondly to the saving of time which is commonly lost in passing from one species of work to another; and lastly, to the invention of a great number of machines which facilitate and abridge labour, and enable one man to do the work of many.[45]

As Myint elaborated: "In the comparative costs theory 'specialisation', conceived as a reallocation of resources, is a completely reversible process. The Adam Smithian process of specialisation, however, involves adapting and reshaping the productive structure of a country to meet the export demand, and therefore not easily reversible."[46]

Given the foregoing rich literature on the subject – empirical and theoretical – one is tempted to conclude that there is considerable agreement concerning the sources of long-term structural transformation and technological development during early industrialization in the eighteenth and nineteenth centuries. Yet, such a conclusion is not fully borne out by the major books of the twenty-first century on the subject.[47] These books show lingering unresolved issues. The rest of this section of the chapter presents pertinent summary positions of these books to identify these unresolved issues that warrant further consideration.

Kenneth Pomeranz's *Great Divergence* has contributed immensely to stimulating further interest in the Industrial Revolution and comparative economic history. Its emphasis on the role of the Americas in the Industrial Revolution places it on the side of trade. But the argument sounds more like a supply-side analysis – New World raw materials and domestic supply of coal solved the critical problem of ecological constraint. Pomeranz does not deal at all with the sources of technological development, not because he subscribes to the exogenous theory, but rather because he believes we do not know the sources of technological development.[48] Unlike *Great Divergence*, Joseph Inikori's *Africans and the Industrial Revolution in England* deals extensively with the sources of technological development, with emphasis on markets and their rates of expansion over long time periods. But, rightly or wrongly, a highly complimentary reviewer believes the analysis is incomplete.[49] Perhaps the most provocative book of the twenty-first century on the subject is Gregory Clark's *A Farewell to Alms*. Clark's explanation of the Industrial Revolution is based almost entirely on the greater survival rate of rich people in England (compared with the poor). As the offspring of the rich inherited the socio-economic norms and ingenuity of their parents, Clark argues, the greater survival rate of the rich spread those attributes far more widely in England than anywhere else on the globe. As one reviewer puts it, "Rich people proliferated, and by a social Darwinian struggle the poor and incompetent died out, leaving a master race of Englishmen to conquer the world."[50] There is no direct analysis of the sources of technological development. We are left to infer that the greater preponderance of the attributes of rich people, transmitted genetically and environmentally to their descendants in England, were the sources of technological development during the Industrial Revolution. The reviews have not been charitable.[51] Findlay and O'Rourke's *Power and Plenty* assigns a considerable role to overseas trade in explaining the Industrial Revolution. As the authors put it: "Domestic inventiveness was required to make the technological breakthroughs of the period, but the key question for us is what would have been the effects of those breakthroughs in the absence of international trade, and what would this in turn have implied for future technological progress. . . . We argue that international trade was a key reason why the British Industrial Revolution was different."[52]

However, Findlay and O'Rourke do not show the sources of inventiveness and technological change. Their argument implies technological change was exogenous, contrary to the empirical and theoretical literature reviewed earlier in this section of the chapter. For Findlay and O'Rourke, international trade became a key element at the point of technological diffusion.

Robert Allen's *The British Industrial Revolution in Global Perspective* traces the sources of technological development during the Industrial Revolution firmly to international trade. The analysis centres on British high wages, which made labour-saving technology profitable. In turn, British high wages resulted from Britain's disproportionate share of global trade between the mid-seventeenth and the mid-nineteenth centuries. Resource endowment, such as coal, was important only in the context of success in global trade: "We habitually describe coal as a 'natural' resource. It is true that there would have been no coal trade had there been no coal in the ground. That much was a fact of nature. But the mere presence of coal was not sufficient to cause the coal trade. It was only activated by the growth of the international economy. Coal was a social artifact as well as a natural fact."[53]

Joel Mokyr's *The Enlightened Economy* takes a different track. While recognizing the contribution of other factors, Mokyr sees technological development during the Industrial Revolution as exogenous and its main source as the Enlightenment: "This book . . . argues, in short, that in addition to standard arguments such as geographical factors and the role of markets, politics, and society, the beginnings of modern economic growth depended a great deal on what people knew and believed, and how those beliefs affected their economic behavior. The eighteenth century was the Age of Enlightenment – and the economic ramifications of that fact need to be fully confronted."[54]

McCloskey's *Bourgeois Dignity* embraces Mokyr's ideological and cultural argument and turns it into a monocausal explanation. Exogenous technological development powered the Industrial Revolution and gave rise to modern economic growth. The source of technological development, McCloskey argues, was ideological and cultural change which permitted the endorsement and celebration of bourgeois values. Markets and trade played no role. For countries struggling with the daunting task of achieving modern economic growth and lifting hundreds of millions of people from poverty, the solution rests with persuading the people in those countries to adore bourgeois dignity and liberty:

> The Big Economic Story of our own times is that the Chinese in 1978 and then the Indians in 1991 adopted liberal ideas in the economy, and came to attribute a dignity and a liberty to the bourgeoisie formerly denied. And then China and India exploded in economic growth. The important moral, therefore, is that in achieving a pretty good life for the mass of humankind, and a chance at a fully human existence, ideas have mattered more than the usual material causes.[55]

As we can see from these seven books, two on ideology and culture (Mokyr and McCloskey) are close together at one end; four with somewhat differing emphasis on markets and trade (Pomeranz, Inikori, Findlay and O'Rourke, and Allen) are close together at the other end; and one on the survival rate of the rich (Clark) stands alone in between. The arguments of the four books with differing emphasis on trade are clearly much easier to reconcile with the evidence and theoretical logic of the literature reviewed earlier in this section of the chapter than those of the other three. Statistically, we can say that the trade and market argument, which re-emerged in the mid-1980s as the dominant explanation of the Industrial Revolution, continues to be the dominant paradigm.[56] But the disagreements among these authors point to lingering issues not fully resolved to the level of satisfaction that would allow a majority of scholars to establish a consensus, especially the issue of the role of culture and ideology. This chapter proposes that a comparative analysis of the development experiences of England's major counties constitutes the best methodological approach that can move the debate closer to a consensus.

A major weakness in the arguments of all but one of our seven books is their exclusive focus on national history in their explanation of the Industrial Revolution.[57] Mokyr identifies two separate problems in "explaining the Industrial Revolution and the origins of modern economic growth" – first, a "big problem": why western Europe achieved modern economic development and the rest of the world did not; and second, a "little problem": why Britain took the lead in western Europe.[58] In fact, there is a third and more directly relevant problem: why did the Industrial Revolution occur in Lancashire and the West Riding of Yorkshire and not in East Anglia or some other region in southern England? We need to reorder Mokyr's problems and call the first a "mega-problem", the second a "big problem" and our third the "little problem". It is the "little problem" that is far more helpful in weighting the contending factors in the explanation. Given this reformulation of the issue, Pomeranz's highly important questions also need to be altered. Instead of asking why England was not the Yangzi Delta and why the Yangzi Delta was not England, we have to ask why Lancashire and the West Riding were not the Yangzi Delta or East Anglia, and why the Yangzi Delta was like East Anglia and not Lancashire and the West Riding.

Allen's argument on high wages as the main source of technological development during the Industrial Revolution is based on aggregate British wages, the "big problem". However, Allen recognizes the inherent problem in the use of national measurements:

A very serious issue is whether countries are appropriate units of analysis. One question is whether they are homogeneous enough. Was there an "English" or an "Italian" wage, for instance? In many respects, the countries were internally heterogeneous, and I represent them with averages. However, if world empires or agrarian institutions were powerful enough to remake societies, their effects should show up in the average experience of the nations concerned. And they do.[59]

Allen's reasoning is certainly consistent with his specific line of argument. However, it leaves out a comparative county analysis that strongly supports his high wage argument and the critical role of overseas trade. For centuries, Lancashire and the West Riding of Yorkshire (treated here as a county for practical purposes) were very poor counties with very low wages. As late as 1767–70, they were among eleven counties with the lowest wages in England. But, by 1794–95, they were among eleven counties with the highest wages, with the West Riding having the highest wages in England.[60] The mechanism through which these changes were brought about by overseas trade, and their causal link to technological development, will be elaborated upon in the third section of this chapter, where we demonstrate the critical role of the Atlantic economy through its impact on the major Atlantic-trading counties of England. But before we get to that central subject, it is important, for purposes of clearer understanding of the main arguments of the chapter, that we clarify some conceptual issues concerning the key concepts – import-substitution industrialization and export-led growth – in the section that follows.

Import-Substitution Industrialization and Export-Led Growth

Import-substitution industrialization is a concept familiar to development economists dealing with long-run development in developing countries.[61] It is not well known to mainstream economists and most historians. Even though the concept originated among classical economists dealing with the long-run development of the British economy in the eighteenth century, its serious application by modern scholars to explain the Industrial Revolution is relatively recent.[62] Hence, the literature contains elements of misunderstanding[63] that need some clarification.

ISI, as applied by development economists to long-run development processes in the developing countries, is a very complex concept. It involves the evolution of markets, the growth of incomes and domestic markets, the creation of taste for manufactures, the growth of passion for their regular consumption and the "industrious revolution"[64] that goes with it, as well as the ultimate process of industrial development that follows, with all its complexities and varieties.[65] There is not just one monolithic ISI process in history and theory, but several. There have been successes and failures in ISI processes. Development economists and economic historians familiar with the process have identified the factors responsible for success and failure. To eliminate the prevailing confusion and misunderstanding, I will summarize the current state of knowledge concerning the twin concepts, ISI and export-led growth.

Table 9.1 shows the various phases and varieties of the ISI process. The primary products export phase is extremely important. It is the period during which taste formation and the "industrious revolution" occur, and the domestic market for manufactures is established and grows.[66] This domestic market created by imports presents the necessary conditions and opportunity for governments committed to long-run development to initiate the process of industrialization through the ISI strategy – that is, phase 2 (ISI_1). In the first few years, given state protection and other incentive-creating policies, industrial output expands rapidly through the production of mass consumer goods to meet the pre-existing domestic demand. Once expansion reaches the limit of the pre-existing domestic demand, further growth of output (based entirely on the domestic market) depends on the national product's growth rate (known historically to usually be slow at this point) and the pattern of its social distribution. Because of the characteristically slow growth of income and the associated domestic demand (no matter the pattern of distribution), the early fast expansion of industrial output is followed by stagnation.

As stagnation sets in, one of two options is usually adopted: (1) move to ISI_2 – the production of consumer durables and intermediate goods for the domestic market; or (2) continue with the production of mass consumer manufactures and struggle to secure export markets for some of the output, so that the growth of exports helps to sustain continued expansion of industrial production. For purposes of clear understanding, it should be noted that this is what analysts familiar with the ISI process call export-led growth, as shown in table 9.1.

If the first option is adopted, industrialization will continue to depend

Table 9.1: Phases in Import Substitution Industrialization Strategy

Phase	Economic Structure	Core Policies
1. Primary product phase (PPE)	Raw materials or food exports, traditional agriculture, handicraft production, and limited manufactures	Free trade and foreign investment, gold-standard exchange-rate policy
2. Import substitution Phase 1 (ISI1)	Growing manufacturing activity, consumer goods	Protection, fiscal and financial supports to industry
3. Import substitution Phase 2 (ISI2)	Industrial deepening in consumer durables and intermediates	Same as ISI1, plus new role for state-owned enterprise and MNCs
OR		
Export-led growth Phase 1 (ELG1)	Manufacturing growth led by exports of labour-intensive goods	Devaluation, selective liberalization, financial and fiscal supports to export industry
4. Import substitution Phase 3 (ISI3)	Continued deepening, including capital goods	Same as ISI2
OR		
Export-led growth Phase 2 (ELG2)	Industrial deepening coupled with upgrading of exports	Targeted industrial policies

Source: Adapted from Stephan Haggard, *Pathways from the Periphery: The Politics of Growth in the Newly Industrializing Countries* (Ithaca, NY: Cornell University Press, 1990), table 2.1, 25.

virtually on the domestic market, and ISI_2 is followed by ISI_3, with all sectors of manufacturing dependent on the domestic market. Under these circumstances, the rate of growth of industrial production, the growth of manufacturing employment, overall technological development and contribution of manufacturing to per capita income growth will all depend on the size of the domestic market and the rate at which it expands over time. This situation builds inefficiency into the production structure and prolongs state protection indefinitely.

As already stated, the adoption of the second option, if successful,[67] leads to industrialization strongly sustained by the production of manufactures for export, which will, over time, include both ISI_2 and ISI_3 – the production of machinery and transport equipment. A major advantage of the second option is that the production of mass consumer manufactures for both the domestic and export markets helps to create a large domestic market for capital goods industries – industries producing intermediate goods, machinery and so on. Because the production of the latter goods entails considerable economies of scale, the large domestic market so provided helps to make the extension of domestic manufacturing to their production economic,[68] thereby facilitating the upgrading of manufactured exports to include them. In addition, competition on the international market compels the building of efficiency into the organization and technology of manufacturing quite early, eliminating the necessity to prolong state protection. The Industrial Revolution in Lancashire and the West Riding (and also, to a lesser extent, in the West Midlands) belongs to this variety of the ISI model. So, too, is the "Asian model".[69] It was largely Atlantic markets that offered the English counties mentioned here the export opportunities. In the next section, we conduct a comparative analysis of the industrialization process in England's major counties to demonstrate the critical role of the Atlantic economy in the extraordinary outcome of the ISI process in Lancashire and the West Riding.

Atlantic Trade and the Industrial Revolution:
A Comparative County Analysis

There can be no doubt that import-substitution industrialization accurately describes the long, drawn-out process of industrialization in England. In the first three-quarters of the last millennium, the development of manufacturing in England followed the path created by imports and re-exports of foreign manufactures. The substitution of domestically produced manufactures for previously imported ones started with woollen textiles in the late medieval period; metals and other textiles came much later, in the late seventeenth and early eighteenth centuries. Over this time period, the ISI phases shown in table 9.1 – from the production of primary commodities for export to ISI and export-led growth – can be found in the English economy at different points.

For much of the medieval period, England exported raw wool to the manufacturing centres in western Europe (Flanders, in particular), where it was manufactured into cloth and exported back to England. The process of import substitution in cloth production started in the fourteenth century. Between the 1330s and 1340s, aided by wartime state policy, English producers struggled successfully to secure the domestic market from continental suppliers. Thereafter, they moved aggressively into cloth production for export.[70] Their success made the industry export-dependent from the fifteenth century, just as raw wool production had depended on exports for centuries. To illustrate, total annual average production of raw wool in England in 1540–47 was 50,723 sacks. Of this total, 5,025 sacks were exported, 28,790 sacks were employed to produce cloths for export and 14,395 sacks were employed to produce cloths for the domestic market.[71] On this evidence, 66.7 per cent of total cloth production during the period was exported.[72] The share of exports fell to 40 per cent in the late seventeenth century, before increasing to 67 per cent in the late eighteenth century.[73]

Because every county in England produced some quantity of raw wool, even in the early eighteenth century,[74] government policy on the wool trade encouraged the early development of cloth production as a sort of agro-allied industry across the counties. However, in the sixteenth and seventeenth centuries, large-scale cloth production was concentrated in the southern counties, especially East Anglia and the West Country.[75] The bulk of the cloth exported in the sixteenth and seventeenth centuries was produced in the latter two regions, making them the most industrialized regions of England during that period.[76] In 1660, Suffolk (one of the three counties in East Anglia) was one of the wealthiest counties in England, second only to Middlesex, whose wealth ranking is inflated by the inclusion of the capital city of London.[77] In 1695, the southern counties accounted for 70 per cent of the total cloth output in England and Wales (£3.5 million out of £5 million); while the West Riding of Yorkshire had 20 per cent (£1 million).[78]

A reversal of fortune occurred in the regional distribution of the industry from the late seventeenth to the nineteenth century. For several centuries, northwest Europe (Germany, Holland, Flanders and France) and northern Europe (Norway, Denmark, Iceland, Greenland and the Baltic) were the main export markets for English woollen textiles. From the second half of the seventeenth century, English producers lost much of those markets as local production expanded in those regions, sometimes under mercantilist policies. From 1699–1701 to 1772–74, English woollen cloth exports to northwest Europe and northern Europe declined absolutely by 37.4 per cent and 38.9 per cent, respectively; from 1772–74 to 1804–6, exports to northwest Europe declined further by £647,000, just about made up by increases in exports to northern Europe (£686,000). In all, English woollen cloth exports to northwest Europe and northern Europe decreased absolutely from £1,544,000 in 1701 to £1,002,000 in 1806.[79] These developments had far-reaching adverse effects on the woollen industry in southern England, particularly the main export-producing regions of East Anglia and the West Country.

The loss of markets in northwest and northern Europe occurred at the same time that Atlantic markets for English woollen cloth expanded phenomenally. Exports to the Americas and West Africa increased from £185,000 a year in 1699–1701 to £1,148,000 in 1772–74; £3,413,000 in 1804–6; and £5,177,000 in 1854–56. Exports to the Americas and West Africa moved from 6.1 per cent of English woollen exports in 1699–1701 to 50.2 per cent in 1804–6, moving down to 40.7 per cent in 1854–56.[80] Exports to Portugal and Spain, which were part of the Atlantic markets for all practical purposes,[81] also grew during the period, particularly during the Brazilian gold-export boom of the first six decades of the eighteenth century. To illustrate, the average annual export of English woollen goods to Portugal in 1750–55 was £778,930, approximately 20 per cent of total exports during the period.[82] Thus, for much of the eighteenth and early nineteenth centuries, Atlantic markets (including Portugal and Spain) must have absorbed about 60 per cent of total English woollen exports.

The new Atlantic markets were captured largely by producers in the West Riding of Yorkshire. The older export-producing regions in the south, particularly East Anglia and the West Country, were outcompeted. Scholars have presented competing explanations.[83] What is not disputed is the fact that the southern producers did poorly in the new Atlantic markets, while those in the West Riding excelled, decades before the adoption of the new technologies. Much of the growth in total English woollen exports in the eighteenth century (from £3 million in 1701 to £6.8 million in 1806) was, therefore, concentrated in the West Riding, the bulk of whose total output was exported. A well-informed contemporary stated in 1772 that no less than 72 per cent of West Riding's total output was exported.[84] Following the rapid expansion of exports, the industry became increasingly concentrated in the region, rising from the 20 per cent mentioned earlier to about one-third in 1772, and 60 per cent in 1800.[85]

As their production for export declined absolutely, East Anglia, the West Country and the rest of the south concentrated on producing for their own regional markets, which they continued to dominate, protected by internal transportation costs and other factors. The cumulative adverse effects of decreased exports on wages and population growth (to be shown later in the chapter) depressed the domestic market, leading to industrial decline, especially in East Anglia.

Similar to the West Riding, but ultimately more revolutionary, cotton textile production for export to Atlantic markets was central to the transformation of Lancashire – virtually the most backward of England's counties for centuries – into the first capitalist industrial society in the world. Cotton textile production in England started as an import-substitution industry in the late seventeenth and early eighteenth centuries. The domestic market for cotton textiles had been created in the seventeenth century by the East India Company's import of Indian cottons.[86] Government restrictions on the import of the Indian cottons, in response to pressure from woollen and silk producers, gave rise to domestic production in several regions in Great Britain in the early eighteenth century.[87]

For the first three decades of the eighteenth century, the growth of the industry depended entirely on the domestic market. Once the pre-existing domestic demand was fully met, growth became sluggish, as retained raw cotton imports (in weight) indicate: 1.48 million pounds (annual average) in 1711–20, which rose dramatically to over 2 million pounds in 1723, following the prohibitive law of 1722, then fell to 1.72 million pounds in 1731–40.[88] It was in the mid-1730s that some of the producers moved into production for export.[89] Thereafter, retained raw cotton imports began to increase significantly: 2.14 million pounds (annual average) in 1741–50, and 2.76 million pounds in 1751–60.[90] Initially, the exports went almost entirely to West Africa and the Americas, where they competed with Indian cottons. Between 1700 and 1774, West Africa and the Americas absorbed between 79.6 per cent and 94 per cent of total British cotton textile exports; in 1784–1806, it was between 52.3 per cent and 69.2 per cent.[91] When exports to Portugal and

Spain are included, the share of Atlantic markets increases further, especially in 1784–1806.

Lancashire took advantage of its low wages and the early development of Liverpool as a leading English port in British trade with Africa and the Americas to capture the Atlantic export markets for English cottons.[92] For this reason, the industry concentrated increasingly in Lancashire before the county became the centre of technological development in the industry. In 1787, the county had close to one-half of the capital value of all cotton mills in Great Britain; in 1820, 165,000 (68.8 per cent) of the 240,000 handloom weavers in Britain were in the county.[93] The great concentration of cotton textiles production in Lancashire meant that the industry's explosive growth between 1760 and 1851 – total British gross output increased from £600,000 in 1760 to £5.4 million in 1784–86 (annual average), £11.1 million in 1798–1800, £30 million in 1815–17 and £48.6 million in 1851[94] – was equally concentrated in the county. Like the West Riding, the bulk of Lancashire's total output was exported.

The rapid growth of industrial production and commerce in Lancashire and the West Riding gave rise to growth of employment, which in turn induced rapid population growth in both regions. They had the highest birth rates among all England's counties between 1750 and 1831. Table 9.2 shows the geographical area and population of selected English counties in selected years from 1600 to 1831. Computing from the figures in the table, the population of England increased by 42.3 per cent in 1600–1750, 46.4 per cent in 1750–1801 and 51 per cent in 1801–31. Comparable figures for the three counties of East Anglia, combined, for the same periods are 25.4 per cent, 26.9 per cent and 34.4 per cent, respectively; for the West Riding, they are 62 per cent, 82.5 per cent and 65.4 percent, respectively; for Lancashire, they are 72 per cent, 121.7 per cent and 90.1 per cent, respectively. It is clear from these figures that the population of East Anglia stagnated over the period, being considerably below the national growth rate. On the other hand, the growth rates for the West Riding and Lancashire were far above the national rate and several times that of East Anglia. It is significant that, in 1750, the counties of East Anglia had a combined population of 588,800 and Lancashire had 317,200; in 1831, the comparable figures are 1,004,000 and 1,336,900, respectively.

As mentioned earlier, the explosive growth of population in Lancashire

Table 9.2: Area and Population of Selected English Counties, 1600–1831

County	Area	Population (in Thousand)s				
	(Acres)	1600	1700	1750	1801	1831
Lancashire	1,117.3	183.7	232.5	317.2	703.1	1,336.9
West Riding (Yorkshire)	1,629.9	199.7	242.0	323.5	590.5	976.4
Essex (East Anglia)	979.0	156.6	164.7	188.5	237.9	317.6
Suffolk (East Anglia)	918.8	139.9	159.2	166.7	223.9	296.3
Norfolk (East Anglia)	1,292.3	173.1	230.9	233.6	285.4	390.1
Stafford	736.3	78.4	114.9	150.8	254.7	410.5
Nottingham	525.8	79.0	92.2	88.4	146.6	225.3
Warwick	567.9	66.2	87.4	132.5	215.9	336.6
Kent	972.2	153.4	160.7	183.7	322.5	479.2
Surrey	474.5	85.8	124.3	151.0	279.9	486.3
Middlesex	179.6	283.3	522.4	584.6	852.9	1,358.3
England	31,770.6	4,161.8	5,210.6	5,921.9	8,671.4	13,091.0

Sources: Population figures for 1600, 1700, 1750 and 1801 are from E.A. Wrigley, "Rickman Revisited: The Population Growth Rates of English Counties in the Early Modern Period", *Economic History Review* 62, no. 3 (2009): table 3, 721. The population figures for 1831 and the area figures are from *1831 Census*, enumeration abstract, II, *Parliamentary Papers*, 1833, 36, 832–33.

Notes: Essex, Norfolk, and Suffolk make up England's southeast region, known as East Anglia. Kent, Surrey and Middlesex are the Home Counties (counties adjacent to the capital city, London). Stafford and Warwick are West Midland counties, and Nottingham is one of the East Midland counties.

and the West Riding occurred at the same time that wages were rising in association with growing demand for labour in industries experiencing the expansion of production for Atlantic markets. Therefore, the domestic market in both regions also experienced considerable expansion during the period. It was this combined expansion of export markets and the regional domestic markets that created market conditions for the growth of the factory system and the development and diffusion of new technologies in Lancashire and the West Riding. Factory employment in the West Riding woollen industry was 50.3 per cent of England's total in 1835; and it was 65.1 per cent in 1850.[95] Lancashire overwhelmingly dominated the mechanization of cotton weaving from the 1830s: 56.5 per cent of power looms employed in cotton weaving in Great Britain in 1835 were in Lancashire; in 1850, the proportion was 70.9 per cent.[96] Early nineteenth-century census data, presented in tables 9.3 and 9.4, indicate a general concentration of the nation's technological development in Lancashire and the West Riding during the Industrial Revolution, thus providing further support for the patent and other evidence discussed earlier in this chapter.

As we can see in table 9.3, 97,517 of the 314,106 adult males employed in factory manufacturing in England in 1831 were in Lancashire, totalling 31.05 per cent; while 74,669 (23.77 per cent) were in the West Riding. Thus, approximately 55 per cent of all adult males employed in factories in England in 1831 were in Lancashire and the West Riding. Table 9.4 shows a combined total of 52,390 (16.68 per cent) for the three Midland counties of Stafford, Nottingham and Warwick (over one-half in Stafford). These five counties had 71.5 per cent of the national total. The remaining thirty-six counties (taking the subdivisions of Yorkshire as counties for practical purposes) were overwhelmingly dominated by handicraft and retail trade – 10:1 (handicraft and retail trade to factory employment) in East Anglia; and 18:1 in the home counties (Kent, Surrey and Middlesex). Factory employment exceeded employment in handicraft and retail trade only in Lancashire, the West Riding and Stafford. In fact, on the eve of the railway age in 1831, the census data clearly show that employment in the national economy was still overwhelmingly dominated by retail trade and handicraft: national employment in retail trade and handicraft dwarfed factory employment 3:1. Hence, England's national economy was not yet an industrial capitalist economy in 1831. Only the regional economies of Lancashire and the West Riding were truly industrial capitalist economies, by definition, in 1831.[97] As Wrigley stated eloquently, the new technologies of the Industrial Revolution were brought into being not by handicraft and retail trade, but by factory industry:

> There were industries in which both productivity per head and employment were rising rapidly in the first half of the [nineteenth] century. Cotton and iron

Table 9.3: England's Counties, Economies in Comparative Perspective, 1831 Census

	Selected Counties in England					
	Lancashire	Yorkshire (West Riding)	Essex	Suffolk	Norfolk	England
Area (acres)	1,117,260	1,629,890	979,000	918,769	1,292,300	31,770,615
Population	1,336,854	976,359	317,597	296,317	390,054	13,091,005
Males 20 Years Plus:	313,097	231,666	79,023	71,376	93,498	3,199,984
(a) Employed in manufacture or in making manufacturing machinery	97,517	74,669	871	676	4,740	314,106
(b) Employed in retail trade or in handicraft as masters or workmen	86,079	60,109	18,953	18,167	26,543	964,177
Occupiers employing labourers	6,658	7,096	4,561	4,526	5,229	141,460
Occupiers not employing labourers	9,714	10,636	888	1,121	2,718	94,883
Labourers employed in agriculture	20,949	24,502	38,234	33,040	37,466	744,407
Labourers employed in labour, not agricultural	60,546	33,685	6,727	5,336	6,577	500,050

Source: 1831 Census, enumeration abstract, II, *Parliamentary Papers,* 1833, 36, 832–33.

Notes: Essex, Norfolk and Suffolk make up England's southeast region known as East Anglia, being compared in this table with that part of northern England comprising Lancashire and the West Riding of Yorkshire. Although the enumerators intended the term *manufacture* to apply only to factory manufacturing, some proto-industrial production may have been included, as they noted that separating manufacture from handicraft was difficult.

Table 9.4: England's Counties, Economies in Comparative Perspective, 1831 Census

	Selected Counties in England					
	Stafford	Nottingham	Warwick	Kent	Surrey	Middlesex
Area (acres)	736,290	525,800	567,930	972,240	474,480	179,590
Population	410,512	225,327	336,610	479,155	486,334	1,358,330
Males 20 Years Plus:	101,632	56,582	83,239	115,655	119,565	358,521
(a) Employed in manufacture or in making manufacturing machinery	26,755	14,260	11,375	476	2,065	11,064
(b) Employed in retail trade or in handicraft as masters or workmen	24,766	14,683	32,579	34,257	44,139	163,220
Occupiers employing labourers	3,781	2,643	2,838	4,361	1,873	1,050
Occupiers not employing labourers	3,649	2,414	1,142	2,152	727	490
Labourers employed in agriculture	16,812	11,799	15,644	36,113	16,761	11,376
Labourers employed in labour, not agricultural	22,690	5,628	10,358	15,245	24,878	79,735

Source: 1831 Census, enumeration abstract, II, Parliamentary Papers, 1833, 36, 832–33.

Notes: Kent, Surrey and Middlesex are the Home Counties (counties adjacent to the capital city, London). Stafford, Warwick and Nottingham are Midland counties.

manufacture fall into this category. . . . But there was also a host of industries [retail trade and handicraft, such as baker, blacksmith, bricklayer, butcher, carpenter, mason, publican, shoemaker, shopkeeper and tailor], which collectively employed a very large proportion of adult men, and in which employment was fully keeping pace with the increase in the labour force, yet where it is improbable that there were any major changes in productivity per man in this period. *The tools and methods of work of tailors, butchers, blacksmiths, carpenters and bricklayers changed very little. . . . They were scattered over the country, working for the most part as isolated individuals or in tiny production units very much as in earlier generations, serving only a local market. They were beneficiaries of greatly enhanced productivity elsewhere in the economy rather than contributors to it.*[98]

Interpreted in this manner, the census data confirm the conclusions drawn from the patent records and other evidence that the development of the new technologies of the Industrial Revolution was driven by market expansion, and that it occurred largely in Lancashire and the West Riding, with the Midlands (especially the West Midlands) coming a distant third.

Conclusion

The evidence presented in the chapter compels us to conclude that arguments based exclusively on national history, or what we have called mega-history (western Europe as a unit of analysis), cannot capture the real relative weights of the contending factors in the long, drawn-out historical process which produced the Industrial Revolution. The relative contributions of the factors can be observed more clearly when we focus our analysis on micro-regions, what we called "the little problem" in our reordering of Mokyr's problems. The weakness of the varieties of arguments which treat culture as the central factor comes out clearly when confronted with the question why the Industrial Revolution and its new technologies were situated in England's socially and economically backward regions of Lancashire and the West Riding of Yorkshire, instead of the more progressive southern counties which were the real centres of the Enlightenment and bourgeois values. Need we say bourgeois values are generally a latent force waiting for opportunities to blossom in every society in the modern world? A Presbyterian missionary extolling the virtues of bourgeois values to his congregation in southeastern Nigeria in 1848 was surprised by the reaction he observed. A member of the local elite had to explain to him that the people already knew and practised everything he said, as a matter of everyday life.[99] It is difficult to believe that some unexplained sudden change in Chinese and Indian culture occurred in the late twentieth century to bring about the endorsement and celebration of bourgeois values and produce the technological change and explosive growth still continuing.

A micro-regional study of England's counties has allowed us to escape the unwarranted tyranny of the small-ratios argument. The impact of Atlantic trade was not evenly spread across western Europe. It was not even spread equally among England's forty counties. The emphasis of Findlay and O'Rourke on military might is well placed, because Britain's naval power helped to secure the plum territories of the Americas for British trade, and the commercial influence of British America in intra-American trade helped to link British Atlantic trade to the rest of the Americas. British domination of Atlantic commerce was completed by diplomatic successes secured, again, through military power, which helped to link British Atlantic trade to Brazil and Spanish America through Portugal and Spain.[100] In terms of its volume and value, no previous expansion of trade in the world came close to the growth of Atlantic commerce in 1650–1850, and no nation engrossed, directly or indirectly, the benefits of seaborne commerce as large as Britain did in the Atlantic world during the period. And those huge benefits were concentrated initially in a few English counties. Lancashire and the West Riding initially exploited their relatively cheap labour (and possibly other advantages) to capture a disproportionate share of Atlantic trade and markets. This helped powerfully to move their import-substitution industrialization process in the direction of export-led growth. Subsequently, the growth of their manufactured exports to expanding Atlantic markets transformed them into high-wage regions. Their rising wages and rapidly growing population added large, fast-growing regional domestic markets to their expanding export markets. Ultimately, a combination of large and fast-growing markets, fast-rising wages and competition in export markets induced inventive activities and technological development in both regions (more so in Lancashire), which in turn expanded the export markets further.

To argue that trade expansion had occurred somewhere before without producing an industrial revolution misses the point.[101] What the major Atlantic-trading regions of England experienced between the mid-seventeenth and mid-nineteenth centuries was truly exceptional. We may recall the question and answer articulated by Eric Hobsbawm several decades ago concerning the seventeenth-century economic crisis in Europe: "Why did the expansion of the later fifteenth and sixteenth centuries not lead straight into the epoch of the eighteenth and nineteenth century Industrial Revolution? What . . . were the obstacles in the way of capitalist expansion?" As Hobsbawm explained, technical and organizational capabilities were not wanting; and there was no shortage of capital. In Hobsbawm's view, the real obstacle was lack of adequate economic opportunity.[102] For Lancashire, the West Riding and the West Midlands, Atlantic trade helped to clear that obstacle, thanks partly to Britain's military might.

There can be no doubt that Lancashire and the West Riding were linked more closely to the Atlantic economy than they were to the other regions of England before the railway age. The bulk of their manufacturing output between the mid-eighteenth and the mid-nineteenth centuries was sold in Atlantic markets. When the amount sold in their own expanding regional markets is added to the exports, it is clear that what was sold to consumers in the other regions of England was a small fraction of their total output. Those who argue that what was sold abroad could have been sold at home in the absence of overseas markets[103] need to revisit John Williams's critique of Mill:

> What Mill overlooked was the entire absence, under assumptions of predominant foreign trade, of comparable alternatives in purely domestic production. . . . He failed to see, indeed, that but for specialisation in world trade such concentration of labour and capital on little land would not be possible. What is more significant, perhaps, he failed to see the relation of international trade to national economic development, spread over time. . . . He failed to see that England's capital and labour were *products* (results) of international trade itself, but for which they would not have existed in any comparable degree.[104]

In general, the economic problems of Lancashire in the late twentieth century, following the loss of overseas markets, even with the integrated national economy that did not exist before the railway age, prove John Williams's point.

The evidence presented in this chapter also suggests the need to revise the

Atlantic trade analysis by Acemoglu, Johnson and Robinson.[105] In general, their analysis is consistent with and further strengthens earlier arguments stressing the importance of Atlantic trade in European development from 1500 to 1850. Their argument, that the volume of Atlantic trade during the period was not large enough to directly cause, by itself, the simultaneous full development of the economies of the Atlantic-trading European nations, also mirrors some earlier arguments explaining why the Industrial Revolution occurred in England, and not simultaneously in several European countries.[106] However, Acemoglu, Johnson and Robinson have not taken into account the fact that the economic benefits of Atlantic trade during the period were not shared out evenly among the Atlantic-trading nations of Europe and among the regions within those nations, as the English evidence shows. Hence, while the absolute volume of Atlantic trade may appear not large enough to bring about simultaneous development across Europe, the disproportionate concentration of the direct impact of the trade on a few countries and on a few regions within those countries, in the first instance, magnified the long-run impact, as the initial regions and countries extended that impact in all sorts of ways to other regions and countries in the larger region of western Europe and the rest of the continent.[107] A consideration of this disproportionate distribution is also important in explaining why Atlantic-trading countries, such as England and the Netherlands, with similar institutional trajectories, did not industrialize simultaneously.

Similarly, the comparative regional evidence presented in this chapter compels some revision in the comparative analysis by Pomeranz.[108] The analysis centres on the question why England (one of the areas of western Europe with the greatest potential for successful industrialization in modern times) did not end up like the Yangzi Delta (the area of China with the greatest potential for successful industrialization during the same period). With Pomeranz's evidence and analysis, China's Yangzi Delta looks very much like England's East Anglia. The Yangzi Delta lost the markets for the products of its proto-manufacturing industries in China's western provinces as they developed their own proto-manufacturing industries in the eighteenth century, the same way East Anglia lost much of the markets for its manufactures in northern and northwest Europe during the same period. And the long-term consequences were about the same. It would seem, therefore, that the Pomeranz question would be analytically more fruitful for our current purpose if reframed: why was East Anglia very much like the Yangzi Delta, and Lancashire and the West Riding of Yorkshire were not? This question helps to focus attention on the importance of large and expanding export markets for technological development, instead of the supply of land-intensive raw materials that occupied centre stage in the Pomeranz analysis. East Anglia had all the land-intensive raw materials it needed for its industries, but the absolute diminution of its export markets prevented industrial growth and technological development. The capture of large and expanding Atlantic markets for mass consumer manufactures made all the difference for Lancashire, the West Riding and, to a lesser extent, the West Midlands. Our micro-regional evidence is consistent with conclusions drawn from patent records that inventive activities and technological development during the Industrial Revolution and early industrialization in the United States depended largely on access to large and expanding markets for manufactures. There may be some room for improvement, but, in general, endogenous theory of technological development is consistent with our empirical evidence, while exogenous theory is not. We believe the way forward is more micro-regional studies ("the little problem") and less mega-history and focus on "the big problem" (national history).

NOTES

1. As defined in the literature, proto-industrialization was the first stage in the process. This early stage was characterized by the transformation of previously independent, small-scale producers of manufactures into semi-wage workers by merchant capitalists who took over the supply of raw materials (and also tools in many instances), the organization of production and the marketing of the final product in distant markets. The producers working at home received payment on a contracted piece rate; hence, they were semi-wage earners. See Joseph E. Inikori, "English versus Indian Cotton Textiles: The Impact of Imports on Cotton Textile Production in West Africa", in *How India Clothed the World: The World of South Asian Textiles, 1500–1850*, ed. Giorgio Riello and Tirthankar Roy (Leiden and Boston: Brill, 2009), 87–89.

2.   Peter Kriedte, *Peasants, Landlords and Merchant Capitalists: Europe and the World Economy, 1500–1800* (Leamington Spa, Warwickshire: Berg, 1983), 13.

3.   Sidney Pollard, *Peaceful Conquest: The Industrialization of Europe 1760–1970* (Oxford: Oxford University Press, 1981), 14–20; Donald C. Coleman, "Proto-Industrialization: A Concept Too Many", *Economic History Review* 36 (1983): 435–48; Brian Short, "The De-industrialisation Process: A Case Study of the Weald, 1600–1850", in *Regions and Industries: A Perspective on the Industrial Revolution in Britain*, ed. Pat Hudson (Cambridge: Cambridge University Press, 1989), 156–74; Frank Perlin, "Proto-Industrialization and Pre-colonial South Asia", *Past and Present* 98 (February 1983): 30–95. For the historical development of the concept, see Franklin Mendels, "Proto-industrialisation: Theory and Reality, General Report", paper presented at the Eighth International Economic History Congress, Budapest, 1982, 69–107.

4.   Kristine Bruland, "Industrialisation and Technological Change", in *The Cambridge Economic History of Modern Britain*, vol. 1: *Industrialisation, 1700–1860*, ed. Roderick Floud and Paul Johnson (Cambridge: Cambridge University Press, 2004), 117.

5.   Christine MacLeod, *Inventing the Industrial Revolution: The English Patent System, 1660–1800* (Cambridge: Cambridge University Press, 1988); Christine MacLeod, "The European Origins of British Technological Predominance", in *Exceptionalism and Industrialisation: Britain and Its European Rivals, 1688–1815*, ed. Leandro Prados de la Escosura (Cambridge: Cambridge University Press, 2004), 111–26; see also two other chapters in the same book: James Thomson, "Invention in the Industrial Revolution: The Case of Cotton", 127–44, and Rainer Fremdling, "Continental Responses to British Innovations in the Iron Industry during the Eighteenth and Early Nineteenth Centuries", 145–69; Richard J. Sullivan, "England's 'Age of Invention': The Acceleration of Patents and Patentable Invention during the Industrial Revolution", *Explorations in Economic History* 26 (1989): 424–52; Trevor Griffiths, Philip A. Hunt and Patrick K. O'Brien, "Inventive Activity in British Textile Industry, 1700–1800", *Journal of Economic History* 52, no. 4 (December 1992): 881–906; Patrick O'Brien, Trevor Griffiths and Philip Hunt, "Technological Change during the First Industrial Revolution: The Paradigm Case of Textiles, 1688–1851", in *Technological Change: Methods and Themes in the History of Technology*, ed. Robert Fox (Amsterdam: Harwood Academic, 1996), 155–76; Patrick K. O'Brien, "The Micro Foundations of Macro Inventions: The Case of the Rev. Edmund Cartwright", *Textile History* 28, no. 2 (1997): 201–33; G.N. Tunzelmann, "Technological and Organizational Change in Industry during the Early Industrial Revolution", in *The Industrial Revolution and British Society*, ed. Patrick O'Brien and Ronald Quinault (Cambridge: Cambridge

University Press, 1993), 254–82; Nick von Tunzelmann, "Technology in the Early Nineteenth Century", in *The Economic History of Modern Britain since 1700,* vol. 1: *1700–1860,* ed. Floud and McCloskey, 2nd ed. (Cambridge: Cambridge University Press, 1994), 271–99; Prasannan Parthasarathi, "Rethinking Wages and Competitiveness in the Eighteenth Century: Britain and South India", *Past and Present* 158 (1998): 79–109; Prasannan Parthasarathi, "The Great Divergence", *Past and Present* 156 (August 2002): 275–93; E.A. Wrigley, "The Divergence of England: The Growth of the English Economy in the Seventeenth and Eighteenth Centuries", *Transactions of the Royal Historical Society* 6, no. 10 (2000): 117–41; Maxine Berg, "From Imitation to Invention: Creating Commodities in Eighteenth-Century Britain", *Economic History Review* 55, no. 1 (2002): 1–30; Maxine Berg, "In Pursuit of Luxury: Global History and British Consumer Goods in the Eighteenth Century", *Past and Present* 182 (2004): 85–142; Maxine Berg, "Consumption in Eighteenth- and Early Nineteenth-Century Britain", in *Cambridge Economic History of Modern Britain,* vol. 1, 357–87; Bruland, "Industrialisation and Technological Change", 117–46.

6. Kenneth L. Sokoloff, "Inventive Activity in Early Industrial America: Evidence from Patent Records, 1790–1846", *Journal of Economic History* 48, no. 4 (December 1988): 813–50; Kenneth L. Sokoloff and B. Zorina Khan, "The Democratization of Invention during Early Industrialization: Evidence from the United States, 1790–1846", *Journal of Economic History* 50, no. 2 (June 1990): 363–78; B. Zorina Khan and Kenneth L. Sokoloff, " 'Schemes of Practical Utility': Entrepreneurship and Innovation among 'Great Inventors' in the United States, 1790–1865", *Journal of Economic History* 53, no. 2 (June 1993): 289–307.

7. Sokoloff, "Inventive Activity in Early Industrial America", 814.

8. Ibid., 816–17.

9. Ibid., 817–18.

10. Sokoloff and Khan, "The Democratization of Invention", 364.

11. Khan and Sokoloff, " 'Schemes of Practical Utility' ", 290. According to Khan and Sokoloff, 150 of these inventors, "who were also patentees received 1,178 patents, or somewhat less than 2 percent of the total awarded over the period".

12. Sokoloff, "Inventive Activity in Early Industrial America", 819.

13. Douglass C. North, *The Economic Growth of the United States, 1790–1860* (1961; reprint, New York: W.W. Norton, 1966).

14. Sokoloff, "Inventive Activity in Early Industrial America", 813.

15. Ibid., 819.

16. Ibid., table 1, 824, 825.

17. We may recall here Douglass North's point on the role of Southern cotton exports in the expansion of income and the growth of domestic markets in the United

States during this period: "In this period of rapid growth [1830s], it was cotton that initiated the concomitant expansion in income, in the size of domestic markets, and creation of the social overhead investment (in the course of its role in the marketing of cotton) in the Northeast which were to facilitate the subsequent rapid growth of manufactures. . . . *Direct income from the cotton trade was probably no more than 6 per cent of any plausible estimate of national income which we might employ, but when income from cotton exports, including shipments to textile mills in our own Northeast, grew from $25 million in 1831 to $70 million in 1836, it set in motion the whole process of accelerated expansion which culminated in 1839.* Certainly the views of contemporaries, northern observers as well as southerners, support the position that in this period cotton was indeed king" (North, *Economic Growth*, 68–69; emphasis is mine).

18. Ibid., 813, and table 6, 844, 845.
19. Ibid., 846–47; emphasis is mine.
20. Sokoloff and Khan, "The Democratization of Invention", table 2, 369.
21. Ibid., table 2, 369.
22. Ibid., 377–78.
23. Khan and Sokoloff, "'Schemes of Practical Utility'", 292, 294, 295.
24. Ibid., 289.
25. MacLeod, *Inventing the Industrial Revolution*; Sullivan, "England's 'Age of Invention'".
26. Griffiths, Hunt and O'Brien, "Inventive Activity in the British Textile Industry", 882.
27. Ibid., 882.
28. Ibid., 884–85.
29. MacLeod, *Inventing the Industrial Revolution*; Sullivan, "England's 'Age of Invention'"; Bruland, "Industrialisation and Technological Change".
30. MacLeod, *Inventing the Industrial Revolution*, 7.
31. Ibid., table 8.1, 148.
32. Griffiths, Hunt and O'Brien, "Inventive Activity in the British Textile Industry", 896.
33. MacLeod, *Inventing the Industrial Revolution*, 148–49.
34. Sullivan, "England's 'Age of Invention'", table 2, 441.
35. MacLeod, *Inventing the Industrial Revolution*, table 8.2, 150.
36. Ibid., 153–54.
37. Ibid., 116.
38. O'Brien, Griffiths and Hunt, "Technological Change during the First Industrial Revolution".
39. Ibid., 171.

40. MacLeod, *Inventing the Industrial Revolution*, 124; emphasis is mine.

41. O'Brien, Griffiths and Hunt, "Technological Change during the First Industrial Revolution", 167; emphasis is mine.

42. Paul M. Romer, "Increasing Returns and Long-Run Growth", *Journal of Political Economy* 94, no. 5 (1986): 1002–37; Paul M. Romer, "The Origins of Endogenous Growth", *Journal of Economic Perspectives* 8, no. 1 (1994): 3–22; Gene M. Grossman and Elhanan Helpman, "Trade, Innovation, and Growth", *American Economic Review* 80, no. 2 (May 1990): 86–91; Gene M. Grossman and Elhanan Helpman, *Innovation and Growth in the Global Economy* (Cambridge, MA: MIT Press, 1991).

43. H. Myint, "The 'Classical Theory' of International Trade and the Underdeveloped Countries", *Economic Journal* 68 (June 1958): 317–37.

44. See, for example, Joel Mokyr, *The Enlightened Economy: An Economic History of Britain, 1700–1850* (New Haven, CT: Yale University Press, 2009), 4–5; E.A. Wrigley, "The Divergence of England: The Growth of the English Economy in the Seventeenth and Eighteenth Centuries", *Transactions of the Royal Historical Society* 6, no. 10 (2000): 126–28.

45. Adam Smith, *An Inquiry into the Nature and Causes of the Wealth of Nations*, Modern Library Edition, ed. Edwin Cannan (1776; reprint, New York: Random House, 1994), 7.

46. Myint, "The Classical Theory of International Trade", 30–31.

47. I consider the following to be the major books of the twenty-first century on the subject: Kenneth Pomeranz, *The Great Divergence: Europe, China, and the Making of the Modern World Economy* (Princeton, NJ: Princeton University Press, 2000); Joseph E. Inikori, *Africans and the Industrial Revolution in England: A Study in International Trade and Economic Development* (Cambridge: Cambridge University Press, 2002); Gregory Clark, *A Farewell to Alms: A Brief Economic History of the World* (Princeton, NJ: Princeton University Press, 2007); Ronald Findlay and Kevin H. O'Rourke, *Power and Plenty: Trade, War, and the World Economy in the Second Millennium* (Princeton, NJ: Princeton University Press, 2007); Robert C. Allen, *The British Industrial Revolution in Global Perspective* (Cambridge: Cambridge University Press, 2009); Joel Mokyr, *The Enlightened Economy: An Economic History of Britain, 1700–1850* (New Haven, CT: Yale University Press, 2009); Deirdre N. McCloskey, *Bourgeois Dignity: Why Economics Can't Explain the Modern World* (Chicago: University of Chicago Press, 2010). There is one important book on the related subject of taxes, but it does not get directly involved in the debates discussed in this chapter: William J. Ashworth, *Customs and Excise: Trade, Production, and Consumption in England, 1640–1845* (Oxford: Oxford University Press, 2003). Some equally important and pertinent books of the period may have escaped my attention. No disrespect is intended.

48. Pomeranz, *Great Divergence*, 194.

49. Kevin H. O'Rourke, "Review of Africans and the Industrial Revolution in England: A Study in International Trade and Economic Development", EH.net, October 2003, accessed 3 July 2015, http://eh.net/book_reviews/africans-and-the-industrial-revolution-in-england-a-study-in-international-trade-and-economic-development. As O'Rourke puts it: "Inikori hasn't answered all the questions, then: so much the better for the rest of us."

50. Deirdre N. McCloskey, "'You Know, Ernest, the Rich Are Different from You and Me': A Comment on Clark's *A Farewell to Alms*", *European Review of Economic History* 12, no. 2 (August 2008): 138. Of the seven articles in this issue of the journal, five are for a symposium on *A Farewell to Alms*, 138–99.

51. Kenneth Pomeranz presents evidence that challenges the basic tenet of Clark's argument: the mechanism for the transfer of bourgeois traits to descendants was weak; and empirical demographic evidence shows that the population of the poor grew faster than that of the rich in eighteenth-century England. See Kenneth Pomeranz's review of *A Farewell to Alms*, *American Historical Review* 113, no. 3 (June 2008): 775–79.

52. Findlay and O'Rourke, *Power and Plenty*, 338–39.

53. Allen, *British Industrial Revolution in Global Perspective*, 90.

54. Mokyr, *Enlightened Economy*, 1.

55. McCloskey, *Bourgeois Dignity*, xiii.

56. Inikori, *Africans and the Industrial Revolution in England*, ch. 3, 89–155, where a discussion of the historiography of the Industrial Revolution shows changes over time in the dominant explanations.

57. Comparative county history features only in Inikori, *Africans and the Industrial Revolution in England*.

58. Mokyr, *Enlightened Economy*, 10.

59. Allen, *British Industrial Revolution*, 108.

60. E.H. Hunt, "Industrialisation and Regional Inequality: Wages in Britain, 1760–1914", *Journal of Economic History* 46, no. 4 (December 1986): table 6, 965–66. In their recent article, Broadberry and Gupta linked the technological breakthrough in Lancashire, from the last quarter of the eighteenth to the first half of the nineteenth century, directly to the fast increases in wages as the producers competed on the global market with cotton exporters in India. The authors' analysis, however, does not include Lancashire's low-wage period and its role in the early development of the English cotton industry, especially its concentration in Lancashire: Stephen Broadberry and Bishnupriya Gupta, "Lancashire, India, and Shifting Competitive Advantage in Cotton Textiles, 1700–1850: The

Neglected Role of Factor Prices", *Economic History Review* 62, no. 2 (2009): 279–305.

61.   Albert O. Hirschman, *The Strategy of Economic Development* (New Haven, CT: Yale University Press, 1958); H. Myint, *The Economics of Developing Countries* (London: Hutchinson, 1967); Hollis B. Chenery, "Patterns of Industrial Growth", *American Economic Review* 50 (1960): 624–54.

62.   Inikori, *Africans and the Industrial Revolution in England*, 10–14, 125–26, 126n110. It is fair to say, for good or ill, that the concept was elaborately employed for the first time in this book.

63.   Maxine Berg, "From Imitation to Invention: Creating Commodities in Eighteenth-Century Britain", *Economic History Review* 55, no. 1 (2002): 1–30; Maxine Berg, "In Pursuit of Luxury: Global History and British Consumer Goods in the Eighteenth Century", *Past and Present* 182 (2004): 85–142 (particularly 102–3); Maxine Berg, "Consumption in Eighteenth- and Early Nineteenth-Century Britain", in *Cambridge Economic History of Modern Britain*, vol. 1, 357–87; McCloskey, *Bourgeois Dignity*, 197–238; Dani Rodrik, "Getting Interventions Right: How South Korea and Taiwan Grew Rich", *Economic Policy* 10, no. 20 (April 1995): 53–107 (including comments by Gene Grossman and Victor Norman).

64.   Jan de Vries, *The Industrious Revolution: Consumer Behaviour and the Household Economy, 1650 to the Present* (Cambridge: Cambridge University Press, 2008).

65.   Remarkably, the classical economists employed the concept with the eighteenth-century British economy in about the same manner. See Inikori, *Africans and the Industrial Revolution in England*, 125–26, 126n110, for David Hume's formulation of the concept.

66.   What has been treated in the recent consumerist literature as novel (in particular, by Maxine Berg and Jan de Vries) will be found, with little or no difference in essence, in works (going as far back as the 1950s and 1960s) by development economists, such as Myint, applying David Hume's ideas to deal with two related historical issues: explaining the expansion of export production of primary commodities in the less developed countries of Asia and Africa in the nineteenth and early twentieth centuries; and the later development of import-substitution industrial strategy. For the first issue, imported manufactures are presented as incentives that operated to encourage the employment of previously unemployed and underutilized resources (including labour) to produce them for export. Simple products, like gas lamps, bicycles, textiles, corrugated iron sheets for residential housing and so forth – consumer goods whose possession heralded material success to neighbours – featured extensively in the analyses. For example, see Myint, *Economics of Developing Countries*.

67.   Because securing export markets depends on factors that are not entirely within

the control of producers – foreign governments may impose protective measures; producers' governments may help secure overseas markets diplomatically or by military force – success is not always easily predictable.

68. This is consistent with MacLeod's evidence on the growth of inventive activity in the capital-goods sector during the period 1790–1830, induced by the expansion of industries that employed such equipment in production. See quotation with note number 33, and the preceding statement, above (page 233, this volume). The export of English consumer manufactures grew considerably in 1783–92 and 1815–30.

69. Inikori, *Africans and the Industrial Revolution in England*, 10–14, 56–88. ISI in Latin America followed the first option until the late 1960s (for Brazil in particular); India followed the same option until the 1990s. Ultimately, it was the demonstration effects of the Asian model's success that moved everyone, including even China, to the second option. For comparative discussions of the varieties of ISI and their outcomes, see Haggard, *Pathways from the Periphery*; Bela Balassa, *The Process of Industrial Development and Alternative Development Strategies* (Princeton, NJ: Princeton University, Department of Economics, International Finance Section, 1981); Jacques Hersh, *The USA and the Rise of East Asia since 1945: Dilemmas of the Postwar International Political Economy* (London: Macmillan, 1993). Export-led growth analysis for South Korea and Taiwan is disputed by Rodrik, "Getting Interventions Right". The dispute, in my view, arises from a conceptual misunderstanding of what ISI analysts mean by export-led growth, as elaborated in this section of the chapter.

70. E.M. Carus-Wilson, "Trends in the Export of English Woollens in the Fourteenth Century", *Economic History Review* 3 (1950): 162–79; T.H. Lloyd, *The English Wool Trade in the Middle Ages* (Cambridge: Cambridge University Press, 1977); Peter J. Bowden, *The Wool Trade in Tudor and Stuart England* (London: Macmillan, 1962).

71. Bowden, *Wool Trade*, 37–38.

72. Bowden's figures do not quite add up: raw wool export figures added to raw wool employed to produce cloth for export and for the home market equal 48,210 sacks, 2,513 sacks less than the total (50,723). Bowden does not account for the difference. Assuming the difference was part of production for the domestic market, cloth exports would still be roughly two-thirds (63 per cent) of total cloth output for the period.

73. Phyllis Deane, "The Output of the British Woolen Industry in the Eighteenth Century", *Journal of Economic History* 17 (1957): 221.

74. In 1700, 35 counties (out of the total of 40) produced one thousand packs of wool or more each; 24 produced two thousand and above; 13 produced three thousand

and more; the largest producers (Lincoln, Kent, Dorset, Northampton, Sussex and Northumberland) produced between four thousand and six thousand packs each (Bowden, *Wool Trade*, 40).

75.   Sidney Pollard and David W. Crossley, *The Wealth of Britain, 1085–1966* (London: B.T. Batsford, 1968), 101–2.

76.   Julian de Lucy Mann, *The Cloth Industry in the West of England from 1640 to 1880* (Oxford: Clarendon Press, 1971), xii–xiii; D.C. Coleman, "Growth and Decay during the Industrial Revolution: The Case of East Anglia", *Scandinavian Economic History Review* 10, nos. 1 and 2 (1962): 115–17.

77.   Inikori, *Africans and the Industrial Revolution in England*, table 2.4, 64.

78.   Deane, "Output of the British Woolen Industry", 220; Mann, *The Cloth Industry in the West of England*, 26–36; R.G. Wilson, "The Supremacy of the Yorkshire Cloth Industry in the Eighteenth Century", in *Textile History and Economic History: Essays in Honour of Miss Julia de Lucy Mann*, ed. N.B. Hart and K.G. Ponting (Manchester: Manchester University Press, 1973), 226–35; Derek Gregory, *Regional Transformation and Industrial Revolution: A Geography of the Yorkshire Woollen Industry* (Minneapolis: University of Minnesota Press, 1982), 41–44.

79.   All figures computed from Ralph Davis, "English Foreign Trade, 1700–1774", *Economic History Review*, 2nd ser., 15 (1962): 99–120; and Ralph Davis, *The Industrial Revolution and British Overseas Trade* (Leicester: Leicester University Press, 1979).

80.   Inikori, *Africans and the Industrial Revolution in England*, table 9.1, 414.

81.   Portuguese and Spanish export and import trade with their European partners in the eighteenth century depended largely on their American colonies. The imports (a large percentage of which was re-exported to the colonies) were paid for largely with re-exports of colonial goods. See Inikori, *Africans and the Industrial Revolution in England*, 203–8, 413–15, 420.

82.   Ibid., 413–14.

83.   Wilson, "Supremacy of the Yorkshire Cloth Industry", 235–44.

84.   Ibid., 230, 230n15.

85.   Deane, "Output of the British Woolen Industry", 215, 220; Wilson, "Supremacy of the Yorkshire Cloth Industry", 228.

86.   Bal Krishna, *Commercial Relations between India and England, 1601–1757* (London: G. Routledge, 1924), 141, 301.

87.   P.J. Thomas, *Mercantilism and the East India Trade: An Early Phase of the Protection v. Free Trade Controversy* (London: P.S. King, 1926).

88.   Brian R. Mitchell, *Abstract of British Historical Statistics* (Cambridge: Cambridge University Press, 1962), 177.

89.   Inikori, *Africans and the Industrial Revolution in England*, 433–34.

90. Mitchell, *Abstract of British Historical Statistics*, 177.

91. Inikori, *Africans and the Industrial Revolution in England*, table 9.9, 448.

92. John K. Walton, "Proto-industrialisation and the First Industrial Revolution: The Case of Lancashire", in *Regions and Industries: A Perspective on the Industrial Revolution in Britain*, ed. Pat Hudson (Cambridge: Cambridge University Press, 1989); John K. Walton, *Lancashire: A Social History, 1558–1939* (Manchester: Manchester University Press, 1987); D.A. Farnie, *The English Cotton Industry and the World Market, 1815–1896* (Oxford: Clarendon Press, 1979); A.P. Wadsworth and J. de L. Mann, *The Cotton Trade and Industrial Lancashire* (Manchester: Manchester University Press, 1931).

93. Ian Inkster, *Science and Technology in History: An Approach to Industrial Development* (New Brunswick, NJ: Rutgers University Press, 1991), 65, 320n17; Geoffrey Timmins, *The Last Shift: The Decline of Handloom Weaving in Nineteenth-Century Lancashire* (Manchester: Manchester University Press, 1993), 25, 26, 37, 39. As of 1820, handloom weaving was still overwhelmingly dominant in weaving in Britain. Scotland had 47,000 out of the 240,000 weavers (19.6 per cent). In 1820, handloom weavers constituted 25 per cent of the total labour force in Lancashire.

94. Phyllis Deane and W.A. Cole, *British Economic Growth, 1688–1959: Trends and Structure* (Cambridge: Cambridge University Press, 1962), tables 42, 43, 185, 187.

95. Gregory, *Regional Transformation*, table 2.11, 61.

96. Timmins, *Last Shift*, table 1.1, 20.

97. For a discussion of the conceptions of capitalism by Karl Marx, Max Weber, R.H. Tawney and others, see Joseph E. Inikori, *Slavery and the Rise of Industrial Capitalism: The 1993 Elsa Goveia Memorial Lecture* (Mona, Jamaica: Department of History, University of the West Indies, 1993), 2–9. In the course of the nineteenth century, aggregate factory employment in England and Wales grew steadily at the expense of handicraft, retail trade and agriculture: the number of adult males employed in factory manufacturing in England and Wales increased from 320,324 in 1831 to 479,774 in 1841 (49.8 per cent increase); that of those employed in retail trade and handicraft, from 1,007,403 to 1,282,120 (27.3 per cent increase); and in agriculture, the number declined absolutely from 1,075,912 to 1,041,980 (3.2 per cent decrease). *1831 Census*, enumeration abstract, II, 832–33, and *1841 Census*, occupation abstract, preface, 26.

98. A.E. Wrigley, "Men on the Land and Men in the Countryside: Employment in Agriculture in Early-Nineteenth-Century England", in *The World We Have Gained: Histories of Population and Social Structure, Essays Presented to Peter Laslett on His*

Seventieth Birthday, ed. Lloyd Bonfield, Richard M. Smith and Keith Wrightson (Oxford: Basil Blackwell, 1986), 335–36; emphasis added.

99. John Iliffe, *The Emergence of African Capitalism* (Minneapolis: University of Minnesota Press, 1983), 44. As the missionary reported, "I preached the way of wealth from the word of God, industry, honesty, economy, temperance, knowledge, and the blessing of God; warning against idleness, sloth, gluttony, drunkenness, ignorance, waste, and bad company, as the sure way to poverty and ruin. Seeing the company did not look pleased, I asked the king what ailed them. He said, that they knew all that themselves already."

100. Inikori, *Africans and the Industrial Revolution in England*, 156–214; Joseph E. Inikori, "Africa and the Globalization Process: Western Africa, 1450–1850", *Journal of Global History* 2, no. 1 (2007): 70–79.

101. McCloskey, *Bourgeois Dignity*, 197–206.

102. Eric J. Hobsbawm, "The General Crisis of the European Economy in the 17th Century", *Past and Present* (1954): 39.

103. C. Knick Harley, "Trade: Discovery, Mercantilism and Technology", in *Cambridge Economic History of Modern Britain*, 191–92.

104. John J. Williams, "The Theory of International Trade Reconsidered", *Economic Journal* 39 (June 1929): 204–5; emphasis in original. Some other points in John Williams's critique should be noted: "It is the writer's [Williams's] view . . . that the relation of international trade to the development of new resources and productive forces is a more significant part of the explanation of the present status of nations, of incomes, prices, well-being, than is the cross-section value analysis of the classical economists, with its assumption of given quantums of productive factors, already existent and employed."

105. Daron Acemoglu, Simon Johnson and James Robinson, "The Rise of Europe: Atlantic Trade, Institutional Change, and Economic Growth", *American Economic Review* 95, no. 3 (June 2005): 546–79.

106. Inikori, *Africans and the Industrial Revolution*, 210–14, 473–86.

107. The economic logic here is somewhat similar to that of income distribution and long-run development. While a lopsided social distribution has adverse effects, sharing out the national product (including business profits) equally among all the people will reduce capital formation virtually to zero.

108. Pomeranz, *Great Divergence*.

Contributors

Colin A. Palmer has taught at Oakland University, the University of North Carolina at Chapel Hill, the Graduate Center of the City University of New York, and Princeton University, where he was Dodge Professor of History. His numerous publications include *Freedom's Children: The 1938 Labor Rebellion and the Birth of Modern Jamaica; Cheddi Jagan and the Politics of Power: British Guiana's Struggle for Independence; Eric Williams and the Making of the Modern Caribbean;* and the six-volume *Encyclopedia of African American Culture and History.*

Selwyn R. Cudjoe is Professor of Africana Studies, Wellesley College, Wellesley, Massachusetts. His most recent books include *Beyond Boundaries: The Intellectual Tradition of Trinidad and Tobago in the Nineteenth Century* and *Caribbean Visionary: A.R.F. Webber and the Making of the Guyanese Nation.*

Ronald Findlay is Ragnar Nurkse Professor of Economics, Columbia University, New York. He is the author of *Factor Proportions, Trade and Growth* and *Eli Heckscher, International Trade, and Economic History.*

Joseph E. Inikori is Professor of History, University of Rochester, New York. His publications include *Africans and the Industrial Revolution in England: A Study in International Trade and Economic Development.*

Franklin W. Knight is Leonard and Helen R. Stulman Professor Emeritus of History and Academy Professor, Johns Hopkins University, Baltimore, Maryland. His most recent major publication, co-edited with Ruth Iyob, is *Dimensions of African and Other Diasporas.*

Lydia Lindsey is Associate Professor of Empire and Commonwealth History,

North Carolina Central University. She has published several articles on twentieth-century British social history with a special focus on West Indian women in the British Isles.

Rafael Marquese is Professor of History, University of São Paulo, Brazil. His most recent publications include the co-authored book *Slavery and Politics: Brazil and Cuba, 1790–1850*.

Kevin Hjortshøj O'Rourke is Chichele Professor of Economic History, All Souls College, Oxford, UK. His publications include *Globalization and History* (with Jeffrey G. Williamson) and *Power and Plenty* (with Ronald Findlay).

Arnold Rampersad is Sara Hart Kimball Professor Emeritus in the Humanities, Stanford University, Palo Alto, California. His recent books include *Ralph Ellison: A Biography* and, as co-editor, *Selected Letters of Langston Hughes*.

Dale Tomich is Professor of Sociology and History and Deputy Director of the Ferdnand Braudel Center, Binghamton University. He is the author of *Through the Prism of Slavery: Labor, Capital, and World Economy* and numerous other publications on Atlantic history and world-economy.